VOLUME 1 | FOUNDATIONS OF
THE DIGITAL WORLD

F**KUP ALMANAC

WHEN LOGIC, TIME AND TRUST GO WRONG

ADAM KORGA

FUCKUP ALMANAC
Volume I: Foundations Of The Digital World
© 2026 Adam Korga

First Edition, 2026

ISBN: 978-3-912499-00-1

Published by QuackFoundry Books
www.adamkorga.com

This book is a work of non-fiction. It examines real events, systems, and failures drawn from historical records, technical analyses, and publicly available sources. Some dialogue, internal reasoning, or simplifications may be reconstructed or paraphrased for narrative clarity, but the events themselves are real unless explicitly stated otherwise.

Any opinions expressed are those of the author and are intended to highlight systemic patterns rather than assign individual blame.

Printed on demand and distributed worldwide by IngramSpark.

TABLE OF CONTENTS & INTRODUCTION

TABLE OF CONTENTS

NOTE ON THE TONE

While planning the Fuckup Almanac series, I spent a long time wondering whether stories tied to real trauma should appear in a work that doesn't shy away from irony, sarcasm, and the occasional silly comparison. In the end, I decided they must — because the lessons they carry are far too valuable to leave out. Some failures make us laugh; others make us stop mid-sentence. Both deserve to be understood.

Across the series, you'll encounter stories that range from harmless absurdities to events that cost lives, reshaped industries, or scarred entire communities. These aren't just anecdotes about bad code or corporate ego; some are tragedies written in steel, fire, and human error. In those moments, the humor stops. The tone shifts to clarity and respect for the people affected, focusing on lessons rather than laughs. Such stories are clearly marked with a black ribbon: pages containing serious cases display a ribbon icon in the header, and the cases themselves are subtly framed with ribbon markers at the beginning and end of the story.

At a broader level, the rule is simple: humor ends where tragedy begins. When the cost of failure is measured in lives, trauma, or cultural scars, the goal is no longer to entertain but to understand. The irreverence returns only once the story allows space for it—when the distance of time, scale, or context makes reflection possible without disrespect.

Across all volumes, the rule is the same: unpack mistakes, teach lessons, and keep it readable. When there's a conflict between being clever and being clear, teaching wins. Every time. If a sarcastic aside would cloud the lesson or disrespect the gravity of what happened, it gets cut. These books exist to educate, not to trivialize. Sometimes that means awry observation; other times, it means letting the failure speak for itself.

ABOUT THIS SERIES

In my previous book, *IT Dictionary*, I poked fun at what doesn't work in IT. The goal there was satire: to say out loud what everyone secretly feels, to strip away the doublespeak, and to make visible the absurdities that otherwise hide behind corporate jargon. It was meant as a catharsis, a survival guide disguised as a dictionary, and—judging by the laughter of readers—it served its purpose.

Fuckup Almanac is the natural sequel. After exploring what doesn't work, we now ask a deeper question: **why do things sometimes go spectacularly wrong?** Not just in IT, though you'll find plenty of that. We look beyond software into engineering at large, into corporate blunders, and into the messy intersection where ambition, technology, and human fallibility collide. The disasters range from laughably small to devastatingly large, but the connecting thread is the same: every one of them carries a lesson. Think of this series as *Murphy's Law in long form, with footnotes.*

During the research and writing process, I realized that the amount of material went far beyond what could fit into a single book. Every category of failure opened new branches—technical, organizational, human, and even philosophical. What began as one project quickly grew into a larger body of work: a multi-volume exploration of how things break, and why we keep rebuilding them the same way.

WHY FAILURE FASCINATES US CULTURALLY

Before we get to the practical lessons, let's pause on why failure grips us so tightly. Whole cultures have been shaped by tales of downfall. Greek tragedies are essentially long-form post-mortems set to verse. Fairy tales often smuggle in warnings: *don't do this, or bad things will happen.* Modern news thrives on calamity because, let's face it, nobody clicks on "Bridge remains structurally sound for 80th consecutive year."

There's something magnetic about collapse. It reassures us that our own mistakes are survivable—at least compared to an exploding rocket. It gives us a shared moment of humility: if NASA, Toyota, or the French railway system can screw up, then maybe we shouldn't be too hard on ourselves for burning dinner. That mix of fascination and relief is why "disaster porn" works. But fascination isn't enough. The point of this work is to channel that curiosity into learning.

LEARNING FROM FAILURE

Let's be honest: some readers come for the spectacle, and that's fine. There's a strange satisfaction in reading about bridges collapsing, projects imploding, or billion-dollar companies undone by a semicolon—the punctuation equivalent of a banana peel. You'll get your fix. But I hope you'll also see the deeper layer. Each case study is more than a screw-up; it's a window into how systems break, how assumptions fail, and how humans—with all our blind spots, biases, and good intentions—create the conditions for disaster.

That's the real purpose of *Fuckup Almanac*: to turn other people's mistakes into your free education. Every example ends with a short summary of the lessons it offers—a personal library of post-mortems, minus the awkward meeting and cold donuts.

This series is, in essence, one giant cross-disciplinary post-mortem. Some entries read like autopsies of projects, products, or entire organizations. Unlike in medicine, no one here is squeamish about poking at the guts. And as you'll see, the same logic applies to bridges, satellites, or corporate takeovers: **you can't fix what you don't understand.**

CONTEXT MATTERS

To truly understand *why* something failed, you often need to understand the building blocks behind it. Sometimes that means a networking protocol. Sometimes it's a piece of physics that determines how a structure held —or didn't hold. Other times it's an organizational pattern or process that quietly set the stage for collapse. And occasionally, it's just someone making a decision at 3 a.m. after too much coffee and not enough sleep.

That's why throughout this series you'll see me step back and explain not just *what happened*, but also *the mechanics behind it*. The catalog of failures will therefore be interwoven with explanatory sections that break down the key ideas, technologies, and phenomena at play. My goal is to give you enough knowledge to follow along, even if you've never touched the field before.

This does not mean I'm writing another dry textbook. Quite the opposite: this is meant to be accessible to anyone, regardless of prior knowledge or professional experience. I'll lean on analogies, strange metaphors, and deliberate simplifications. But here's the key: I simplify without distorting.

The core of the problem will remain intact, free of factual errors—at least I hope so. And if somewhere along the way I do get something wrong, consider this my preemptive apology. After all, *Fuckup Almanac* is about failure; it would be almost suspicious if I didn't manage to sneak in a couple of my own.

And if there's a side effect, I hope it's this: by the time you finish reading, you'll be armed with enough understanding to make sense of the next headline about something blowing up—without having to run to Wikipedia. You may even start spotting the oversimplifications in articles you read, because you'll know the hidden layers underneath. Bonus: you might become that annoying friend who interrupts the news to say, *"Well actually..."*

My Promise About Explanations

Every explainer in these books aims to be clear, simplified, and still factually correct. Specialists may occasionally think, *"You could also mention X or Y here,"* but ideally never *"That's wrong."* This isn't meant to replace a textbook—it's meant to make one less intimidating.

If you're a curious mind who just wants to understand how things fit together, these explanations should serve you well. You'll get the essence without the academic gibberish.

And as a bonus—if you happen to be learning the topic right now and the term sounds like pure dark magic, I hope these pages will make it feel human again. The goal is simple: you'll grasp the big picture and be able to dig into the details later, armed with context instead of confusion.

Think of it as a friendly map to the territory, not the detailed topographic map.

THIS REALLY HAPPENED

No matter how absurd the stories across *Fuckup Almanac* may sound — they all happened. None of this is myth or dramatization.

Every event, failure, or blunder described in the series has been verified and documented in an online archive, which includes all sources with clickable links. There's no bibliography at the end of each volume, because I decided not to send readers on a noble yet pointless quest of retyping hundreds of URLs from footnotes — everything lives in one easily searchable document.

 **You can find the full reference archive here** ↵
https://adamkorga.com/books/fuckup-almanac/vol1/sources/

Whenever possible, that archive references official documents, technical reports, or regulatory filings. However, many of these stories never received public explanations or official post-mortems (see: "Types of Post-Mortems" in Chapter 0). In such cases, sources may be less formal — press articles, engineering forums, or firsthand accounts from platforms like Reddit and X (formerly Twitter). In every case, I've done my best to verify them through a mix of my modest expertise, an oversized dose of skepticism and nitpicking, and the invaluable help of early readers who pointed out inconsistencies or dead ends.

Occasionally, I'll also include smaller incidents from my own experience. They never made headlines, but they add texture and honesty — and sometimes the most humbling failures happen on a small scale.

A Note On Recurring Names

Throughout this series—especially in the IT-related stories—you may notice a familiar pattern. The same names show up again and again: **Google, AWS, Meta, Cloudflare, Microsoft,** and a few others.

Part of this is simply the curse of scale. When you operate the infrastructure of the modern world, you don't get to fail quietly. If a startup crashes, it's a bad Tuesday; if a cloud giant stumbles, half the internet goes dark. We see them because they are everywhere, and statistically, at that size, the improbable happens before lunch.

But there is a deeper, more important reason for their presence here.

These organizations embody a standard that this work deeply respects: a rigorous, transparent post-mortem culture. Unlike many others who bury their mistakes under NDAs and PR fog, these companies tend to fail *in the open*.

When something breaks, they document it. They publish it. They dissect it in technical detail. Their engineering blogs and incident write-ups are masterclasses in honesty and professional accountability. They don't hide their failures; they teach with them.

I'll admit with some embarrassment that I don't always maintain their standard myself. But that's precisely why this series exists: to celebrate those who set the bar high, and to learn from them.

So if you see their names appear with suspicious frequency, don't mistake this for incompetence. Their visibility here is a compliment. We learn far more from the giants who openly share their scars than from the ones who pretend they never bleed.

Treat their stories with respect. They earned their place here not just by failing, but by having the courage to tell us *how*.

HOW TO READ THESE BOOKS

The *Fuckup Almanac* series is designed so that each volume stands firmly on its own. You don't need to start from Volume I to gain value; every book offers a self-contained set of stories and lessons. Still, reading the entire collection reveals recurring themes, familiar blind spots, and a pattern that stretches far beyond any single field. The lessons are, as it turns out, *easily transferable*.

Read these books like an anthology of cautionary tales — one part storytelling, one part therapy, one part crash course in humility. You'll find humor where it fits, empathy where it's due, and the occasional reality check disguised as a joke.

How To Read This Series

When I first started this project, I didn't expect it to grow quite this much—but here we are. *Fuckup Almanac* turned into a four-volume journey through how complex systems fail, recover, and repeat the same mistakes on larger scales. Each volume widens the scope, moving from circuits and code to concrete and conscience. Together they form one long narrative about complexity built faster than understanding.

1. Volume I — Foundations of the Digital World

We start at the foundations of the modern world: the digital infrastructure that quietly rules our daily lives. From broken math and unreliable timekeeping to fragile data, false safety, and the illusion of resilience, this volume explores the machinery of the 21st century—and how it occasionally sets itself on fire.

2. Volume II — Stuff We Built on Top

Once we mastered computing, we stacked abstractions on top of it—algorithms, automation, and collaboration at scale. This volume looks at how those layers magnified small mistakes into planetary ones: data collection gone wrong, bias industrialized by machine learning, and open-source foundations held together by duct tape and goodwill.

3. Volume III — Hard Engineering & Physics

Here the digital meets the physical. Bridges, reactors, pipelines, aircraft—systems that don't just crash but collapse. We'll see what happens when the real world ignores our abstractions and gravity files a bug report. The same logic still applies; only the units have changed from bytes to tons.

4. Volume IV — The Human Factor & Hubris

Finally, we reach the root cause behind them all: people. This volume examines ego, shortcuts, and organizational decay—how pride, pressure, and denial turn good systems into bad legacies. It's where every technical failure finds its human reflection.

VOLUME I. INTRODUCTION

This first volume focuses on the digital bedrock beneath everything else. It explores the hidden mechanisms that make our world function — and occasionally malfunction — at scale. From clock drift to data decay, from buffer overflows to backup illusions, these stories show what happens when the smallest errors ripple through global systems.

Structure Of Volume I

- **Part I — Digital Foundations of Failure**
What happens when math, time, and logic betray us — the world of bits, clocks, and arithmetic gone rogue.

- **Part II — The Internet's House of Cards**
How our global network of duct-taped optimism keeps running until it doesn't.

- **Part III — The Fragility of Data**
Where information decays, gets misplaced, or quietly self-destructs.

- **Part IV — The Illusion of Safety**
Our attempts to protect what we built — and how those very defenses become new points of failure.

- **Part V — The Illusion of Resilience**
Why "don't worry, we have redundancy" is the most dangerous phrase in technology.

Parts I – III cover how machines **compute**, **communicate**, and **store** data — the three basic verbs of every digital system. Parts IV and V explore our attempts to make those verbs safer, and the myths that follow.

So buckle up. You're about to explore the digital underbelly of the modern world — from the smallest bit flip to the grandest systemic meltdown. Some stories will make you laugh, others will make you cringe, and a few might make you rethink the systems you rely on every day. But all of them have one goal: to make the invisible foundations of our digital civilization a little more visible — and a lot more human.

If nothing else, you'll finish this volume armed with enough cautionary tales to make your coworkers question every system update and every "it's just a minor change" ever uttered.

But before we start, there's one thing to clarify...

Production Note: In an ironic twist of fate, the DTP phase of this book hit a systemic failure: proprietary font licensing. Once it became clear that licensing them would cost roughly as much as a used car, I decided to practice what this book advocates: remove unnecessary complexity before it turns into a failure mode. The result is a set of open-source fonts you can read without funding anyone's yacht — unless, of course, this book turns out to be spectacularly successful.

CHAPTER 0:
THE ANATOMY OF A POST-MORTEM

This entire book is essentially a collection of autopsies, so it's only fair we start by defining the process itself: the post-mortem. Consider this the theory class before the field trip. Don't worry, we won't be dissecting every case in this book with a full formal process. Instead, we'll focus on the story itself and then jump straight to the conclusions and the lessons that flow from it. But it's worth understanding what a post-mortem is and why it matters.

Etymologically, the word *post-mortem* comes from Latin and literally means "after death." Originally, it referred to autopsies: examining a body after life had ended. In the corporate or engineering context, it's the same idea—except the "body" is a project, a system, or an organization that just suffered a collapse. In short: a post-mortem is what you do once something has already gone spectacularly wrong and you're left poking at the remains to figure out why.

At its core, a post-mortem is an analysis conducted after something has gone wrong. Different industries call it by different names—Root Cause Analysis, accident investigation, incident review—but the goals are consistent: understand what broke, and make sure it doesn't happen again. Whether it's an airplane crash, a power outage, or a factory mishap, the terminology varies, but the principles are universal: stop, rewind, analyze, and learn.

What a Post-Mortem Is Not

Just as important is what a post-mortem is *not*. It is not a witch-hunt, not a trial, and not a convenient way to find someone to fire or to scapegoat in a press release. Done correctly, a post-mortem focuses on situations, not individuals. It asks *how* and *why* something happened, not *who* to punish.

Sadly, many organizations get this wrong. They confuse the noble art of learning from failure with the cheap thrill of finding someone to blame. The result? A meeting where everyone glares at the intern until the crying begins, or a report that triumphantly concludes "the outage was caused by human error," as if that phrase magically explains everything. Spoiler: it doesn't. "Human error" is not a root cause—it's the starting point of the investigation, not the end.

That doesn't mean people never make mistakes. In fact, as you'll see throughout this book, human error shows up again and again. But a proper analysis goes beyond "she screwed up" or "he pushed the wrong button." Well-designed systems account for human fallibility: fatigue, distraction, lack of knowledge, even the occasional act of sabotage. The real question is: why did the system allow a single human slip to cascade into catastrophe, and how can we prevent that next time?

Why Blameless Matters

You might have noticed the buzzword *blameless post-mortem* floating around in tech culture. It isn't corporate fluff—it's a survival strategy. When people feel that admitting mistakes will get them fired, they clam up. Instead of honesty you get silence, defensiveness, or the classic: *"I have no idea what happened, maybe the database just... felt sad."* In a well-run investigation the truth comes out anyway, but the longer it takes the more expensive it gets. Worse, a blame-heavy culture kills the willingness to take reasonable risks, which in turn kills innovation.

A blameless approach doesn't mean we pretend nobody ever screwed up. It means the focus is on understanding the *systemic* factors that allowed a single misstep to snowball into a disaster. When people know they won't be burned at the stake for speaking up, they actually tell you what went wrong. That psychological safety builds trust, improves learning, and—believe it or not—helps teams feel like a team rather than a firing squad.

And when psychological safety is absent, the opposite happens. People hide problems, delay reporting, or even falsify data to protect themselves. Famous disasters—from space shuttles to nuclear plants—were made worse because engineers felt ignored, managers feared punishment, and truth got buried under politics. Blame culture doesn't just backfire; it actively breeds the very conditions for repeat failures.

Types Of Post-Mortems

Not all post-mortems are created equal. Broadly, you'll encounter three flavors:

- **Public incident reports:** polished documents released after high-profile disasters (think aviation accident reports or Post Mortems from big cloud providers). They're meant to reassure the public that the situation is under control, while also demonstrating transparency.

- **Internal post-mortems:** detailed analyses circulated only within an organization. These often contain more brutal honesty—because nobody wants to admit to the world that Bob forgot to plug in the backup generator.

- **Customer-facing reports:** somewhere in between, especially in B2B contexts. Clients affected by an outage expect an explanation, but you don't necessarily want to air *all* your dirty laundry. These reports tend to be diplomatic, balancing honesty with just enough PR polish to avoid panic.

Different audiences, different levels of candor, but the underlying purpose is the same: identify what broke and how to stop it from happening again.

It's also worth noting that some technical details simply *cannot* leave the organization—or at most get shared with a very limited group of "trusted" partners. And let's be real: in corporate speak, "trusted" is usually defined not by friendship but by legal agreements and NDA[1] clauses. In plain English: *"I could tell you, but then Legal would have to kill me."*

Likewise, customer-facing reports aren't always delivered out of goodwill. Sometimes they're required by contract, with deadlines and penalties attached. In those cases, transparency is less about virtue and more about compliance paperwork.

A Short History Of Post-Mortems

Post-mortems are not some Silicon Valley gimmick cooked up to justify free pizza after outages; the practice has deep roots across multiple domains. In medicine, 19th-century doctors gathered for what were bluntly called "morbidity and mortality" conferences. Imagine a room full of physicians saying, "Well, that didn't go as planned," and then arguing over scalpels. Brutal? Yes. Effective? Also yes.

The military and naval world had its own flavor. As far back as the 1700s, inquiries were convened after shipwrecks or failed campaigns. Early on, these often turned into ceremonial witch-hunts against commanders —"string him up and the sea will be calmer next time."

---

[1] **NDA (Non-Disclosure Agreement)** — the corporate equivalent of "What happens in Vegas, stays in Vegas"... until it takes down half the Internet and you still can't talk about it.

Over time, though, they evolved into more structured boards of inquiry, realizing that blaming one captain wasn't nearly as useful as fixing the systemic flaws that kept sinking ships.

Then came aviation, which gave us perhaps the most iconic tool of systematic learning from disaster: the flight data recorder, better known as the "black box." After World War II, this tiny device transformed crash investigations from speculative finger-pointing into evidence-based science. Suddenly, investigators could replay the last moments of a flight and know exactly what happened—data that would save countless lives. It also killed the classic defense of "trust me, the pilot sneezed."

Manufacturing, meanwhile, turned failure into a lifestyle choice. The rise of quality movements in the 20th century—Deming's principles, Six Sigma, and endless clipboards—embedded the idea that every defect was a chance to tighten the system. Factories learned to love their post-mortems almost as much as their stopwatches.

And finally, the tech industry picked up the baton. Inspired by aviation and manufacturing, large internet companies like Google, Amazon, and Microsoft began formalizing incident reviews in the late 20th and early 21st centuries. With entire slices of the internet depending on their uptime, the cost of brushing off an outage was too high. Today, even startups dabble in post-mortems—though let's be honest, some of those read more like creative writing exercises than actual analysis.

Across all these fields, the lesson repeats: writing things down and poking at the problem afterward beats shrugging and hoping it won't happen again. Or, put another way: denial may be comforting, but it doesn't keep planes in the air or servers online.

The Black Box (And Its Cousins)

Since we've already mentioned aviation's black box, it deserves its own spotlight. Despite the name, a "black box" is not black at all—it's usually painted in a vivid, almost neon orange. The reason is simple: crash sites are chaotic, and investigators need every advantage to locate the recorders quickly. Orange stands out against debris, smoke, and even snow. The box itself is engineered to survive extremes—fire, salt water, crushing impacts—because if it fails, the entire investigation fails.

So why call it a *black* box? The term has two origins. One is colloquial: engineers often use "black box" to describe any system where you can observe inputs and outputs without knowing the internal details. The other comes from accident investigation jargon, where "black" implied secrecy or inaccessibility. Ironically, in modern aviation, the point of the box is the opposite: to spill its secrets.

That leads to a broader metaphor that also shows up in analysis:

- **Black-box analysis:** you only look at inputs and outputs, without knowing (or caring) what's inside. Useful when internals are unknown or too complex.

- **White-box analysis:** you know every detail of the system and trace causes through full transparency.

- **Grey-box analysis:** the messy middle ground, where you have partial knowledge and mix inference with facts.

Real-world post-mortems almost always end up in the grey zone. Pure black-box approaches risk oversimplification ("the server was slow"), while pure white-box analysis is often impractical (no team has infinite time and resources). The art lies in balancing the two—digging deep enough to find useful lessons without disappearing down every rabbit hole.

And speaking of digging ahead: black boxes are what help us understand the past, but some teams try to anticipate the future. Enter the pre-mortem.

Pre-Mortems

As a quirky cousin to the post-mortem, some organizations experiment with what's called a *pre-mortem*. Instead of waiting for disaster to strike, a team imagines the project has already failed spectacularly, then brainstorms all the possible reasons why. It's like playing "spot the doom" in advance.

This approach isn't free—designing safeguards for every nightmare scenario is costly. But in high-stakes environments (NASA, nuclear power, space exploration), it's been worth the effort. The technique gained traction in the mid-20th century, popularized by NASA, and it's often tied to Murphy's Law[2]: *anything that can go wrong, will go wrong*. A pre-mortem simply asks, "Okay, *how* exactly will it go wrong, and what can we do now to stop it?"

---

[2] **Murphy's Law**

Credit (or blame) goes to **Edward A. Murphy Jr.**, an Air Force engineer working on rocket sled tests in 1949. When a technician wired all the sensors backward, Murphy allegedly muttered the immortal line: *"If there's a way to do it wrong, he'll find it."*

The phrase spread through test pilot circles faster than jet fuel fumes and eventually evolved into the universal constant of engineering despair:

"Anything that can go wrong, will go wrong — and probably right before the weekend."

Murphy wasn't being cynical — he was just the first to publish peer-reviewed evidence that the universe hates deadlines.

Root Cause Analysis

To get there, investigators use different tools. One of the simplest and surprisingly effective is called the "5 Whys." The idea is straightforward: keep asking "why" until you reach the real root cause. Rarely is the first answer the correct one. You have to dig. It's essentially the grown-up version of that childhood game where a kid bombards you with an endless chain of "but why?" questions—except now it's socially acceptable in the workplace, and occasionally saves billions of dollars.

Take a mundane example: you were late to a meeting.

- Why? Because you were stuck in traffic.

- Why were you stuck in traffic? Because you left home late and hit rush hour.

- Why did you leave home late? Because you overslept.

- Why did you oversleep? Because you went to bed too late.

- Why did you go to bed too late? Because you were binge-watching Netflix.

Suddenly, the problem isn't "traffic"—it's your questionable self-control in front of a glowing screen. That's the value of digging deeper: uncovering the underlying causes that aren't obvious at first glance.

Of course, the "five" in "5 Whys" is just a convention. Sometimes you get to the root cause in three questions; sometimes it takes seven. The point isn't to hit a magic number but to keep digging until you actually understand what happened.

Crucially, this isn't an automatic or mechanical exercise. You *could* keep asking forever—"Why did you binge-watch Netflix?" "Because the show was too good." "Why was it too good?" "Because Netflix invested in strong writing and acting." At some point you're no longer uncovering useful causes, you're just blaming television executives. The art lies in recognizing when you've hit the layer that actually gives you an actionable lesson, not when you've milked the word "why" dry.

Another frequent failure mode is stopping too soon or, conversely, padding out the answers just to reach the magic five. I've seen reports where authors bent over backwards to invent sub-points just to hit exactly five, and others where they triumphantly stopped at the fifth "why"... precisely when things were finally getting interesting. That's process theater, not investigation.

And keep in mind: the 5 Whys are just one tool in the kit. The moment you forget the actual goal—finding real causes—you risk turning it into yet another cargo cult ritual[3], where form trumps substance and the box-checking matters more than the learning.

A More Realistic Example

Take aviation. Ever wondered why airplane windows are round? In the 1930s, many aircraft—like the Dewoitine D.332, D.333, or D.338—had rectangular windows, just like in your living room. It looked elegant... until the windows started cracking.

Back then, flying was mostly low-altitude and cabins weren't fully pressurized, so a cracked window was treated as a maintenance issue rather than a looming disaster. The attitude was basically: *no one died, just call the*

---

[3] **Cargo cult ritual** — a process faithfully copied from smarter people without grasping why it works, producing the same ceremonies, none of the miracles.

More details: https://en.wikipedia.org/wiki/Cargo_cult

glazier and move on. Warnings existed, but without fatalities they didn't trigger systemic investigation.

Fast forward to the jet age after World War II. The de Havilland Comet 1, the world's first commercial jet airliner, soared at 12 km where pressurization was non-negotiable. It sported large, nearly square windows with only gently rounded corners—a design that looked elegant but proved fatal. Then, catastrophic failures struck—crashes like BOAC Flight 781 and South African Airways Flight 201, where cabin decompression tore fuselages apart. Cracks weren't just drafts; they were death sentences.

Investigators eventually performed pressurized-water tank tests at Farnborough, which showed the real culprit: sharp corners in rectangular windows (and antenna mounts) became stress concentrators, turning metal fatigue into a countdown clock. Every flight cycle weakened the structure until, one day, the plane literally tore itself apart midair.

The fix was simple but revolutionary: remove the corners. Round the windows. That design change, along with stronger fuselage standards, became the template for modern aviation safety.

So next time you're staring out of an oval window, remember it's not just a design choice—it's a monument to the power of post-mortem thinking, and a reminder that ignoring early warnings because "nobody died" can be the most dangerous error of all.

Common Pitfalls

Before we move on, it's worth noting the mistakes that crop up again and again:

- Stopping at "human error" and calling it a day.

- Writing the report just to satisfy compliance, with zero intent to change anything.

- Turning the process into a blame-fest rather than a learning exercise.

- Skipping documentation entirely because "we're too busy putting out fires."

If you recognize these patterns in your workplace, congratulations: you've already identified your next failure waiting to happen.

Another critical aspect often overlooked: **action items.** A well-run post-mortem doesn't end with a tidy PDF or Confluence page. It ends with a concrete plan of improvements—technical, organizational, procedural—that someone is actually responsible for carrying out. And yes, those improvements should be tracked, prioritized, and reviewed.

Balancing Rigor And Reality

Now, let's be clear: not every cut deserves stitches. Just as a doctor won't run a full autopsy on a paper cut, an organization doesn't need to launch a 30-person task force because the office printer jammed. Some incidents are worth deep dives; others deserve only a note in the logbook. The trick lies in knowing the difference.

Similar logic applies to action items. Do all of them need to be implemented? Of course not. They compete with new features, customer demands, and limited resources.

Sometimes business reality wins and the fix gets postponed—or dropped. That can be a reasonable decision, but it must be made consciously and justified properly.

Pretending the risk no longer exists just because the document is filed is the worst possible outcome. If your

strategy is basically "clench fists, cross fingers, and hope,"
you don't need a post-mortem. You need a prayer circle.

This "chapter zero" exists to clarify what I mean when I
call this book one giant post-mortem — and, let's be
honest, to justify the educational value of writing
hundreds of pages of disaster gossip. In the chapters
ahead, we'll dissect failures big and small, spectacular and
mundane. The point isn't to gawk at wreckage, but to
understand it — and to make sure the same mistakes don't
get repeated.

Think of this book as a highlight reel of failure.
Readable, digestible, and just ironic enough to make you
smirk while learning something that might save you one
day.

And to be clear: this isn't a full-scale forensic exercise.
Complete post-mortems of major failures often aren't
even possible — most internal details never see daylight,
especially the juiciest ones that stay locked behind NDAs
and corporate firewalls. Even if they did, the result would
be a tome so long and dry that nobody (including me)
would finish it. The goal here is to give you a mental
toolkit, not a classified dossier. As you read the coming
chapters, try applying what you've learned in this one:
imagine what might have been happening beneath the
surface, where the processes, incentives, or sheer human
chaos aligned just right to make things go wrong.

Or, if you'd rather, grab some popcorn and enjoy the
show.

I. DIGITAL FOUNDATIONS OF FAILURE

Welcome to the bedrock of modern chaos: the digital layer. Before we get to collapsing bridges, exploding factories, or corporate scandals, we need to start with the zeros and ones. Because let's face it: without software, most of today's spectacular disasters wouldn't even get off the ground. Sometimes quite literally—rockets have a way of following whatever bad math you feed them.

This part is about the kinds of failures that live entirely in silicon and logic: bugs, time bombs, runaway growth, and the delightful surprises that emerge when the digital world's abstract perfection collides with the messiness of reality. These are the failures born not of rust or concrete fatigue, but of misplaced semicolons, arithmetic quirks, and the universal law that software will always do exactly what you told it to do—whether or not that was remotely sensible.

Or, to put it in office terms: remember the manager yelling "Do what I mean, not what I say"? Computers don't play that game. They'll do exactly what you said, with zero sympathy for what you meant.

We'll start with numbers that betray their masters: floating-point divisions gone wrong, arithmetic errors that cost millions, and the infamous rocket that veered off-course thanks to a single missing hyphen. Then we'll turn to our collective attempts at measuring time—a supposedly basic concept that has confused everyone from medieval calendar reformers to modern operating systems. And finally, we'll look at scale: how exponential growth makes a mockery of even the most carefully designed systems[4], whether it's a worm spreading across the internet or a telecom network collapsing under its own genius design.

Why begin here? Because these failures are deceptively pure. Strip away the politics, the concrete, and the corporate mismanagement, and you're left with logic itself betraying us. They remind us that human fallibility doesn't only live in boardrooms or construction sites—it's also baked into algorithms, timestamps, and protocols that we naïvely assume are flawless. And when the foundations are shaky, everything built on top of them is already halfway to the blooper reel.

Think of this part as a guided tour of the operating system of failure. It's where the rules of digital fragility are laid bare. By the end, you'll understand why "computer error" can mean anything from a typo in code to a multi-million dollar hardware bug, why exponential curves should terrify you more than any horror movie, and why modeling time is a lot less straightforward than your wall calendar suggests.

So here we go—the original sin of the digital world: perfect logic in the hands of imperfect humans. A match made in hell, now playing on every screen.

---

[4] **System** – this word will be conjugated through every possible case throughout the entire series, so let's clarify it (not to be confused with define it, which would imply false precision). A system is any collection of components that cooperate toward some purpose—you can think of it like a box where you throw stuff in and get stuff out, though what comes out may bear zero resemblance to what went in. The concept is intentionally broad enough to encompass everything from a coffee machine, through a server, to the internet, or the entire European power grid. Engineers love it because it sounds significantly more dignified than "contraption" or "that whole mess over there."

And yes, you guessed it: systems are composed of subsystems, which are composed of sub-subsystems, turtles all the way down until you hit something that technically counts as atomic but probably isn't.

CHAPTER 1:
WHEN NUMBERS LIE

Numbers are supposed to be the one thing we can trust. Politicians spin, managers obfuscate, but math? Math is supposed to be solid. Unfortunately, once you ask computers to handle numbers, things get... wobbly. The very tools we designed to enforce precision turn out to have blind spots, quirks, and the occasional catastrophic meltdown.

This chapter is about the moments when numbers quietly betray us—and then laugh as everything built on top of them collapses. Sometimes it's the universe reminding us that physics isn't as clean as we'd like. Sometimes it's the computer reminding us that memory isn't infinite. Sometimes it's just a tiny flaw that sneaks past all the clever people in lab coats. And occasionally, the absurdity happens so close to home that you end up staring at your own code wondering if arithmetic itself is gaslighting you.

What ties these stories together is a simple, unsettling truth: numbers may look perfect on paper, but once they hit the real world of sensors, processors, and half-baked assumptions, they become tricksters. They can mislead, overflow, distort, or quietly shave off just enough precision to ruin your day.

This is where the comedy of errors begins—before politics, before concrete, before management decisions. When numbers lie, everything else is already compromised.

Mariner 1
The Most Expensive Missing Line In History

Date: July 22, 1962

Impact: NASA's first Venus probe was destroyed 293 seconds after launch, ending in a fiery failure that cost $18.5 million in 1962 (≈ $197 million in 2025, adjusted for inflation).

Root Cause: A missing over-bar symbol in the guidance equation caused the autopilot to misread noisy data as real course deviations, steering the rocket off track.

It was the height of the Space Race. On July 22, 1962, NASA launched Mariner 1, its first probe bound for Venus. A shining symbol of technological ambition, designed to prove that America could match the Soviet Union beyond Earth's orbit. The plan was simple: launch, slingshot, and make history. Except the rocket never got past our own atmosphere. Less than five minutes after liftoff, it veered so far off course that the range safety officer had no choice but to press the button. Boom. Mission over.

So what went wrong? Not sabotage, not faulty fuel, not even Soviet interference. Just... math. Or rather, the lack of one tiny symbol in it. In the shorthand version, Mariner 1 wasn't destroyed by flames or by hostile powers, but by the absence of a line on a page.

The real world is messy. Sensors don't measure things perfectly — they pick up noise, glitches, random spikes. Engineers deal with this by smoothing the data, averaging it out so the guidance system doesn't panic every time a signal burps. It's the difference between noticing the overall curve of a road versus slamming the wheel every time a pebble jiggles your tires. The flight equations for Mariner 1 included exactly such a smoothing step. At least, they were supposed to.

And here comes the technical jargon: the missing symbol was an over-bar on $\dot{R}$ — the time derivative of radius vector. Sounds intimidating, right? Translated from math-phys gibberish into human: that's just velocity.

This story is often told as a "missing hyphen," but that's a convenient simplification. It wasn't a dash in the middle of text, it was a small line above a letter — a detail that looks similar but means something very different.

The bar meant: apply smoothing to this value, don't trust it raw. Without that tiny decoration, the software basically thought every random twitch in the telemetry was a crisis. One micro-glitch? Correct it. Another half a second later? Correct it the other way. Engineers call it "overreacting to noise." Ordinary people call it "flailing."

Imagine you're driving on a highway, and instead of steering smoothly, your car violently jerks the wheel every time the GPS momentarily loses signal. One blip to the left? Full correction. A second later, a blip to the right? Full correction the other way. That's what Mariner 1 looked like in flight: less like a precision spacecraft and more like a drunk skier weaving down a slope, burning fuel to chase ghosts.

The mistake wasn't mathematical — it was clerical. A handwritten formula from the physics team lost a tiny overbar when transcribed into code. That single omission changed the meaning of the equation and made the rocket overreact to minor fluctuations. In other words: handwriting and rocket guidance don't mix well.

By T+293 seconds, the situation was irrecoverable. The range safety officer pressed the destruct switch. Better to sacrifice the probe than risk it crashing into populated areas. Eighteen and a half million dollars, gone in less time than it takes to boil pasta.

Arthur C. Clarke later quipped that Mariner 1 was "destroyed by a hyphen" — calling it the most expensive hyphen in history. In truth it wasn't a hyphen at all but a missing over-bar. But honestly, "hyphen" makes for a better headline when you're explaining to Congress why a mission to Venus turned into confetti over the Atlantic.

In the end, Mariner 1 didn't fail because it malfunctioned. It failed because it worked too well. It took a flawed equation and executed it with suicidal precision, proving that computers are the ultimate bureaucrats: they will enforce the rules exactly as written, even if it means steering a multimillion-dollar rocket straight into the Atlantic. It was the first expensive lesson in digital malicious compliance: the machine will always do what you say, never what you mean.

LESSON LEARNED

- Precision in specification isn't optional; one missing symbol can kill a mission.
- Handwritten notes and sloppy transcription are a dangerous combo.
- Noise is real. If you don't smooth your data, your rocket might smooth itself... into the ocean.
- Small errors don't stay small at rocket speed — they compound into fireballs.

If you ever doubt the power of punctuation, remember: it once cost NASA a rocket.

Ariane 5
When A 16-Bit Integer Destroyed A $370M Rocket

Date: June 4, 1996

Impact: Ariane 5 exploded 37 seconds after launch, destroying four satellites and dealing a $370 million loss in 1996 (≈ $785 million in 2025, adjusted for inflation).

Root Cause: A 64-bit floating-point value was forced into a 16-bit integer slot from Ariane 4's reused code, triggering overflow in both redundant Inertial Reference Systems.

The Ariane 5 was Europe's pride: a brand-new heavy-lift launch vehicle, years in the making, meant to show off ESA's[5] engineering might. After all the tests, all the budgets, and all the political promises, the rocket rolled out to the pad carrying four expensive satellites. Then, 37 seconds into flight, it turned into the world's most costly fireworks display.

The culprit? A conversion. Specifically, a 64-bit floating-point number that was forced into a 16-bit integer box — a container far too small and meant for something entirely different.

Here's how it happened. Engineers reused flight control code from Ariane 4, the previous generation rocket. That software had been reliable for years, so reusing it seemed like a smart, low-risk choice. The problem: Ariane 5 accelerated much faster and reached higher horizontal

---

[5] **ESA — European Space Agency.** Europe's answer to NASA, but with more languages and fewer launchpads. Founded in 1975 to pool together the continent's scientific ambitions (and budgets), ESA oversees programs like Ariane, Rosetta, and Gaia. It's living proof that international cooperation works — eventually — after half a dozen translations, a few dozen committee meetings, and at least one polite argument over who gets their flag on the rocket.

velocities than its predecessor. Numbers that comfortably fit into Ariane 4's calculations now became much larger.

Before that fateful launch, Ariane 5 had gone through years of simulations and validation campaigns, including the so-called "battleship" tests in 1992–1993. These verified the rocket's mechanical and control systems under ground-based conditions, but the simulated trajectories still mirrored Ariane 4's gentler ascent profile. The steeper, faster trajectory of Ariane 5 introduced entirely new dynamic ranges that the reused code had never encountered. In short, the system was tested—just not for the world it was actually going to fly through.

And one subsystem—the Inertial Reference System (SRI[6])—tried to stuff those large floating-point values into a tiny integer slot that wasn't meant to store them at all.

The box wasn't just too small; it was meant to hold something entirely different. Imagine trying to pour 10 kilograms of sand into a net designed for two kilograms of potatoes. Even if you somehow glue the grains together so they don't slip through the holes, the bag will still burst long before it fits.

How does this relate to computers?

Computers don't use decimal numbers like we do. They speak binary: strings of 0s and 1s. A "bit" is just one of those digits, but how those bits are interpreted is another story. That's called encoding. Think of it like language.

In Polish, the word "ja" means "I." In German, "ja" means "yes." Same letters, totally different ideas. Likewise, the German word "dick" means "thick" or "fat,"

---

[6] Most documentation on Ariane 5 sticks to the French acronym **SRI (Système de Référence Inertielle).** The English equivalent, **IRS**, would be technically correct but politically unwise. No aerospace engineer wants their inertial guidance system associated with the U.S. tax office — rocket failures are stressful enough without invoking *that* kind of terror.

but say it to an English speaker and you'll get a very different reaction.

Same symbols, wildly different meanings — and computers aren't any better at guessing context than tourists with phrasebooks.

That's exactly what happened in Ariane's code. The system knew how to represent floating-point numbers (real values with fractions) and integers (whole numbers), but the conversion between them was handled carelessly. For small values, the system could still manage. It had dedicated logic for this conversion, roughly speaking storing a number like 12.5 as 125 and 3.14 as 314, keeping a side note on whether to divide the value by 10 or 100 when decoding it again. In other words, it could "clump the sand together" just fine for small piles.

But this dynamic handling had its limits. Once the encoded value grew beyond what a 16-bit box could handle, it no longer fit at all. The software tried to squeeze that oversized, pre-compressed real number into a tiny integer slot—a completely different encoding. The result wasn't just a rounding error; it was unreadable garbage.

The SRI, which handled the rocket's sense of position and movement, couldn't make sense of the corrupted data and crashed. Ironically, the overflow check actually existed — but only for the vertical velocity. Engineers had explicitly protected that component from conversion errors, while the horizontal velocity, the one that turned out to be problematic, was left unguarded. It's hard to find a better illustration of Murphy's Law than a system that defends against gravity but not momentum. The main computer switched to the backup SRI, but in a perfect demonstration of redundant design gone wrong, that one had the exact same flaw. Duplicating a mistake twice doesn't make it safer—it just makes the explosion symmetrical. (We'll revisit this theme in Part V, when we dive into the myth of "redundancy equals safety.")

Within seconds, both systems failed, and the rocket began receiving nonsense data. To its computer brain, it looked as if the rocket was tumbling out of control. The automatic safety system triggered self-destruct.

At 37 seconds after launch, four satellites and $370 million in European ambition disappeared in a single fireball over French Guiana.

LESSON LEARNED

- Reused code is not free: past reliability doesn't guarantee future safety. Context matters.
- Redundancy must mean diversity: two identical systems fail identically.
- Validation must cover new operational ranges: old assumptions die hardest.
- Conversions between number types are not trivial: understand how data is encoded and what happens when it crosses boundaries.
- In software as in rockets, you need to fully understand the limits of the data you work with, and the consequences when those limits are crossed.

All that thrust, precision, and math—undone by a number that didn't fit in the box.

From My Own Burn File
The Day `floor(3+5)` Turned Into 7

Date: Around 2007

Impact: Confused developer, baffled invoices, no actual rocket explosions (thankfully).

Root Cause: Binary representation of 8.0 stored as 7.99999999998; the `floor()` operation rounded down to 7 — a tiny numerical error with potentially massive implications.

Back in 2007, I was writing a billing system for a company. The details of the project don't matter, but one moment from that experience is burned into my brain. I stared at a result that seemed absurd: `floor(3.0+5.0) = 7`.

On the surface, this should be impossible. The math is clear: 3 + 5 = 8, and the floor of 8 is 8. Yet here I was, debugging[7] a program that insisted otherwise.

For the uninitiated: `floor(x)` is a mathematical function that returns the greatest integer less than or equal to x. In plain terms: `floor(2)= 2`, `floor(3.5)= 3`. It's simple. Elegant. Predictable. Until it isn't.

It took me a while to understand what was going on. The culprit wasn't my arithmetic skills but the way computers handle real numbers — the infamous floating point. Under the hood, real numbers aren't stored exactly; they're

---

[7] The term **debugging** will appear many times in this book. It simply means the process of analyzing a program to locate and fix an error (a "bug").

The word itself comes from a very literal incident: an actual moth that got fried on the lamp of one of the first computers in history (Harvard Mark II, 1947), shorting a circuit and disrupting signal flow. Engineers removed it, logged it in their notes as *"First actual case of bug being found,"* and a metaphor was born.

approximated, following a standard called IEEE754. I don't recommend reading it unless you need a cure for insomnia.

Here's the key: computers are great at handling discrete values — integers, counts, on/off states. But continuous values? That's where the trouble begins. Every real number you feed a program gets squeezed into a finite binary representation. Most of the time it's "close enough." But occasionally, the cracks show. My innocent-looking 8.0 was actually more like 7.99999999998. And when you take the floor of that, you get 7. Perfectly correct from the computer's perspective, completely maddening from mine.

Now, before you rush to open your browser console to fact-check me: yes, if you type `floor(3.0 + 5.0)` today, you'll get 8. But in my case, those numbers weren't fresh literals typed by a human — they were the battered survivors of a long chain of earlier calculations. Fractions added, multiplied, rounded, and nudged until they drifted just enough to break reality. To the human eye, the variables looked like clean, innocent 3.0 and 5.0. Deep in floating-point memory, however, one of them was more like 2.99999999999. And `floor()` is merciless: it doesn't round, it simply chops. So my neat, expected 8 quietly became a 7.

This wasn't a disaster — no satellites were lost, no skyscrapers collapsed — but it was a sharp reminder. Floating point math is an approximation game. Forget that, and you're bound to get burned. That's why programmers often compare values with a margin of tolerance (are these numbers "close enough"?) rather than strict equality. Some languages even bake that behavior in, sparing developers from nasty surprises.

> **LESSON LEARNED**
>
> - Always understand the data format you're working with — even the boring parts.
> - "Natural" operations may not behave the way you expect when computers are involved.
> - Computers are obedient, not wise. They'll happily repeat design decisions made decades ago, whether or not they make sense in your use case.
> - If you're working with floating point, assume approximation. Absolute truth is not on the menu.

On the bright side, at least I'm not the only one who's been betrayed by floating-point math — as we'll see in the next story...

Intel Pentium FDIV Bug
When Your Cpu Couldn't Do Math

Date: 1994

Impact: Shaken trust in Intel's "gold standard" CPUs, recalls worth $475 million in 1994 ($\approx$ $1.04 billion in 2025, adjusted for inflation)

Root Cause: Five missing entries in the processor's lookup table for floating-point division (FDIV), causing rare but measurable errors and undermining confidence in hardware reliability.

In 1994, eagle-eyed users began noticing something strange: their brand-new Intel Pentium processors occasionally gave the wrong answers when dividing floating-point numbers. Not wild errors, but subtle ones —

like 1 ÷ 824633702441.0 returning something just a little off. A tiny discrepancy, but enough to undermine confidence in the very thing computers were supposed to guarantee: reliable math.

The culprit was the FDIV instruction, short for "floating-point division." You see, computers are excellent at addition, subtraction, and multiplication — those they can do almost on virtual fingers. But division? That's slower and more complicated. Think of it as the CPU sitting down with a pencil to do long division on a very imaginary sheet of paper.

To speed things up, Intel's engineers added a kind of mathematical cheat sheet — a lookup table of precomputed partial results. It wasn't a full list of answers, just about a thousand reference points to guide the long-division process. Think of it as a shortcut: faster than working everything out by hand, but dependent on having every key value in place.

The problem? Imagine a multiplication chart where 6×7 has been erased, so someone glances over, sees 6×6=36, and calls it good enough. That's roughly what the Pentium did — except its table was a thousand entries deep, and five of them were missing. The odds of hitting those gaps were tiny, but not zero, and when it happened, the chip confidently produced the wrong answer. To a casual user crunching spreadsheets, the chance of hitting the bug was minuscule. To anyone doing scientific or financial computing, the idea that their CPU couldn't divide correctly was terrifying.

At first, Intel brushed it off. The company called it a "statistically insignificant error," estimating that most users would only encounter the problem once every 27,000 years of typical computing. That might have been technically true, but it was a catastrophically bad sales pitch. Because when you sell chips whose *entire job* is math, the last thing customers want to hear is: "don't worry, it's only wrong sometimes."

The issue became public after Professor Thomas Nicely, a mathematician at Lynchburg College, published his findings. He had been running computations involving prime numbers when he noticed recurring inaccuracies. Instead of staying quiet, Nicely went public — and the story spread quickly. Scientists, financial analysts, and journalists amplified the case. What started as an obscure academic observation snowballed into a PR nightmare.

Intel initially offered replacements only to users who could *prove* they needed high precision, a move that enraged customers further. The public backlash grew until Intel was forced to backtrack and offer free replacements to anyone affected. The recall ultimately cost around $475 million — and more importantly, it cracked Intel's aura of infallibility. If the most trusted name in CPUs could get division wrong, what else might be hiding under the hood?

LESSON LEARNED

- Hardware bugs are just as real (and just as costly) as software bugs.
- Downplaying a flaw as "statistically insignificant" is PR suicide when accuracy is the product's entire promise.
- Trust, once shaken, is expensive to rebuild.
- Always assume some professor with a calculator and too much free time will check your work.

Joke of the era:
Q: What's 2 + 2?
A: 3.999999998 — according to Intel.

Vancouver Stock Exchange
The Index That Ate Itself

Date: January 1982 – November 1983

Impact: The exchange's main index fell nearly 50%, misleading investors and shaking confidence until a sudden overnight correction.

Root Cause: A persistent downward bias from truncating rather than rounding, compounding over thousands of recalculations to halve the index.

In January 1982, the Vancouver Stock Exchange launched what it proudly called a *modern* index to track its resource-heavy market. The starting point: `1000.000`. The mission: precision. The result: unintentional slow-motion suicide by arithmetic. After every single trade, the index recalculated and lopped off anything beyond the third decimal place. Not rounded — *lopped off*. That's not precision; that's accounting with a machete.

Rounding adjusts numbers with some sense of fairness. Truncation, its sociopathic cousin, behaves like an accountant with scissors or a banker who skims fractions of a cent and calls it "operational efficiency." `520.1267` should become `520.127`, but truncation insists it's `520.126`, and it does this with every trade, every day, forever. Think of it as financial sandpaper — imperceptible on one pass, catastrophic after a few thousand. After 22 months of this numerical manslaughter, the index had fallen to `524.811`, while the real market was partying above 1000.

On November 25, 1983, engineers finally noticed that gravity seemed unusually aggressive in Vancouver. The market resurrected itself over the weekend faster than most startups fix their login pages, as teams rebuilt the data from scratch. By Monday, the index "miraculously" jumped to `1098.892`. Investors rejoiced. Journalists gasped. Somewhere, a programmer quietly learned the difference between `truncate()` and `round()`. It was the first recorded case of a stock market performing an exorcism.

This wasn't the last time numbers plotted against their human overlords. In finance, even the tiniest math bug can outlive CEOs. This drove modern finance to demand precision of at least nine decimal places — but fifteen or seventeen is common — especially in high-frequency trading, where even tiny miscalculations can implode economies one decimal at a time.

If all this sounds familiar, you've probably seen *Office Space* (1999). Its plot? A programmer decides to steal fractions of cents from transactions — the same kind of rounding residue that doomed the Vancouver index. Unfortunately, he misplaces a decimal and starts robbing the company blind. Fictional justice, real-world math lesson: never underestimate a tiny number with bad intentions.

LESSON LEARNED

- Truncation isn't rounding — it's slow financial self- harm with extra decimals.
- Small numerical errors can quietly tank a market faster than a scandal.

> - Always document and test rounding behavior — before your index needs a resurrection.
> - Precision isn't pedantry; it's the firewall between confidence and chaos.

If you ever feel insignificant, remember: so did each of those decimals—until they took down an entire stock exchange.

CHAPTER 2:
TIME IS BROKEN

Time might just be the worst bug humanity inherited from the Solar System. Handling it in computing sounds straightforward, but in practice it's one of the messiest problems you can run into. Calendars, time zones, leap years, leap seconds — each layer adds a new dimension of confusion. To show just how bizarre this gets, let's start with a little background.

Sit back and get ready for a rollercoaster. I apologize in advance for the flood of dates and details — don't worry, there won't be a test. The goal is just to show the scale of the mess we're dealing with.

 **Not-So-Tech Explainer:**
Time is Broken

Let's start with a deceptively simple question: how long does it take Earth to orbit the Sun?

Most people will say: 365 days. The pedants upgrade it to 365.25, hence leap years. Both are wrong. The real number is 365.24219 days[8]. That's 365 days, 5 hours, 48 minutes, and 45.22 seconds. Those missing 11 minutes? They stack up. Think of them as cosmic compound interest, except instead of money you get calendar chaos.

---

[8] I'll admit this one: in the first draft of this manuscript I mixed up the *sidereal year* (365.256363004 days) with the *tropical year* (365.24219 days), the one the Gregorian calendar is actually based on. That's a 20-minute annual difference. I'll spare you the explanation of *why* the universe thought this was a good idea, but it serves as a perfect illustration of just how profoundly messed up "time" really is.

Cue the leap year circus. The rule isn't just "every 4 years add a day." No, it's: every year divisible by 4 is a leap year... unless it's divisible by 100... unless it's also divisible by 400. That's why 2000 was a leap year, 1900 wasn't, and 2100 won't be. The system looks like it was designed by a medieval lawyer billing by the clause.

But wait, we're just getting warmed up. Add time zones: neat one-hour offsets? Ha. India is +5:30. Nepal is +5:45. And China? A country that geographically spans four time zones but insists on using Beijing Time everywhere. In the far west, the sun can rise at 10 AM. Great if you're a vampire, less so if you want breakfast.

History didn't help. Julius Caesar introduced the Julian calendar in 45 BCE with a leap year every 4 years. Sounds tidy, but his math was slightly off. Fast forward to 1542 and spring equinox had drifted to March 11 instead of March 21. Enter Pope Gregory XIII with the Gregorian reform. To fix the drift, he straight-up deleted ten days in October 1582. October 4 was followed immediately by October 15. Imagine trying to explain that to HR when your timesheet shows you worked negative five days.

Naturally, not everyone signed up right away. Protestants held out until 1752. Russia only switched in 1918—so yes, the "October Revolution" actually happened in November. Greece dragged its feet until 1923, when it had to delete 13 days in one go. And you thought your daylight savings shift was rough.

Meanwhile, Earth itself refused to cooperate. Our planet doesn't spin like a Swiss clock; it wobbles and slows down thanks to the Moon's gravity and other cosmic bullies. Enter the leap second. Every few years, the International Time Lords (okay, officially the International Earth Rotation Service) insert an extra second: after 23:59:59 comes 23:59:60. The last one was December 31, 2016. The next might land June 30, 2026. Surprise! Nothing says "happy new year" like debugging a second that technically doesn't exist.

The fun part? In 2022, the General Conference on Weights and Measures decided to eliminate leap seconds by 2035. Translation: we'll just let time drift and hope future generations deal with it. That's not science, that's cosmic procrastination.

Now, why should you care? Because in the past, none of this mattered. In the 18th century, two towns could disagree by half an hour and life rolled on. Today? A 30-second misalignment can tank a financial trade, ground planes, or scramble GPS. It's hard to run a global digital empire when your clocks think it's 1901.

Oh, and all this mess only applies to Earth. The moment we go interplanetary, it gets even dumber. NASA already maintains conversion tools between Earth time and Mars time, because "Tuesday at 3 PM" means something very different when the day is 24 hours and 39 minutes long.

BOTTOM LINE

If you ever feel the urge to write your own time-handling code from scratch—don't. Sit quietly until it passes.

Time is already a cosmic prank. No need to add your bugs to the universe's collection.

Y2K Bug
When Two Digits Weren't Enough

Back when computerization was still in diapers, standards were few and far between. One common way of storing dates was simply as text. And because memory was more limited than the attention span of a modern TikTok scroller, saving space was essential. A classic shortcut: storing years with just two digits (e.g., 97 instead of 1997). In the 1980s or even early 1990s, nobody worried about the day when "19" would flip into "20."

As the 1990s drew to a close, panic set in: on January 1, 2000, computers might go haywire. Nobody knew exactly what would happen or how widespread the problem was, but the fear was universal. Companies worldwide poured billions into patching their systems ahead of the so-called Judgment Day.

January 1, 2000, arrived — and... nothing exploded. Planes didn't fall from the sky. Power plants didn't shut down. The only casualties were mathematicians wincing as TV anchors declared the start of the third millennium. Spoiler: the year 2000 was the *last* year of the second millennium; 2001 started the third — but that's trivia for pedants (yes, I count myself among those pedants).

The hidden problem was that many companies hadn't really "fixed" the bug — they had applied a trick called *windowing*. This meant: if the year was 00–09 (or sometimes 00–19), treat it as 2000-something. That bought time to implement real solutions... in theory. In practice, some organizations happily moved on to shinier projects and new features.

And then January 1, 2010, rolled around. Cue the first aftershocks.

2010 Glitches (Y2K10)

- **Symantec/Norton Endpoint Protection:** Their antivirus license checks used a two-digit year window (1930–2029). In 2010, "10" overflowed their logic, breaking license validation and real-time protection until a hotfix shipped.

- **SpamAssassin Email Filter:** One open-source spam filter had a rule to flag suspicious dates. Unfortunately, it treated 2010 as invalid, so legitimate emails dated that year ended up in junk folders until the rule was fixed.

- **Payroll Systems:** Older HR and payroll platforms (many running on 1980s mainframes) used windowing logic that misdated 2010 entries, sometimes shifting them to 2016 due to century rollovers. Pension calculations and tax filings were among the affected, and vendors like ADP had to push quick patches.

- **Embedded Medical Devices:** Some patient monitors and other 2010-era medical devices with two-digit date fields mislogged data, occasionally interpreting 2010 as 2016 when the base year was misaligned. The FDA[9] noted isolated recall cases.

---

[9] **FDA — Food and Drug Administration.** The U.S. agency responsible for regulating food, drugs, medical devices, and other health-related products. In short: if you can eat it, inject it, or rub it on your skin, the FDA probably has a form about it.

- **Industrial Control Systems:** Manufacturing SCADA[10] systems with Y2K windowing fixes reported log anomalies in 2010. Date stamps could shift by six years (2010 to 2016) if the pivot window misaligned with a 2006 base year.

At this point you might notice something odd — the timeline jumps from 2010 straight to 2016, skipping half a decade as if history took a coffee break. Don't worry, that's not a typo. There's a good reason for it, and it's one of those cases where the detour is worth the wait. We'll get to it in just a moment.

2010 produced many such oddities. Some were just Y2K windowing leftovers, but others stemmed from a different bug — one we'll dig into in more detail shortly.

2020 Glitches (Y2K20)

The next big wave hit January 1, 2020. Two decades after Y2K, some of those quick fixes were still lurking in production.

- **NYC Parking Meters:** Over 14,000 Parkeon meters rejected credit cards due to outdated anti-fraud checks misreading the year. Coins or apps were the only option until manual firmware updates rolled out.

- **McKesson Healthcare Software:** Used in U.S. hospitals, it stumbled over date validation on Jan 2, 2020, delaying patient records until patched.

---

[10] **SCADA — Supervisory Control and Data Acquisition.** A family of industrial control systems used to monitor and operate critical infrastructure like power grids, water treatment, or pipelines. In theory, they bring efficiency and automation; in practice, many still run on hardware old enough to remember dial-up. Here's a twist: the very systems keeping the lights on often rely on machines that panic when they see a USB stick.

- **ServiceNow Time Tracking:** Logs reverted to Dec 31, 2019, across time zones, throwing off billing and technician records.

- **Novitus Delio Fiscal Printers (Poland):** Thousands of cash register printers couldn't set the date to 2020 due to a clock error, blocking receipt printing with correct dates. Each device required physical delivery to service centers for manual fixes—remote patching was impossible.

These are just a sample of the chaos. The specifics varied, but the underlying pattern was the same: quick fixes had simply kicked the can down the road.

Despite these hiccups, it's important to stress that we avoided the doomsday scenario many feared in 2000. The billions spent weren't wasted — for every delayed fix that resurfaced later, countless systems were properly repaired and carried on without drama.

An attentive reader may have noticed: Symantec's "fix" only handled years up to 2030. We can only guess how many other companies quietly did the same.

LESSON LEARNED

- Quick fixes are band-aids, not cures. They're valid emergency tactics, but they must be followed by real fixes.

- Investing billions to dodge catastrophe in 2000 paid off — but many organizations learned the hard way in 2010 and 2020 that shortcuts have expiration dates.

- If you think "this code will be gone by then," you're probably wrong. It will be running production workloads long after you've left the company.

If the same date bug keeps coming back every decade, it's not the computers that failed the test of time — it's us.

Y2K10
When 0X10 Meant 2016

January 1, 2010. Instead of fireworks, millions of Germans got silence from their ATMs, Belgians couldn't log into online banking, and Australians were asked to pay cash like it was 1985. The culprit? Not hackers, not power outages, but the humble number 10.

A Short Detour: How Many is 10?

At first glance, 10 obviously means ten. That's true—*if* you're thinking in **decimal** (base-10), the system humans instinctively use. Why base-10? Because we learned to count on ten fingers. It's cultural, not cosmic law.

Fun fact: even that's not universal. The ancient **Sumerians** used *two* systems—**base-12** and **base-60**. Sounds odd? Not really. Twelve comes from the number of finger segments on one hand: the thumb acts as a pointer, not part of the count. And sixty? That's just five times twelve. Picture an ancient accountant tallying bundles of grain—using one thumb to track finger bones on a single hand, and the fingers of the other hand to mark each completed dozen. The result was a system that felt natural, efficient, and remarkably elegant from a mathematical standpoint.

The echoes of it still shape our world today: twelve months in a year, sixty minutes in an hour, and even in language—*dozen* for twelve, *threescore* for sixty. From a practical perspective, base-12 and base-60 were arguably better: more divisible, easier to split evenly into halves, thirds, and quarters. Humanity just happened to stick with the system that matched its hands, not its logic.

So why do other number systems exist at all? Because not all counting problems are created equal. Machines, engineers, and mathematicians each optimized for different kinds of efficiency:

- **Binary (base-2):** the natural language of computers—just ones and zeros. Compact for logic circuits, miserable for humans. Here, 10 means *two*.

- **Octal (base-8):** a mid-century compromise that mapped neatly onto early 3-bit hardware. Once practical, now mostly a museum piece. Here, 10 means *eight*.

- **Decimal (base-10):** our cultural default. Easy on the eyes, terrible for binary arithmetic. Here, 10 means *ten* (finally something intuitive).

- **Hexadecimal (base-16):** a programmer's shorthand. One hex digit equals four bits—half a byte—which keeps memory addresses readable without needing a magnifying glass. This notation is also widespread outside code, such as in color definitions like #FF9900. Here, 10 means *sixteen*.

- **BCD (Binary-Coded Decimal):** an awkward hybrid where each decimal digit is stored as a separate 4-bit binary number. It looked clever on paper—then computers got faster, and nobody wanted it anymore. Here, 10 technically means... nothing, because it needs four bits for every single digit.

We'll skip the full lecture on number theory. For our purposes, it's enough to know that multiple systems are in common use—and that confusion between them is fertile ground for disaster.

So how do we tell them apart in code?

- `10` → **decimal** (base-10).

- `010` → **octal** (base-8). In older languages like C, a leading zero meant octal; modern syntax like Python's `0o10` makes that explicit.

- `0x10` → **hexadecimal** (base-16). To represent digits above nine, hexadecimal uses letters A through F, so values like `0x0a` (*ten*) are perfectly valid and even common in code.

- `0b10` → **binary** (base-2).

This convention is older than most programming languages still in use today, but it's hardly divine law. And even within those conventions, there's room for chaos. Ever noticed what's missing from the list above? Right— there's no clear way to mark **BCD**. And that's a nuance we need to explain...

What Happened

For decades, financial systems, telecom protocols, and embedded devices used BCD to store dates. Combined with legacy windowing "fixes" from the Y2K era, this worked fine through the 2000s.

But then came 2010. In BCD, the year "10" was supposed to mean ten. Unfortunately, some newer libraries treated the same prefix (`0x10`) as hexadecimal— where it means sixteen. Stack the Y2K windowing hack on top of that, and suddenly systems jumped forward six years. Overnight, the world lurched from 2009 into... 2016.

The fallout was swift and widespread:

• **German Bank Cards:** Up to 30 million Sparkasse and partner bank debit/credit cards refused to work at ATMs, stores, or online. The chips rejected "future" expiration dates, effectively bricking half the country's cashless economy.

• **Citibank Belgium Digipass Tokens:** Hardware security devices used for online banking authentication stopped generating valid one-time passwords. The tokens' clocks thought they were in 2016, making every session invalid.

• **Australian EFTPOS[11] Terminals:** Thousands of retail payment terminals spat out errors, misreading card dates as "expired in 2016." Shops resorted to cash-only transactions.

Elsewhere, smaller glitches surfaced too: SMS timestamps in Windows Mobile jumped into the future, spam filters flagged emails from "the year 2016," and various embedded devices started acting like time travelers.

Why It Failed

On the surface, this was "just a date bug." Underneath, it was a perfect storm of:

• **Ambiguous Standards:** Legacy systems used 0xYY for BCD dates long before 0x became the standard prefix for hexadecimal. By 2010, software libraries no longer agreed on how to interpret it.

---

[11] **EFTPOS – Electronic Funds Transfer at Point of Sale.** The system handling debit and credit card payments. Invisible when it works, national emergency when it doesn't.

- **Windowing Debt:** Quick fixes from Y2K (e.g., "if year < 20, assume 2000s") were never replaced with real solutions. Kicking the can forward only postponed the chaos.

- **Interoperability Assumptions:** Banking, telecom, and retail systems assumed everyone would parse dates the same way. They didn't.

Just as in 1582, when the Gregorian reform erased ten days from the calendar, here six whole years simply "evaporated" from the digital consciousness of countless systems. Different century, same story: when your timekeeping method changes, reality bends with it.

Humans handle ambiguity with context. Computers handle it by breaking things. When systems can't agree on what a number means, reality doesn't negotiate—it splits.

LESSON LEARNED

- Prefixes and encodings matter. Ambiguity in standards is a time bomb.
- Legacy quirks don't die; they hibernate until triggered.
- In tightly coupled systems (finance, telecom), small inconsistencies cascade into national-level outages.
- Dates are hard. If you ever feel like inventing your own way of storing them—don't.

Who needs time travel when your payment terminal already thinks it's six years in the future?

PSN 2010
The Phantom Leap Day Bug

Date: March 1, 2010

Impact: PS3 Fat bricked for one day (approx 0.4% of consoles)

Root Cause: Console OS error treating year 2010 as leap year.

2010 wasn't finished handing out date-related headaches. If broken bank cards and login tokens weren't enough, Sony delivered its own "bonus level" in the form of a PlayStation Network meltdown.

March 1, 2010. Instead of grinding trophies or fragging friends online, thousands of PlayStation 3 owners found themselves staring at error screens. The culprit? A day that didn't exist.

Sony's PlayStation Network (PSN) suddenly became inaccessible for hundreds of thousands of older "fat" PS3 consoles. Affected users couldn't sign into PSN, launch certain games, or sync trophies and saves. The consoles' internal clocks insisted it was still **February 29, 2010**—a date that never existed, because 2010 wasn't a leap year.

The mismatch caused chaos: game launches failed, especially titles with trophy or license checks; online authentication requests were rejected by PSN servers, which expected March 1; save synchronization and DRM validation went haywire. Owners panicked. Forums dubbed it "Y2K 2.0." For many, the only fix was to wait until the real calendar overtook the console's imaginary one.

The exact cause was never officially confirmed by Sony. One plausible hypothesis is that the module responsible for leap year detection misread the year byte `0x10` as 2016—a year that actually was a leap year. This would explain why the PS3 suddenly believed February had 29 days in 2010. In other words, it wasn't a deliberate misapplication of the leap year rule, but a low-level desync in how the clock logic parsed the year. Whether through BCD mishandling or firmware quirk, the result was the same: a phantom day.

The "fix" was anticlimactic. No patch, no hotfix—just the passage of time. On March 2, the clock incremented correctly, the phantom day vanished, and consoles rejoined reality. Sony called it a "clock functionality bug" and promised newer Slim models weren't affected.

Roughly 0.4% of PS3s worldwide were affected (millions in absolute numbers). Gamers lost access to PSN services, trophies, and some offline games. PR backlash was swift: "Sony's Y2K" trended across tech media.

For a brief moment in 2010, PS3 owners weren't living in the future or the past—they were stuck in a day that never existed.

LESSON LEARNED

- Even entertainment devices are embedded systems— and inherit all the fragility of "serious" hardware.
- Leap year math looks simple but hides subtle traps. Get it wrong, and your calendar becomes fantasy fiction.
- Waiting for a bug to self-resolve is rarely an acceptable fix—but sometimes the only one.
- User trust evaporates faster than leap days. "It'll fix itself tomorrow" isn't a great support message.

When your console believes in days that don't exist, it's not a feature—it's theology.

Z2K9
Microsoft Zune 30Gb, The Day Time Froze

Date: December 31, 2008

Impact: Every 30GB Zune on the planet froze simultaneously, turning thousands of music players into inert plastic until the calendar rolled over.

Root Cause: A leap-year bug in the device's internal clock logic caused an infinite loop when it tried to process the 366th day of 2008.

On the last day of 2008, Zune users woke up to find their devices had entered cryogenic stasis. Screens locked at the loading bar, controls unresponsive, batteries draining as if possessed. The culprit wasn't sabotage, malware, or a global outage — it was time itself. Specifically, the fact that 2008 was a leap year.

Deep inside the Zune's firmware lived a simple counter responsible for tracking the number of days since January 1. In normal years, it looped neatly from day 0 to day 364 — because programmers, for reasons known only to them and their rubber ducks, always start counting from zero. (Mathematicians are still debating whether zero is even a natural number, and they've had a few centuries' head start.) When 2008's bonus day arrived, the code tried to count one step too far, tripped over its own logic, and got stuck in an infinite loop. The music stopped, literally.

It was a perfect storm of hubris and complacency. The bug hid in the Zune's timekeeping component, adapted from another manufacturer's reference code. Its job was to track days. That's it. But when December 31, 2008 rolled around, the logic went into a loop asking itself, "Wait, what day is this again?" forever. The system never got past initialization.

Engineers quickly confirmed that nothing could fix the issue except waiting. At midnight, January 1, 2009, the counter reset, and every Zune spontaneously resurrected itself. Microsoft's official advice was essentially: *do nothing and wait for tomorrow.* Somewhere, a PR manager probably considered rebranding it as a mindfulness feature.

The incident was quickly dubbed **Z2K9**, a tongue-in-cheek nod to Y2K. The parallels were uncanny: both were preventable rollover bugs caused by lazy assumptions about how time works. Only this time, the victims weren't banks or airlines — they were people trying to listen to Linkin Park on New Year's Eve.

For users, the episode was a meme. For engineers, it was a reminder that time remains undefeated. Embedded devices, from routers to thermostats, often hardcode simplified calendars, blissfully unaware that Earth's orbit refuses to play nice with binary counters.

LESSON LEARNED

- Time is hard; anyone who tells you otherwise hasn't debugged a leap year.
- "It only happens once every four years" is not an acceptable mitigation strategy.
- Shared code means shared mistakes — we'll revisit this in Part VI, Volume 2 on open- source fragility.
- Always assume the calendar hates you; it's been trying to confuse humanity since 1582.

If a single leap day can brick your music, just wait until time itself runs out of integers. See you in 2038.

Explainer:
Unix Timestamp

One of the most common standards for storing dates in computing is the **Unix Timestamp**. It's just the number of seconds since the beginning of 1970 — the *Unix Epoch*. The counter runs both ways: positive values for dates after 1970-01-01, negative values for dates before it.

On many systems (especially older or embedded 32-bit ones), this is stored in a signed 32-bit integer. That works fine... until January 19, 2038, at 03:14:07 UTC. At that moment the counter reaches 2,147,483,647; adding one more second overflows it to −2,147,483,648 — which corresponds to **December 13, 1901, 20:45:52 UTC**. Some software will interpret the wrapped value as that 1901 date; others may crash or reset to 1970. Either way, it's chaos. That's the infamous **Year 2038 Problem**.

You might think: "But modern computers are 64-bit!" True. A 64-bit counter pushes the limit so far into the future it's basically science fiction: the year 292,277,026,596. By then, the Sun will be long gone, so we can let future civilizations worry about it.

But here's the catch: not every system has been rebuilt to use 64-bit values. Remember Ariane 5 from the previous chapter? Legacy assumptions die hard. Plenty of software — especially embedded systems — still relies on 32-bit timestamps. Which means the Year 2038 bug is very real.

The good news? Maybe it will save us from another round of half-baked "windowing" fixes. After all, if some companies patched Y2K by extending their logic to 2040 or 2050, the 2038 meltdown might finally flush those shortcuts out of hiding.

—— The Linux Leap Second Meltdown Of 2012 ——

Back in the chapter intro we already met the strange beast called the leap second. We noted that last time the extra second slid in—back in 2016—it was calm. But four years earlier, in 2012, a single second caused quite a bonanza. When the leap second landed then, Linux tripped over it spectacularly.

By 2012, Linux wasn't just an operating system for hobbyists—it was the quiet emperor of the internet. Android phones, routers, servers, cloud platforms... even if you didn't know it, you were relying on Linux every time you scrolled through cat videos or argued with strangers on Reddit. Which meant that when Linux coughed, the whole internet caught a cold.

And cough it did, on the night of June 30, 2012. The occasion? A leap second. Just one extra second slipped into Coordinated Universal Time at midnight. For most people, this passed unnoticed. For Linux, it was like being asked to juggle chainsaws after a few too many drinks.

The bug came from a part of the system called FUTEX. We won't dive into the technicalities here—just think of FUTEX as a kind of conductor or drummer in an orchestra, making sure every musician (or in this case, every program thread) plays in sync, comes in at the right moment, and doesn't drown out the others. When the leap second was added, this timekeeper lost the beat. Instead of calmly adjusting the rhythm, FUTEX sent everyone into a frenzy, with programs waking up instantly, checking the clock, finding nonsense, and spinning in circles at full speed.

The result: servers that didn't crash outright, but melted down in place. CPU cores pegged at 100%. Load averages skyrocketed. The watchdog thought the system was hung and hard-crashed it just to be safe. Some apps became totally unresponsive. Others limped along like drunk marathon runners, burning energy but going nowhere.

And this wasn't just an obscure lab problem—it hit the internet's heavyweights. Reddit went offline for more than an hour. LinkedIn, Foursquare and The Pirate Bay all declared "nope, not today" and stopped working. Qantas Airlines couldn't process some of its systems, leaving staff scrambling for hours. Even big media sites stumbled and newsrooms went dark. For a bug triggered by a single second, the fallout was global.

The fix, embarrassingly enough, was often just: reboot the box and hope your clocks line up again. Patches came later, but by then the damage was done.

LESSON LEARNED

- Leap seconds are rare, but not rare enough to ignore. If your system can't handle them, it will show up at the worst time.

- Linux may run the world, but even the emperor trips over one second of extra time.

- A single glitch in the "timekeeper' of the system can bring down entire services—not with a bang, but with an endless spin loop.

- If your emergency plan is "reboot everything," you're one leap second away from chaos.

The internet didn't end that night, but for a few hours it got very wobbly—proof that even one second can be too much for a global empire of code. More importantly, it showed just how fragile our modern world is when it comes to time. Every transaction, every flight, every social network post depends on clocks being in sync down to the tiniest sliver of a second. That night reminded us that time isn't just something we check on our wrists—it's the invisible glue holding the digital age together.

CHAPTER 3:
THE MEMORY PROBLEM:
TOO MUCH TRASH, NOT ENOUGH WALLS

Computers don't just process data; they live by memory. A running system is a chain of recalls — what instruction to execute next, what variable to update, where the next bit of data is waiting. Lose any of it, and everything unravels. When a program crashes or hangs, it's rarely because it forgot the math; it's because it lost context. The art of computing is, in many ways, the art of not forgetting.

Their efficiency comes down to two factors — whether they remember their tasks, and whether they have enough space to keep those memories while they work. When either runs out, systems start to stumble, freeze, or erase their own to-do list in a moment of digital amnesia.

Let's clear up one simple point first.

 **Explainer:**
Your phone does not have 512GB of memory

A note on terminology

Let's start with a confession: this explainer might sound pedantic, but it's worth clarifying a simple thing about terminology. Especially since it explains why a chapter about memory appears in a part devoted to **compute.**

In everyday language, the distinction between *storage* and *memory* has blurred. Marketing loves to boast about phones with "256GB, 512GB, even 1TB of memory." Sounds impressive — except that's not memory. It's **storage** — long-term data retention, not active workspace.

In reality, memory and storage are two very different beasts.

The Kitchen Analogy

Imagine your computer as a kitchen, and the CPU as the chef. Brilliant, creative, but dependent on ingredients.

- The ones **on the counter** are always within reach — quick to grab, no interruption needed.

- The rest sit **in the pantry** — accessible, but it takes a short pause to fetch them.

At the end of the day, the counter gets cleared: whatever's still good goes back to the pantry; the rest goes in the trash.

Memory is that counter space — fast, expensive, and *volatile*. When you turn the system off, everything on it disappears.

Storage is the pantry — slower, cheaper, but *persistent*. You can power it down, unplug it, or move it elsewhere, and the contents remain. Sometimes it's a small fridge (an SSD in your laptop), sometimes a warehouse-sized cold room (a data center array). The further from the counter, the bigger and slower it gets.

Why This Matters

In computing, memory belongs to the **compute** domain — it works hand-in-hand with processors to handle *active* data. **Storage**, regardless of whether it's flash drives, SSDs, or magnetic tapes, lives in the **storage** domain — the world of *resting* data.

That's why this chapter sits here, not in the data section. Because before anything can be stored, it has to be remembered first.

Your phone doesn't have 512GB of memory. It has 512GB of storage — and just enough memory to remember what it's doing for the next few milliseconds.

Marketing has been confusing RAM with storage for decades—but to be fair, so have most software engineers right before their system runs out of both and starts thrashing the *pantry* for scraps.

Explainer:
What Is a Memory Leak?

Every program requests chunks of RAM when it needs them. When it's done, it should give that memory back to the operating system. Keyword: *should.*

In reality, software forgets. A program stops using a piece of memory but never tells the system it's available again. The program itself may not even remember it still "owns" that space—it's just sitting there, reserved forever, like a ghost reservation.

Think of it like a storage facility where customers rent rooms. Everything is fine and dandy until one absent-minded customer starts losing the keys. They're not using the rooms anymore—in fact, they've already moved on and started booking new ones—but the manager still thinks the old ones are occupied. It doesn't take a genius to guess what happens next: the storage fills up with rooms no one is actually using, yet none of them can be rented out.

That's a memory leak. Modern programming languages try to fight this using something called a **garbage collector** —a built-in system that periodically searches memory for these ghost reservations and frees them. Think of it this way: the *tenant* (the program) hires an internal administrator whose job is to keep track of which keys still matter and which rooms were forgotten.

But this safety net isn't bullet-proof, and a huge amount of the world's software is still written in languages without garbage collectors[12].

Operating systems try to help too — just in a different way. Think of the *storage facility manager* hiring a night guard whose job is to walk through the corridors, spot rooms that haven't been touched in ages, and say, "Alright, let's move this stuff to that big warehouse outside the city." In computing terms, that's **swap**: shifting rarely-used (but still technically "in use") memory pages onto the disk to free up valuable space in RAM. And just like hauling forgotten junk to a warehouse outside the city, getting it back later takes a whole lot longer than if it had stayed nearby.

But in the end, there's only one guaranteed way to reclaim everything: shut the program down. Just like the storage manager finally giving up and declaring, "Right, everybody out," the operating system wipes the slate clean and all memory becomes free again.

You've seen this before, though you might not have known it had a name. Most of this chapter is about exactly that: computers forgetting how to forget.

---

[12] In 2022–2023, NSA (National Security Agency) and CISA (Cybersecurity and Infrastructure Security Agency) urged developers to ditch memory-unsafe languages like C/C++—because manual memory at scale is a decades-long game of Russian roulette. By 2026, vendors must roadmap the switch or face scrutiny.

Chrome Memory Leak Saga

Date: 2010–Ongoing

Impact: Browser bloat normalized worldwide; multi-GB RAM consumption on everyday workloads; performance degradation, crashes and user frustration.

Root Cause: Multi-process architecture, incomplete cleanup of renderer processes, fragmentation across Blink/ V8 heaps, and extensions misbehaving as unmonitored background services.

Let's start with something painfully familiar: you open three tabs, feel productive, and suddenly Chrome is inhaling RAM like it's training for a competitive eating contest. You haven't done anything special—maybe glanced at documentation, doom-scrolled a bit—but one glance at your computer's "this is fine" spinning fan tells you Chrome has quietly claimed half your RAM and is negotiating for the rest like a hostage situation gone polite.

Chrome didn't mean to become this way. Back in 2008, it was the spry, minimalist wunderkind promising speed and isolation. Tabs ran in separate processes for safety— great idea! Until it scaled. By 2010, users began noticing classic symptoms of what you now know from the explainer as memory leaks. Tabs closed, but the memory stayed occupied. Chrome kept holding onto RAM it no longer needed—those ghost reservations from the explainer, but at scale. Extensions ran quietly in the background, never checking out. Even when memory was technically freed, fragmentation left it scattered into tiny, unusable scraps.

Google kept shipping fixes, and many of them genuinely helped—but each one also added a new corner of the house that needed cleaning. Over time, Chrome stopped looking like a browser and started feeling like a tiny accidental operating system: almost as complicated as the real thing, just with more bugs and fewer excuses. And the modern web didn't make this easier. Sites grew heavier, apps moved into the browser, and suddenly everything from spreadsheets to 3D tools behaved like full-blown desktop software, only running inside a tab.

Users adapted. Ten tabs became twenty. A hundred became a lifestyle choice. The average person didn't care why Chrome was hungry—only that the laptop felt like it was running a space heater. But deep inside the Chromium bug tracker, engineers faced a much darker reality. By 2020, data revealed that **roughly 70% of high-severity security bugs were actually memory safety issues.** Chrome wasn't just leaking memory; it was losing control of it entirely. This wasn't the result of a single dramatic flaw, but a long chain of reasonable choices that built an unreasonable result.

Memory Saver modes emerged, tabs were allowed to "sleep," allocators were tuned, but let's be honest: the architecture is the architecture. Browsers weren't supposed to become OS kernels, yet here we are—Chrome as the world's most popular, least intentional operating system.

The real punchline? Nothing here is technically broken. It's just the web fulfilling its destiny as a sprawling, ungovernable hotel where every guest demands their own private suite and never checks out.

LESSON LEARNED

- Every layer of isolation trades safety for memory—eventually, that bill arrives.
- A temporary state becomes permanent when no one truly owns its lifecycle.

- Incremental patches can compound complexity faster than they reduce it.
- A browser that becomes an operating system inherits all the problems of one.
- Performance issues at scale are rarely caused by a single leak—they're ecosystems.

Chrome didn't just leak memory—it redefined "normal" for how much memory a browser is allowed to leak.

Windows 98 GDI Leak

Date: 1998–1999

Impact: System-wide UI corruption, application crashes, and forced reboots for millions of users.

Root Cause: GDI (Graphics Device Interface) objects allocated but never freed; a rigid, system-wide 64KB resource heap exhausted by normal usage, regardless of available RAM.

Let's take a brief detour into the ancient past—though if, like the author, you're at the age where keeping paracetamol on your bedside table "just in case" qualifies as a practical life hack, you might actually remember it. So let me tell this story very much *in the spirit of the era.*

It was the late 1990s. Dial-up modems screamed, CRT monitors hummed, and Windows 98 proudly sat at the center of the universe, glowing in 256 colors and asking you every other day if you wanted to run ScanDisk.

On the surface, it looked modern enough: colorful icons, a friendlier Start Menu, and a UI that—while deeply limited by today's standards—felt like a genuine step up from Windows 95. Under the hood, however, lived a time bomb. A very small, very polite, but catastrophically stubborn time bomb called the GDI resource pool.

GDI—the Graphics Device Interface—was responsible for drawing everything on screen: windows, icons, text, menus, scrollbars, the works. To manage these thousands of visual elements, the system relied on a specific, specialized area of memory called a heap. If your RAM is the spacious kitchen counter from our earlier analogy, think of the GDI heap as that narrow magnetic rail above the pass where the chef clips the active order tickets. It is a reserved, high-priority space for the most critical details— tracking exactly which window is where and what button looks like what.

But that rail had a fatal design flaw: it was incredibly short, and it was physically incapable of growing. Due to architectural hangovers from the 16-bit era, this heap was capped at exactly 64 kilobytes. It didn't matter if you installed a massive amount of RAM or upgraded your processor; that magnetic rail remained 64KB long, period. And worst of all, it wasn't one rail per app—it was one single rail for the entire kitchen.

Every program you opened, from Solitaire to Word, had to fight for space on that same tiny strip of metal. Each visual element—window, button, scrollbar—required its own clip on that rail, a small data structure called a handle. These handles tracked what was drawn where, updating constantly as you moved windows or clicked buttons. In theory, closing an application would remove all its handles, freeing up precious rail space for the next program.

Handles were supposed to be released when windows closed. They weren't. Windows 98 leaked GDI objects the way a colander leaks water: slowly at first, then alarmingly, then all at once. Normal usage—opening folders, scrolling through Internet Explorer, running programs that created lots of UI elements—allocated handles that were never properly freed. Third-party apps contributed to the disaster, but the operating system itself was one of the main offenders.

The symptoms were surreal. After a few hours, icons turned pitch black, like they'd been censored. Menus appeared empty. Text vanished. Windows refused to redraw themselves, freezing mid-frame like early digital art experiments. Eventually the entire UI collapsed into an "Out of resources" death rattle that left users staring at a broken desktop with all the enthusiasm of a dying Tamagotchi.

There was only one fix: reboot. Not restart the app, not close a few windows—*full restart*. The OS couldn't reclaim leaked handles without wiping the slate clean. And so an entire generation learned that leaving too many windows open was not a lifestyle choice but an act of self-harm. Meanwhile, power-users on early internet forums proudly posted screenshots of uptimes exceeding a week—as if they'd achieved enlightenment rather than simply avoided opening the Control Panel.

Microsoft acknowledged the issue in knowledge-base articles of the era, with tools like `GDIObj.exe` letting curious users watch the numbers climb toward doom with the same energy as watching a microwave countdown. Patches arrived in Windows 98 Second Edition, and later the NT-based line (Windows 2000, XP) resolved the problem more permanently with better resource tracking and per-process limits.

But the lesson remained: in a world constrained by tiny resource pools and no automated cleanup, even a few forgotten objects could take down an entire operating system.

LESSON LEARNED

- Resource leaks scale badly—small per-object waste becomes catastrophic in fixed pools.
- Allocation without guaranteed cleanup is a slow-motion outage.
- Global resource limits fail globally. One misbehaving app kills the entire system.
- When rebooting becomes routine, something in the architecture has already given up.

Some bugs haunt you for decades. This one taught an entire generation that "Don't open too many windows" was not advice—it was survival.

Meltdown & Spectre

Date: January 2018 → ongoing variants

Impact: Global performance regressions (5–30%), billions in cloud infrastructure costs, erosion of trust in CPU isolation guarantees.

Root Cause: Speculative execution leaking sensitive data through side-channel timing attacks; 20+ years of "speed first, security later" CPU design.

Let's fast-forward from the dial-up 90s to a moment when computers were thousands of times faster, systems had become tangled webs of interdependent abstractions, and humanity kept inventing new and exciting ways to break absolutely everything — including, of course, security.

Before we get there, a quick detour. RAM isn't the fastest memory in your computer—not by a long shot. CPUs have their own tiny, blisteringly fast workspace called cache. Think of it not as the neatly laid-out ingredients on the countertop from the explainer earlier, but as absurd little conveniences like hanging a whole ring of sausage over a chef's shoulder or keeping a salt shaker tucked into a chef's apron pocket. It's right there, instantly reachable—and absolutely central to the story.

In early 2018, the world woke up to a revelation worthy of a conspiracy thriller: for two decades, nearly every CPU on the planet had been quietly cheating. Not cheating *you* exactly—cheating *reality*. And like all good shortcuts, it eventually crashed head-first into the brick wall of physics, security, and wishful thinking.

The trick in question was **speculative execution**, a performance hack so clever it bordered on smugness. Modern processors don't like waiting for decisions, so they guess the future. Literally. If code says, "If X, then do Y," the CPU often starts doing Y *before* it knows whether X is true. If the guess was wrong, it rolls back—no harm done. Well... unless you count the fact that the work wasn't entirely rolled back: the CPU's cache still remembered what it touched.

That tiny detail—an implementation quirk baked into billions of devices—was all attackers needed. Because if you measure how fast the cache responds, you can infer what speculative execution briefly accessed. And once you can do that, you can read anything: passwords, cryptographic keys, the operating system's own memory, data from other processes... even data from entirely different virtual machines in the cloud.

This wasn't a bug you fix with a quick patch. This was the architectural equivalent of discovering your house was built entirely out of crackers.

Meltdown and Spectre arrived as a pair. **Meltdown** punched straight through the wall between user programs and the operating system, letting normal apps read the operating system's own memory as if the doors were politely left open. **Spectre** went for something even more unsettling: tricking programs into *speculating along dangerous paths*, forcing them to leak data they were never supposed to touch. Meltdown was devastating but patchable. Spectre was subtle, elegant, and basically immortal.

The fallout was immediate. Emergency patches went out overnight. Linux introduced KPTI—Kernel Page Table Isolation—which promptly slowed certain workloads by 5–30%. Windows deployed similar fixes. Cloud giants like AWS, Google, and Azure quietly rebooted entire fleets, rewrote the very software layer that keeps customers' systems separated, deployed microcode updates, and spent billions replacing hardware—all while insisting, with the dead eyes of people under NDA, that everything was fine.

Worse: the patches were only the first layer of the onion. New variants kept appearing with increasingly ominous names—Foreshadow, ZombieLoad, RIDL, MDS—each revealing yet another corner where speculation leaked secrets. Engineers eventually realized this wasn't a bug but a design philosophy problem. For twenty years, CPUs had pursued speed with religious devotion, assuming isolation and security were someone else's job. That fantasy died in 2018.

To this day, no one is entirely sure how many variants we'll ultimately discover. Intel's newer chips include partial hardware fixes, but even 2025's processors still rely on software mitigations and microcode band-aids. The performance tax never fully disappeared. Virtualized environments will pay for it forever.

Meltdown and Spectre didn't just break computers—they broke the illusion that hardware was the stable, trustworthy foundation and software was the messy layer on top. Turns out the foundation was made of duct tape and speculation.

LESSON LEARNED

- Speed without safety is a time bomb in silicon form.
- Side-channel attacks aren't academic—they're architecture-level attacks.
- Hardware mistakes become software problems for decades.
- Isolation is a promise, not a guarantee—and in this case, a broken one.
- "Secure by design" means nothing if performance shortcuts rewrite the design.

Some failures crash your system. This one crashed the entire worldview that hardware was trustworthy and software was the messy layer. Turns out the foundation was reading everyone's diary.

Rowhammer

Date: 2014 → ongoing variants

Impact: Bit flips in physical DRAM[13] enabling privilege escalation, sandbox escapes, crypto key leaks, and cross-VM attacks.

Root Cause: Electrical interference between densely packed DRAM cells; repeated accesses ("hammering") to one row cause charge leakage and flips in adjacent rows.

Let's step into a story where physics itself joins the security industry—not politely, not cooperatively, but with all the enthusiasm of a drunk uncle crashing a wedding. The tale begins in the mid-2010s, but its roots reach deeper: for years, memory manufacturers kept shrinking DRAM cells to fit more bits into the same space. That density came with a hidden surprise. It turned out that when cells sit too close together, they start... chatting. Or, more accurately, leaking charge into one another like gossipy neighbors with very thin apartment walls.

That accidental "electrical gossip" is the foundation of **Rowhammer**, a hardware-level exploit that still feels like science fiction. The attack works by repeatedly—and absurdly quickly—accessing the same row of memory over and over ("hammering" it). Do this hundreds of thousands of times in under a millisecond, and the electrical disturbance can flip bits in the rows next door. One moment a bit says 0, the next it quietly turns into 1. This

---

[13] **RAM, but Make It Confusing**

"RAM" isn't one thing — it's a whole category of memory types. The actual chips you use come with weird letter combos in front, because of course they do. The most common one is **DRAM** (sometimes **SDRAM**, but let's not open that box). The "D" stands for **Dynamic**, which in practice means *goldfish memory*: it has to keep reminding itself what it's storing. Stop refreshing it for a moment and — *poof* — everything's gone.

isn't hacking in the Hollywood sense. It's physics filing a bug report.

The trick became public in 2014, when Google Project Zero demonstrated the first bit flips in a lab setting. A year later, researchers showed something far more worrying: those tiny bit flips weren't just a lab curiosity. With the right nudge, they could change data in places they absolutely shouldn't, giving ordinary software the ability to poke holes in the system around it. Suddenly this wasn't a physics demo anymore—it was a security problem with teeth. Then things escalated. In 2016, **DRAMMER** achieved Rowhammer-based Android root without needing a PC at all. By 2018, the family tree included **GLitch**, **Nethammer**, and **Throwhammer**—attacks launched through JavaScript, over the network, or via RDMA. Physics had officially gone remote.

This wasn't a software bug you could fix with clever programming. Perfectly written code couldn't stop electrons from misbehaving. Side-channel defenses didn't help; sandboxes crumbled under bit flips; even virtual machines, supposedly isolated fortresses, could be breached by flipping a few carefully chosen bits.

The consequences were ugly: privilege escalations from user → kernel (we'll explain what that actually means in Chapter 18 of Part IV), theft of cryptographic keys, and even browser sandbox escapes. Billions of devices were vulnerable—from PCs and servers to phones and cloud infrastructure. Pinching pennies by packing DRAM cells closer together had created a global attack surface.

Mitigations arrived slowly and imperfectly. ECC (Error Correction Code) memory helped by detecting and correcting some flips. DDR4 introduced TRR (Target Row Refresh), an automatic "spray bottle" meant to calm overly excited rows—but variants like **Half-Double** and

Blacksmith later found ways around it. Software defenses tried doubling refresh rates, isolating memory allocations, or monitoring access patterns, but you can't out-code the laws of physics.

Rowhammer's legacy is blunt: hardware is now part of the threat model. A security flaw can live not in your app, nor your OS, nor your CPU's microcode, but in the literal physical design of the memory chips.

LESSON LEARNED

- Physics doesn't respect privilege boundaries.
- You can't patch silicon with software—not cleanly, and not forever.
- Hardware miniaturization creates new vulnerabilities as fast as it creates new chips.
- "Reliable" memory can fail spectacularly under adversarial pressure.
- Security has to span the entire stack, down to the atomic level.

Rowhammer didn't just flip bits—it flipped the entire assumption that hardware was a passive bystander. Turns out even electrons have opinions.

CHAPTER 4:
THE RACE THAT NOBODY WINS

We humans are terrible at waiting. We multitask even when we're not aware of it: we breathe, tap our feet while the microwave hums, and check the clock every ten seconds as if it'll move faster under pressure. That's still harmless enough.

The real fun begins when we do it consciously—like when we open Netflix, hit play, and halfway through decide to check our phone notifications. Five minutes later, we have no idea what's happening in the movie or what we just scrolled past. Congratulations, you've successfully context-switched yourself into oblivion.

Naturally, we demanded the same brilliance from our computers: *do everything, everywhere, all at once.* Parallelism sounded noble—tasks sharing resources, running faster, finishing sooner. In practice, it's a group project where everyone edits the same file at the same time. Deadlines don't move; sanity does.

Computers never asked for multitasking. We did. And in chasing speed, we built systems that move exactly like us —frantic, overlapping, and occasionally catastrophic.

 **Explainer:**
Why CPUs Can't Really Multitask

Processors are often described as "doing many things at once," but that's mostly an illusion. A CPU can perform only one operation per core at any given moment. What makes it *seem* like your computer is running hundreds of programs simultaneously is speed—sheer, relentless, context-switching speed. Modern CPUs can switch from one task to another hundreds of thousands of times per second, giving the impression of parallelism while, in reality, performing one thing at a time and juggling the rest in a queue.

This is true for a single core. Multi-core processors expand the illusion... Modern consumer CPUs reach 16+ cores in 2025 models, yet your system's task manager will happily list hundreds of active processes. The trick is scheduling—each core hops between tasks so quickly that humans perceive continuity where there is only frantic alternation.

That illusion has a cost. Every time a CPU switches from one task to another, it must pause, save the current task's state to memory, and load the next one's context. Those microseconds add up. It's like shuffling papers on your desk—no single switch is slow, but doing it thousands of times a second consumes real time.

To visualize it, try a quick experiment: write the alphabet in one column and then numbers in another. Then flip the page and try writing them interleaved—a 1, b 2, c 3, and so on. You'll notice it takes longer. Each switch between letters and numbers forces your brain to refocus, recall where you left off, and resume. CPUs face the same penalty every time they change tasks.

In short: CPUs don't multitask. They time-share—and they're astonishingly good at faking it.

These frantic switches are what crack open the door to race conditions—two tasks sprinting to touch the same memory, and whoever arrives first decides if your program crashes, corrupts, or quietly lies to you.

 **Explainer:**
What Is a Race Condition?

Imagine you and your partner have a simple household arrangement: every morning, they hang a shopping list on the fridge, and you, coffee in hand, take a photo of it before heading to work. After your shift, you stop by the store, buy everything on the list, and come home a hero. Simple. Reliable. Efficient.

Until, one day, timing betrays you.

Your partner posts the updated list half an hour later than usual—or you, trying to be clever, snap the photo the night before because you know the morning will be chaotic. Either way, you end up with an *old* list. On your way home, you dutifully buy milk, bread, and tuna. You arrive, proud of your foresight, only to discover all three already in the kitchen. Meanwhile, the cat litter is gone, the coffee's out, and your partner is very much *not* impressed.

Now scale that to a bank transfer double-charged because two threads both saw $100 and withdrew it—twice.

That's a race condition in a nutshell: two processes—human or digital—accessing the same resource, but out of sync. Each behaves logically in isolation, yet together they produce chaos.

In computing, it happens all the time. Two fragments of an application (what engineers call *threads*) act at the same moment, both thinking they have the latest information. Or two servers update the same record within milliseconds. Or two automated systems each assume the other will wait. The details vary, but the pattern is universal: timing isn't just important—it's everything.

And as we'll soon see, getting it wrong can break far more than a shopping list.

Mars Pathfinder — Priority Inversion: When Low Priority Crashed The Mission

Date: 1997

Impact: System resets, temporary mission data loss

Root Cause: Priority inversion in real-time scheduling, missing priority inheritance

It began with a spacecraft doing exactly what it was told. On July 4, 1997, NASA's Mars Pathfinder landed on the red planet, unfolded its Sojourner rover, and began transmitting data home, a triumph of engineering and one of the first autonomous systems to operate off Earth. But soon, the joy turned into confusion. The lander kept rebooting itself mid-transmission. Out of nowhere, the mission computer would simply reset, erasing unsent data and pausing scientific operations. Nothing on Mars was wrong, except for Pathfinder's software.

Here's the tricky part: not all tasks on a spacecraft—or any computer—are created equal. Some jobs can wait; others can't. The system's scheduler decides which one gets the CPU's attention first. But when software isn't careful, that hierarchy can backfire. A low-priority weather task grabbed a shared bus lock. A medium-priority task then preempted it, starving the high-priority manager that needed the bus to run. Classic inversion: the important job waits while the trivial ones party, like a chef stuck outside the kitchen while waiters keep passing through.

A perfect storm called **priority inversion**. Technically a race condition in the scheduler—three threads racing for CPU time, with the slowest one blocking the fastest.

The watchdog timer, seeing the high-priority task miss its deadline, assumed a total system freeze and issued a hard reset. The lander obediently rebooted, wiping data and wasting precious time. Over and over again.

At NASA's Jet Propulsion Laboratory, engineers eventually replicated the issue on an Earth-based testbed. After days of debugging, they pinpointed the cause and the fix: enabling priority inheritance, an OS feature that temporarily boosts the priority of the low-level process holding a lock so it can finish and release it faster. A simple patch, literally a configuration flag, sent across 200 million kilometers stopped the resets cold. The mission, meant to last a week, kept going for 83 days.

A decades-old scheduling quirk nearly crippled the mission, where the illusion of multitasking met the reality of physics. A planetary mission failed not because Mars is hostile, but because concurrency is. The problem wasn't cosmic rays; it was human assumptions about how computers "multitask."

LESSON LEARNED

- Test under real load and timing—static analysis misses scheduling races.
- Always enable priority inheritance (or at least understand why you didn't).

- A watchdog timer is only as smart as the code it watches.
- Most mission-critical failures come from assumptions, not asteroids.

Mars didn't reboot Pathfinder. A weather report did.

Spider-Man: No Way Home
The Nft That Broke The Box Office

Date: November 29, 2021

Impact: Simultaneous outages across AMC Theatres, Fandango, and Regal during the first hour of sales; queue times exceeding 90 minutes; immediate secondary market with 400x markup.

Root Cause: Marketing-induced DDoS (Thundering Herd) and database lock contention.

When Spider-Man: No Way Home tickets went on sale, someone in marketing decided the first 86,000 buyers should receive a "limited edition NFT[14]." Cute on a slide deck, catastrophic in production. Overnight, a normal premiere became a competitive sport. The psychology flipped instantly: from "I'll buy sometime this week" to "I must be in the first 86,000 or I get nothing." Artificial scarcity transformed casual moviegoers into day traders rushing a single endpoint at midnight EST.

---

[14] **NFT (Non-Fungible Token):** a cryptographic certificate proving you "own" a JPEG everyone else can copy and download. Primarily used to melt servers and investor optimism. Also: proof that people will buy anything if you stop being ashamed of selling nothing.

AMC went down in under sixty seconds. Fandango lasted ninety. Regal collapsed under the refugee wave—everyone fleeing broken platforms, arriving simultaneously, creating a perfect cascade across American ticketing infrastructure. Every graph went vertical. Every backend thread accepted its fate.

The frontend showed spinning wheels and timeouts. While the vendors never released a detailed post-mortem, the symptoms—spinning wheels, inventory timeouts, and queue failures—point to a classic suspect in high-concurrency systems: database lock contention. Under Spider-Man load, it is highly probable that thousands of threads fought over the same tables simultaneously.

Seat selection normally takes microseconds—lock the row, check availability, commit, release. Under Spider-Man load, thousands of threads fought over the same tables simultaneously. What should have been a queue became a demolition derby. Threads waited for locks. Locks waited for commits. Commits waited for other locks. The database wasn't processing reservations—it was refereeing a circular deadlock where every transaction blocked every other transaction.

Row-level locks piled up. Connection pools exhausted. The system ground to a halt not from volume—databases handle tens of thousands of writes per second—but because every write fought every other write for the same microscopic slice of data. Meanwhile, autoscaling spun up more servers, which just meant more threads waiting to fight over those same bytes, faster.

Virtual waiting rooms became eternal purgatory. Users queued for an hour, reached checkout, got booted by 504s. Retry buttons multiplied the disaster. And while humans refreshed frantically, bots executed with mechanical precision, parsing and submitting faster than pages could render.

By 2 AM EST, systems limped back to life. By sunrise, eBay listed NFTs at $10k–$25k. Engineers were exhausted. Fans were furious. Official statements blamed "unprecedented demand"—which is accurate only if telling millions of people to sprint toward the same door counts as "unprecedented" rather than "foreseeable."

This wasn't a capacity problem. It was an incentive design problem that manifested as a database problem. The systems could have handled the traffic if it arrived like traffic instead of like an avalanche. Marketing transformed behavior from "I want tickets" into "I must win this race," and nobody consulted engineering before launching.

LESSON LEARNED

- Artificial scarcity compresses demand into system-killing spikes—"first 86,000 get NFTs" is functionally identical to "please DDoS us at midnight."

- Autoscaling handles load, not lock contention. You can't scale out of thousands of threads fighting over the same database rows.

- When marketing gamifies urgency, engineering inherits a race condition designed by people who've never heard of the CAP theorem.

- A queue in front of the database is a safety feature; a queue inside the database is a crime scene.

Everyone kept saying blockbuster premieres were dead after the pandemic. Few realized the part that died first would be the ticketing systems.

Apple TCC Privacy Bug
When Permissions Raced The Clock

Date: 2021

Impact: Potential privacy bypass affecting millions of macOS users

Root Cause: Race condition in the TCC (Transparency, Consent, and Control) permissions subsystem

Apple built macOS's privacy framework, TCC, to be a gatekeeper between apps and your most sensitive data. It's the invisible bouncer deciding which apps can peek through your webcam, listen through your mic, or rummage through your files. Unfortunately, in 2021 that bouncer was having a bad day. Researchers found that the doors didn't always close fast enough. A race condition—two bits of code competing to move faster—let malicious apps sneak in during the split second between *"Are you allowed?"* and *"Too late, you're already in."*

The flaw, tracked as **CVE-2021-30713**[15], affected macOS 10.15 (Catalina), 11.x (Big Sur), and early 12.x (Monterey). At its core, TCC relied on a small database called TCC.db, which logged every permission grant and denial—essentially a digital guest list. But when too many apps knocked on the door at once, the system's timing fell apart. It wasn't properly synchronized, so a clever piece of code could exploit those nanoseconds of hesitation and slip through before the lock engaged.

---

[15] **CVE** stands for *Common Vulnerabilities and Exposures*—a public catalog of known software security flaws maintained by *MITRE Corporation* and funded by the U.S. government. Those odd-looking numbers, like CVE-2021-30713, are the reason thousands of cybersecurity specialists lose sleep around the world.

In plain terms: the privacy guard was checking IDs at the door, but if you sprinted fast enough, you could walk right past while it was still reaching for the clipboard.

No widespread attacks were confirmed, but the implications were embarrassing. Any unpatched Mac could, in theory, be tricked into granting access to the camera, microphone, or personal files—no popup, no warning, just quiet snooping. The irony? Apple's marketing called privacy a "fundamental right," yet even their watchdog needed a leash. Once again, reality reminded everyone that even billion-dollar security slogans are still written in code, and code has a sense of humor.

Apple patched the issue in September 2021 through Security Update 2021-005 for macOS 10.15 and equivalents for newer systems. The fix introduced stricter validation and locking, making the decision and enforcement steps occur together—finally an atomic operation worthy of the word "secure." No user interaction was needed, aside from the usual *"Please restart to finish installing updates you ignored for three weeks."*

The discovery joined a growing list of TCC hiccups, including earlier bugs exploited by the XCSSET malware. It pushed Apple to rethink concurrency testing in its privacy stack and, predictably, reignited debate about the company's habit of issuing silent patches. Users got the fix without explanation, just a vague "security improvements" —because nothing says transparency like opacity wrapped in an NDA.

LESSON LEARNED

- Privacy promises crumble without atomic checks— make decision and enforcement one step.

- Test privacy and permission systems under concurrency, not just functionality.
- Even privacy frameworks need transparency in patching and disclosure.
- A silent patch fixes code, but not trust.
- The fastest exploit is sometimes just the one that wins the race.

The race wasn't between users and hackers—it was between Apple's own threads.

Ethereum DAO Hack
When Code's Law Met Human Panic

Date: June 2016

Impact: ~$60M (3.6M ETH) drained, Ethereum split into ETH and ETC

Root Cause: Reentrancy race condition in smart contract

Back in 2016, Ethereum was still a shiny newcomer in the crypto world — one of those digital currencies that promised freedom from banks, governments, and boring middlemen. The idea was simple: money without a central bank, running on math instead of trust. A better, fairer, more democratic economy — at least on paper. In practice? Let's just say this series will have more to say about that later.

The DAO, a crowdfunded *"decentralized venture capital fund,"* had raised over $150 million worth of Ether, making it the largest crowdfunding project ever. But on June 17, an attacker discovered that The DAO's smart contract was, quite literally, too trusting.

The culprit was a **reentrancy race condition**—a vulnerability that let a contract call itself repeatedly before finishing a transaction. When The DAO tried to transfer Ether, it sent the money *before* updating the sender's balance. That created a window of opportunity: the attacker's contract simply called back into The DAO again and again, draining funds before the ledger realized anything was missing. By the time the dust settled, roughly $60 million was sitting in the attacker's "child DAO."

In human terms, it was like withdrawing money from an ATM that never updates your balance, and realizing you can just keep pressing the button.

Panic spread faster than the blockchain could process blocks. Ether's price plunged nearly 50% as investors realized that *"code is law"* sounded great—until the law had a bug. The DAO's code was immutable, meaning it couldn't be patched. And in Ethereum's world, immutability wasn't just a feature; it was a religion.

Then came the argument that split an entire ecosystem. One camp said, "The blockchain must stay untouched—code did exactly what it was written to do." The other said, "If we let the thief walk away with $60 million, the whole idea of trustless finance collapses." After weeks of chaos, the developers did what humans always do when ideals meet reality: they hit the reset button. A new version of Ethereum was launched with the stolen money rolled back and refunded. Most users followed that version, now called **Ethereum (ETH)**. A smaller but stubborn group refused and stayed on the old one—**Ethereum Classic (ETC)**—keeping the "original" blockchain alive as a monument to immutability and stubborn pride.

The bug itself was a textbook example of sloppy sequencing: The DAO sent money before cleaning up its own bookkeeping. In more human terms, it was like handing over the car keys before checking if you still had the car. The safer approach is simple—update your own records first, then deal with the outside world. That lesson became known in the community as the *checks-before-actions* rule, now one of Solidity's holy commandments.

Philosophically, though, the DAO hack became something much bigger—a reminder that every supposedly *"trustless"* system still depends on people. Once developers overrode the *"immutable"* code, they proved that decentralization isn't a law of nature. It's a choice—and sometimes, a compromise.

LESSON LEARNED

- Checks before actions: update state before external calls.
- Audit and formally verify smart contracts—because the blockchain doesn't forget.
- Immutability is a social construct; consensus beats purity.
- Race conditions exist even on supposedly deterministic systems.
- "Code is law" works until lawyers get involved.

The blockchain didn't fork. Human faith in '*code is law*' did.

Therac-25
When Software Became Lethal

Date: 1985–1987

Impact: At least six patients killed or seriously injured by radiation overdoses

Root Cause: Software race conditions, lack of hardware safety interlocks, and overconfidence in automation

If there's a patron saint of software engineering ethics, it's probably the six people who died because a computer couldn't keep up with a fast typist. Therac-25 wasn't just a failure—it was the moment the software industry lost its innocence.

Therac-25 was a medical linear accelerator built by Atomic Energy of Canada Limited (AECL). It was designed to deliver controlled doses of radiation to cancer patients —an evolution of earlier machines that had used both mechanical and electronic safeguards to prevent lethal overdoses. But in the mid-1980s, engineers decided the future was software-controlled.

Hardware interlocks were expensive, bulky, and— apparently—unnecessary when you had perfectly reliable code. *IF* you had perfectly reliable code.

Between 1985 and 1987, at least six patients that we know of – the actual number may be higher, obscured by incomplete reporting and corporate opacity – in the United States and Canada received massive overdoses—up to 125 times the prescribed dose. The burns and injuries were catastrophic. Some patients died within weeks. Others suffered severe and permanent damage. Each incident seemed isolated until investigators realized they all had one thing in common: the same machine, the same software, and the same fatal race condition.

The Therac-25's control system ran on a DEC PDP-11 with software that couldn't handle human typing speed. If an operator typed treatment parameters too quickly—correcting a mistake, say, within a fraction of a second—the machine could enter a faulty state where it delivered the electron beam at full power without the protective metal attenuator. The difference between 'therapeutic' and 'lethal' was measured in keystrokes per second. A fast typist could kill someone by fixing a typo.

Compounding the tragedy was a dangerous cocktail of corporate denial and inadequate safety testing. AECL's response was textbook corporate deflection. When hospitals reported injuries, the company blamed operator error. When physicists provided evidence of software failures, AECL insisted their testing had been thorough. The software was proprietary, documentation was sparse, and for years the company maintained that accidents were statistically impossible. Meanwhile, people kept dying.

It took years—and the intervention of both the FDA and independent researchers—before the true cause was identified.

Therac-25 became a defining case in the history of software engineering ethics. It demonstrated that software bugs can be just as deadly as mechanical failures, and that automation without accountability magnifies risk rather than reducing it. Every engineering discipline since has referenced it as a turning point—a stark reminder that trust in software must be earned, not assumed.

LESSON LEARNED

- Never remove a hardware safety mechanism without an equally reliable software substitute.

- Redundant safety systems exist precisely because the primary system will eventually fail.
- Automation can reduce human error—but only if it's designed with human fallibility in mind.
- Transparency and traceability in safety-critical code are not optional.
- Denial is not a mitigation strategy.

Toyota Unintended Acceleration

Date: 2009–2010

Impact: 89+ deaths linked to unintended acceleration; 9 million vehicles recalled; $1.2 billion criminal penalty.

Root Cause: Stack overflow, memory corruption due to recursion, and cyclomatic complexity ("Spaghetti Code"[16]).

Between 2009 and 2010, Toyota faced one of the most devastating safety crises in automotive history. Drivers began reporting that their vehicles were accelerating out of control, failing to respond to the brakes. The incidents weren't just technical anomalies; they were fatal. The crisis reached its horrifying peak with a widely publicized crash involving a Lexus ES350 in California. The final moments were captured in a 911 call that ended with the passenger's desperate plea: *"We're going 120... the accelerator is stuck... there's no brakes... Hold on and pray."* The

---

[16] **Spaghetti code** is a term coined in the 1960s to describe source code that has become excessively complex, unstructured, and difficult to maintain due to poor design, repeated modifications, or lack of modular architecture. It refers to programs where control flow and data dependencies are intertwined in a chaotic manner, making it hard to trace logic or implement changes without unintended consequences.

line went dead as the car struck an embankment, killing all four occupants.

Initially, the industry focus was mechanical. Toyota blamed floor mats trapping the gas pedal and later "sticky" accelerator pedals, issuing massive recalls to address hardware interference. Yet, even after these physical fixes, reports of unintended acceleration persisted. The problem wasn't on the floor of the car; it was in the brain.

While a 2011 NASA investigation failed to identify a specific software trigger, a subsequent 2013 court case (*Bookout v. Toyota*) exposed the reality. Independent embedded software experts from the Barr Group conducted a deep audit of Toyota's Electronic Throttle Control System (ETCS) and found it to be dangerously flawed. The source code was described as "spaghetti code"—an unstructured, tangled mess that violated industry standards for safety-critical systems.

The system relied on over 11,000 global variables, creating a chaotic state where data could be overwritten by any function at any time. Worse, the code violated rules against recursion, allowing functions to call themselves until they triggered a "stack overflow"—essentially running out of memory and crashing critical tasks. The experts demonstrated that if the specific task controlling the throttle (Task X) died due to this memory corruption, the fail-safe "Watchdog Timer" failed to notice. The watchdog continued to be reset by other surviving tasks, tricking the computer into thinking everything was fine while the throttle remained frozen in the "wide open" position.

The court testimony effectively ended the "mechanical only" defense. It showed that a single bit flip in memory, uncorrected by the hardware and exacerbated by bad software architecture, could override the driver's input completely. Toyota eventually agreed to a $1.2 billion settlement, and the automotive industry was forced to accept a grim new reality: mechanical redundancy isn't enough if the code that controls it is too complex to be safe.

LESSON LEARNED

- Isolate critical control loops from non-critical logic to prevent cascading failures.
- High cyclomatic complexity and "spaghetti code" make safety verification impossible.
- Excessive global state creates non-deterministic behavior that cannot be reliably tested.
- A fail-safe watchdog must monitor the health of specific processes, not just the CPU's power status.
- Strict adherence to standards like MISRA-C is the only defense against memory corruption in embedded systems.
- In drive-by-wire systems, a software crash is functionally indistinguishable from a cut brake line.

CHAPTER 5:
SCALE & EXPONENTIAL PAIN

Computers are really good at doing the same thing over and over again, really fast. That's their superpower. But like any superpower, it comes with a catch: they don't know when to stop. Humans tend to think in linear terms —one step, two steps, ten steps. Computers double, triple, and explode their way forward in exponential leaps. And when exponential growth meets fragile infrastructure, things fall apart in ways that feel both absurd and terrifying.

This chapter is about scale: what happens when systems that seem solid suddenly encounter runaway growth. It's about the tipping points where a little too much becomes way too much, and why the curves that look so elegant on paper end up smashing real-world systems. If the first chapters showed how numbers lie and time betrays us, this one shows how growth—innocent-looking on a graph —turns into a wrecking ball.

Underneath all of it is a deceptively simple truth: exponential growth doesn't just add up, it blows up. Whether it's packets flooding routers, processes spawning uncontrollably, or recovery systems stepping on each other's toes, the effect is the same: what seemed manageable at first doubles, doubles again, and before you can blink, the whole system is on fire.

Scale is a cruel teacher, and in the next pages we'll see why computers hate exponential growth with a passion.

The Comair Christmas Meltdown
When A Snowstorm Found Your Integer Limit

Date: December 24–25, 2004

Impact: 1,100 flights canceled; entire fleet grounded; 30,000 passengers stranded

Root Cause: 16-bit signed integer overflow in the crew-scheduling system

Before we dive headfirst into the wild world of exponential growth, let's pause for a delightful reminder: you don't always need a pandemic, a viral cascade, or a runaway algorithm to blow up a system. Sometimes all it takes is weather looking at human infrastructure and saying, *"Oh, you're doing a scale chapter? Cute. Let me play."*

In December 2004, nature decided to join the fun. A massive winter storm swept through the Ohio Valley, hammering Cincinnati—Comair's main hub—with ice, snow, and the sort of conditions that make airlines reconsider their life choices. Delays cascaded, flights were rerouted, crews were shuffled, and everyone involved assumed things were chaotic but manageable.

They were not.

Comair was using a legacy crew-scheduling system built by SBS International. Like many early-1990s enterprise systems, it was designed with the optimism of an era when memory was expensive, CPUs were slow, and no one believed numbers would ever get *that* big. The system tracked crew reassignments using a 16-bit signed integer —a maximum of 32,767 changes per month.

To the designers, this was generous. What kind of catastrophe could possibly require more than thirty-two thousand schedule updates? (Spoiler: a snowstorm.)

On Christmas Eve, after days of disruption, reassignments, reserve activations, and last-minute swaps, the counter ticked from 32,767—the maximum—and wrapped into negative territory" to stay both clear and precise.

And then everything exploded.

A signed 16-bit integer cannot hold 32,768. At that point it overflows, wraps, and becomes negative. The scheduling system—already strained—tried to index a new schedule update into a value that no longer made sense. It didn't just produce the wrong number. The entire database locked itself into a corrupted state. Crew pairings could no longer be validated. Flight assignments could no longer be issued. Every attempt to schedule anything triggered deeper inconsistencies.

The system didn't fail gracefully. It failed like someone had pulled the fire alarm inside the code.

Comair couldn't simply reboot. The corrupted counter meant the system was incapable of generating legal crew schedules, dispatching flights, or even printing pairing lists. Fixing it required shutting down operations entirely while the database was rebuilt from scratch.

On Christmas Day, Comair canceled 1,100 flights—100% of its schedule. Thirty thousand passengers were stranded nationwide. Other airlines couldn't absorb the load due to the holiday surge. Bags piled up in airports. Customer service lines stretched into geological time.

The most painful part? None of this involved exponential curves. Comair didn't get hit by viral growth, runaway recursion, or branching cascades. This was linear growth —a counter ticking up one update at a time until the month happened to include a storm big enough to cross an arbitrary integer boundary.

It was the simplest possible failure, triggered by the simplest possible math.

LESSON LEARNED

- Nature doesn't care about your integer limits, and it will gleefully test them during holidays.
- A 16-bit counter is not "conservative design"—it's future debt waiting for bad weather.
- If your system cannot exceed a threshold without collapsing, it's not a system; it's a countdown.
- Rare events become inevitable when multiplied by time, scale, and holidays.

Everyone prepared for frozen runways. Nobody expected frozen computer systems.

The Buffett Overflow
When Nasdaq Ran Out Of Numbers

Date: May 4, 2021

Impact: Trading disruption for BRK.A; emergency suspension of price broadcasts

Root Cause: 32-bit integer ceiling reached by the world's most expensive stock

Warren Buffett is famous for many things: long-term investing, plain-spoken wisdom, and turning Coca-Cola into a personality trait. What he is not usually accused of is committing an integer overflow—though the pun 'Buffett Overflow' is too good to resist. Yet on May 4, 2021, Berkshire Hathaway Class A (BRK.A) became so absurdly valuable that it punched straight through NASDAQ's numeric limits.

To understand how this happened, we need to clear up one misconception: financial exchanges do not use floating-point numbers. As you already know from the very first chapter, they learned that lesson decades earlier —often the hard way. When your job is to store prices that decide the fate of pension funds and hedge funds, you avoid floats the way pilots avoid thunderstorms. Instead, NASDAQ used scaled integers: store the real price multiplied by 10,000 as an unsigned 32-bit integer. No rounding errors, no drifting decimals, just clean integer arithmetic.

Sound decision. Until the number gets too big.

A 32-bit unsigned integer tops out at 4,294,967,295. Divide by 10,000 (their scaling factor), and you get a maximum representable stock price of $429,496.7295.

For normal companies this ceiling is... generous. For Berkshire Hathaway, it was a Tuesday.

In early 2021, BRK.A traded well above $430,000 per share, casually blowing past the limit like it didn't even notice there *was* a limit. And unlike signed integers, which fail by flipping negative, an unsigned integer overflow wraps around to the bottom. In other words:

> The world's most expensive stock was about to look like a penny stock because math ran out of bits.

Depending on the exact intermediate calculations, NASDAQ's broadcast price would have wrapped to something hilariously low—potentially fractions of a cent or a few thousand dollars. Either way, it would've implied that Berkshire Hathaway went from "buy a house or buy one share" to "grab a coffee or buy one share."

NASDAQ did the only sane thing: they pulled the plug. They halted publication of the BRK.A price, patched the encoder, and upgraded their entire price-transmission pipeline to 64-bit integers, raising the ceiling high enough that even Buffett would have trouble hitting it again. (Probably.)

But the more embarrassing truth is this: none of this happened overnight. Berkshire Hathaway didn't wake up one morning and suddenly leap from $50,000 to $430,000. The climb took years, each new all-time high sending a polite, increasingly urgent memo to NASDAQ's infrastructure: *"Hi, I'm going to break your integers soon."* And NASDAQ, a trillion-dollar exchange operator, had all the time in the world to prepare. Instead, they behaved like someone standing on the tracks, watching a train approach, fully convinced it would swerve out of courtesy.

This wasn't a surprise event. It was a slow-motion arithmetic inevitability, ignored until denial was no longer mathematically sustainable.

It wasn't a system crash. It was something quieter and far more humiliating: a reminder that even the world's largest exchanges can be undone by a literal number being too small.

And yes, engineers noticed the irony: after all the lectures about the dangers of floating-point arithmetic, it was the *safe*, integer-based solution that failed first.

LESSON LEARNED

- If your business depends on numbers, make sure your numbers can count high enough.

- Unsigned overflow doesn't apologize; it just turns $430,000 into pocket change.

- Financial systems outgrow their assumptions long before anyone admits those assumptions were temporary.

> • Upgrading from 32-bit to 64-bit is not "over-engineering" — it's adult supervision.

Everyone feared Buffett's stock would crash someday. No one expected the first thing to hit the floor would be NASDAQ's integer type.

 **Explainer:**
Why Computers Hate Exponential Growth

Let's start our conversation about exponential growth with a puzzle to set your intuition on fire:

Take a giant sheet of paper, just 0.1 mm (0.0039 inches) thick. Imagine you can fold it in half as many times as you like.

Quick reality detour: In real life, of course, you can't fold an ordinary sheet more than seven times. In 2002, Britney Gallivan set the world record by folding a roll of toilet paper 12 times. The roll was 1.2 km (4,000 feet) long, and she needed math and serious determination to pull it off. So yes, with enough toilet paper and stubbornness, you can break records. But let's stay theoretical for now.

Now, average distance from Earth to the Moon? About 384,400 km (238,855 miles). The question: how many folds until your paper stack is thicker than that?

Most people I've asked guess in the thousands. Some, more cautious, say hundreds. A few shoot for around a hundred. The actual answer? Forty-two. Yes, *that* number. Turns out exponential growth reaches the Moon right around the meaning of life, the universe, and everything.

That's right: after 42 folds, a 0.1 mm (0.0039 inches) paper tower explodes to 440,000 km (273,400 miles), soaring past the Moon.

That's exponential growth. It doesn't creep, it explodes. Each fold doubles the thickness, and doubling compounds terrifyingly fast. Our brains, wired for linear thinking, can't keep up.

For a more everyday example, self-help coaches love to say: "Improve yourself 1% every day, and in a year you'll be 37.8 times better." They usually skip the boring caveats like diminishing returns or basic human limits. But hey, it sounds great on a poster.

The point isn't to argue with 5 a.m. gurus. It's to show that exponential growth feels harmless at the start but spirals out of control faster than intuition allows. And in complex systems—computer networks, telecom grids, the entire internet—this curve isn't just scary. It's catastrophic. As the next stories will show, once exponential growth gets loose, the result isn't a graceful slowdown. It's a spectacular crash.

The Morris Worm

Date: November 2, 1988

Impact: ~10% of the entire internet brought to its knees (about 60,000 machines at the time)

Root cause: A self-replicating worm written by a curious grad student — and one very questionable design choice

Robert Tappan Morris, a 23-year-old Cornell graduate student, wasn't out to burn the internet down. He just wanted to measure it. In 1988, that was a genuinely mysterious question: how big was this shiny new network? His solution was a worm — a little program that could spread from machine to machine and report back. Purely academic. What could possibly go wrong? (Hint: everything.)

The worm exploited holes in familiar Unix utilities like `sendmail`, `finger`, and `rsh`. Once inside, it installed itself and went hunting for new prey. Elegant in theory, if you squinted hard enough. But Morris had a nagging worry: what if admins noticed repeat infections and blocked them? His "brilliant" solution was to force a re-infection 14% of the time. Because nothing says "scientific rigor" like Russian roulette with the world's computer network.

That tiny percentage was the butterfly wingbeat that unleashed chaos. Machines didn't get infected once — they got buried under dozens or hundreds of copies. Performance tanked. Networks choked. Servers thrashed and keeled over. Sysadmins stared at screens like doctors facing a patient growing extra limbs: processes multiplying uncontrollably, no obvious cause. Within hours, about 10% of the internet was toast. Remember, this wasn't some war game scenario — this was just Tuesday night in academia.

Usenet — think of it as the proto-Reddit or early Facebook — filled with frantic messages along the lines of "does anyone know why my machine is convulsing?" Universities yanked cables out of walls, admins coordinated by phone like it was a digital fire brigade, and nobody really knew how to stop the bleeding.

Eventually, the worm was dissected, patches were cobbled together, and Morris himself was caught. He became the first person convicted under the brand-new Computer Fraud and Abuse Act. His punishment? Probation, community service, and a fine. Considering he'd just taken down a tenth of the world's most advanced network, you could call that a bargain.

The legacy? Priceless. This was the internet's coming-of-age disaster. It launched the security industry, forced institutions to care about digital hygiene, and proved beyond doubt that scale is merciless. The first global crash didn't come from enemy nations or shadowy hackers. It came from a curious grad student with a compiler and a 14% "just to be safe" clause. Spoiler: it wasn't safe.

LESSON LEARNED

- The first internet-wide crash didn't come from hackers or war — it came from a student with a compiler and too much curiosity.
- Even non-malicious code can wreak havoc at scale.
- "Just 14% chance" is still a terrible idea when the loop is infinite.
- Sometimes the scariest bugs are the ones born out of good intentions and bad math.

Congratulations, you found the scale limit of the early internet. Accidentally.

SQL Slammer

Date: January 25, 2003

Impact: Within 10 minutes, the worm infected 75 000 servers and crippled global Internet traffic; banks, ATMs, and airlines went dark before anyone could even open their incident playbooks.

Root Cause: A buffer overflow in Microsoft SQL Server's "Resolution Service" allowed a 256-byte payload to replicate itself exponentially without writing to disk — a pure in-memory denial of service on a planetary scale.

If the Morris Worm was the internet's first migraine, SQL Slammer was a full-on seizure. The worm wasn't big, it wasn't clever, and it didn't even try to steal data. It was just small, dumb, and brutally fast — the digital equivalent of a toddler with a drum kit.

The entire program fits into 376 bytes. For perspective, this paragraph and the one before it together total 404 — more than the worm itself.

Slammer targeted Microsoft SQL Server and its lightweight cousin, MSDE 2000, via port 1434/UDP, causing a buffer overflow. That's a mouthful — so let's unpack it.

Think of a port as a numbered door into a building; software listens on specific doors for visitors. UDP-style packets (I'll explain this term in chapter 6) are basically "knock-and-run" — you send the packet and don't wait to confirm anyone opened the door.

A buffer overflow? Imagine trying to shove an entire American football team through that door. The players who don't fit spill into the neighbour's yard, knock over the grill, and cannonball into the pool. In computer terms, the excess data overruns adjacent memory and party-crashes other running applications — they start misbehaving, crashing, or executing whatever the overflow carries.

Once Slammer found a vulnerable machine, it stuffed its tiny payload in, hijacked execution, and immediately began spraying copies of itself at random IP addresses. No files encrypted, no ransom notes, no espionage — just bandwidth turned into confetti.

The speed was unprecedented. Within ten minutes of its release, Slammer had infected roughly 75,000 servers worldwide. Internet traffic surged by about 10%, which sounds modest until you realize that meant entire backbones went wobbly. Routers crashed under the flood. ISPs throttled into paralysis. Continental Airlines grounded flights because its ticketing systems were offline. Bank of America ATMs went dark. South Korea basically fell off the internet for half a day. The collateral damage spread far beyond IT: suddenly, a worm the size of a text message had grounded planes and blocked cash withdrawals.

The really infuriating part? Microsoft had already released a patch six months earlier. The vulnerability was documented, the fix was available, but patch management in 2002 was more wishful thinking than discipline. Admins either missed the memo, didn't prioritize it, or assumed nobody would bother writing an exploit. Slammer was the internet's blunt reminder that ignoring patches doesn't mean you're safe — it just means you're waiting your turn.

To make matters worse, Slammer's tiny size gave it a unique advantage. Many firewalls and intrusion detection systems of the time filtered out larger packets but let these 376-byte packets sail straight through. Network defenses optimized for the "big bad attacks" of the day simply weren't ready for a mosquito-sized threat that traveled at jet speed.

Was it malicious? Probably not in the cinematic sense. Code analysis suggests it may have been released accidentally during testing. But intent didn't matter. The result was one of the fastest, most chaotic internet disruptions in history, and a stark lesson in how neglect can be just as dangerous as malice. For many companies, it was the first time executives realized that their IT teams' "patch later" policy could have real-world consequences measured in grounded flights, lost revenue, and public humiliation.

And while Slammer itself burned out quickly — the worm spread so fast that it effectively saturated its own pool of targets in minutes — its legacy lingers. It became the textbook example cited in security trainings, policy documents, and conference talks. If you've ever had a boss breathing down your neck to patch faster, chances are Slammer's ghost was in the room.

LESSON LEARNED

- Speed kills. Propagation can cripple systems before humans even realize what's happening.
- "Patch later" is just another way of saying "get owned soon."
- Small doesn't mean harmless: a 376-byte worm grounded airplanes.
- Intent is irrelevant at scale; chaos doesn't care if you meant it or not.
- Security theater won't save you — timely, boring, unglamorous updates will.

SQL Slammer didn't steal, encrypt, or spy. It just showed how fragile the global internet was in 2003 — and still is, whenever we treat patches like optional updates.

AT&T Long-Distance Outage

Date: January 15, 1990

Impact: A single software update crashed 114 switches nationwide, cutting off long-distance service for an estimated 60 million calls over nine hours — effectively muting America for a day.

Root Cause: A race condition in the recovery code of AT&T's 4ESS switches caused neighboring nodes to simultaneously reset each other in an infinite loop of well-intentioned self-healing.

At 2:25 p.m. on a Monday afternoon, America's proud long-distance phone network decided to take a nine-hour nap. The crown jewels of AT&T's telecom empire—the 4ESS electronic switching systems—collapsed almost in unison. For the better part of a workday, U.S. customers couldn't place long-distance calls. Airlines couldn't confirm tickets. Wall Street traders couldn't yell at each other across states. For a country addicted to phone lines, this was the digital equivalent of a sudden nationwide laryngitis.

Naturally, conspiracy theories erupted. Was it hackers? Terrorists? The Soviets? Nope. The true culprit was more humiliating: a single missing `break` statement in C code. Not a grand cyber offensive, not enemy agents in trench coats—just one lonely punctuation mark gone AWOL. It was the software equivalent of forgetting to put the lid on a blender before hitting *max power*.

Here's how the chaos unfolded. Each 4ESS switch was designed with resilience in mind. If a switch encountered an error, it would reboot quickly and send out a recovery message to its peers. The logic was simple: "I tripped, but I'm back, everything's fine." Except thanks to the bug, that message wasn't a reassuring wave—it was a live grenade lobbed over the fence. Neighboring switches, upon receiving it, keeled over in sympathy, rebooted, and hurled grenades of their own. The result was a synchronized nationwide conga line of collapse: 114 switches stuck in endless crash-reboot cycles, all enthusiastically sabotaging each other in the name of "resilience."

Ironically, AT&T's vaunted self-healing mechanism turned into the accelerant of failure. The faster the switches tried to recover, the faster they knocked their neighbors down. Imagine a fire alarm that, when triggered, activates sprinklers filled with gasoline. Designed to save the system, it instead guaranteed mutual destruction.

The fallout was brutal. An estimated $60 million evaporated in lost business. Airlines scrambled with crippled booking systems. Financial firms found their trades delayed or cancelled. Thousands of ordinary Americans picked up their receivers and met nothing but busy signals. Congress held hearings to demand answers from AT&T execs, who had to explain how the world's most reliable long-distance network had been undone by a missing line of code. Unsurprisingly, "punctuation" wasn't the explanation lawmakers wanted to hear.

The press had a field day. Headlines screamed about "The Most Expensive Typo in History." Conspiracy enthusiasts filled in their own blanks with Cold War paranoia. Surely, they argued, a mere programming error couldn't possibly bring down a national network. Except that's exactly what happened: no sabotage, no foreign agents, just one misplaced line of logic. Humanity had survived the Cold War, only to be brought low by punctuation.

The outage became infamous not just for its cost, but for what it revealed: scale is merciless. At national scale, even a one-line bug becomes a weapon of mass disruption. And resilience isn't free—done badly, it becomes the accelerant of collapse. AT&T's engineers discovered that the hard way.

LESSON LEARNED

- Resilience mechanisms can amplify, not mitigate, failures when misdesigned.
- Scale makes trivial bugs catastrophic: one line of code toppled an entire national network.
- Cascading failures are sneaky: the system fails by trying too hard to fix itself.
- Never underestimate the destructive power of a missing semicolon, brace, or `break`.

One line of code, nine hours of silence, sixty million dollars: the most expensive typo in telecom history.

—— Stack Overflow Regex Outage ——
When One Line Of Text Ddos-Es The Entire Site

Date: 20 July 2016
Impact: 34 minutes of complete downtime
Root Cause: Catastrophic backtracking in a poorly written regular expression triggered by a single user edit

Stack Overflow has survived waves of traffic, controversial Java questions, and endless debates about tabs versus spaces. What finally brought it down—completely, for half an hour—was one user editing one post containing one very stupid thing: around twenty thousand spaces at the end of a line.

Stack Overflow's application servers used a regex to trim trailing whitespace. Nothing fancy. Nothing dangerous. Just: "look at the end of the line and remove extra spaces." Easy.

Without getting ahead of ourselves (we'll cover Regex properly in Part II), here is the simplified version: some patterns are harmless, others are time bombs. To figure out how many spaces to remove, the regex engine had to check many possible combinations of matches. With a handful of spaces, that happens in milliseconds. With 20,000 spaces, the number of combinations grows **exponentially**.

This is exactly the kind of thing this chapter warns about. The input grew linearly (just more spaces), but the time required to process it hit a wall where "slow" suddenly becomes "heat death of the universe."

For that one edit, the regex would have taken years of CPU time to finish.

Instead, it locked up the entire server thread instantly. And not just one server: every web node tried to process the same poisoned input, pegging all CPU cores to 100%. The load balancer watched its servers scream in agony, assumed they were dead, and dutifully took them out of rotation.

Within minutes, Stack Overflow became a read-only ghost town—and then not even that.

This wasn't a database issue. The storage layer was fine. It was the application tier collapsing under its own text-processing logic. Engineers quickly identified the offending regex and replaced it with a simpler, safe version—one that doesn't attempt interstellar mathematics when asked to remove spaces.

LESSON LEARNED

- Regex engines are powerful, but untrustworthy when fed untrusted input.
- Linear-looking problems can hide exponential landmines.
- One user input can be a denial-of-service attack without any malicious intent.
- Always assume someone, someday, will paste twenty thousand spaces.

And the ultimate irony? There is a non-zero chance that the engineer who wrote that faulty regex copied it from a Stack Overflow answer.

 **Explainer:**
Factorial Growth – Worse Than Exponential

If exponential growth scares you, factorial growth is pure nightmare fuel. Exponential means doubling: 2, 4, 8, 16... Factorial means multiplying by every number along the way: 1, 2, 6, 24, 120... By the time you hit 20, factorial growth is already unimaginable.

To make this less abstract, let's use a historical anecdote. In 1736, Leonhard Euler—one of the greatest mathematicians in history—faced the famous "Seven Bridges of Königsberg" problem. The city (then in Prussia, now Kaliningrad in Russia) had seven bridges. The challenge: could you plan a walk that crossed each bridge exactly once?

Seven bridges sounds manageable. But if you try brute force, you need to check all possible bridge orders—7! possibilities. That's 5,040. Many of those paths collapse quickly as nonsense, but you still have to test them. And yes, before you ask: Euler didn't have a laptop at hand (for the historically disoriented, computers wouldn't be invented until the mid-20th century, which somewhat complicated his debugging options in the 18th).

At one second per check, a computer would need under an hour and a half. Add just one more bridge: 8! = 40,320 possibilities, or 11 hours. At 10 bridges, you're at 3.6 million, or 42 days. At 15 bridges, it's 1.3 trillion paths—over 41,000 years. And if you scale up to real cities—Venice with ~400 bridges, New York ~2,000, Hamburg ~2,500, or Chongqing with 13,000—the timescales rocket beyond the age of the universe.

Euler, of course, realized brute force was futile. He invented graph theory, which became a foundation of modern mathematics and computer science. The lesson: raw power can't solve everything. Smarter methods are the only way forward. Or, as a slightly nerdier academic might phrase it: finding more efficient algorithms is the real superpower.

That's why you rarely hear about spectacular factorial disasters. They don't happen because nobody dares to deploy systems that rely on solving them by brute force. Most scientists and engineers would run screaming at the suggestion. And for good reason: exponential growth may break your system, but factorial growth breaks reality itself.

PART I: SUMMARY
DIGITAL FOUNDATIONS OF FAILURE

So what have we learned from this little tour through the digital underbelly? That computers don't usually fail in spectacular fashion because of some cinematic hacker pounding on a keyboard. They fail because of the boring stuff: numbers, time, and growth curves. The things we assume are neutral, universal, safe. The things we trust without thinking.

We've seen how small mismatches or lazy shortcuts can unravel entire systems. Numbers? They overflow, round the wrong way, or refuse to fit into the box you gave them. Time? It drifts, it jumps, it adds a leap second and suddenly airplanes can't take off. Growth? It doubles, doubles again, and before you know it the system isn't scaling, it's imploding. Different stories, different decades, same punchline: complexity plus scale turns minor errors into disasters.

The deeper connection here is humility. Our digital foundations are built on abstractions — formats, protocols, conventions — that only work as long as we stay within their invisible boundaries. Cross them, and the logic doesn't bend, it breaks. Computers are mercilessly literal. They do exactly what we told them to, never what we meant.

And yet, that's the point of this Almanac: to remind us that failure isn't exotic. It's ordinary. It lives in the spaces we don't think about because they seem too small, too trivial, too basic to matter. A missing symbol, an unchecked assumption, a single line of code. That's all it takes to turn "solid infrastructure" into "expensive paperweight."

Part I was about recognizing those hidden fragilities. The digital world isn't built on bedrock — it's built on shifting sand. And if we don't respect that, the next overflow, leap, or cascade is always just around the corner.

II. THE INTERNET'S HOUSE OF CARDS

PART II:
THE INTERNET'S HOUSE OF CARDS

In the previous part, we explored how computers fail on their own—arithmetic betraying physics, time losing its mind, exponential growth quietly turning competence into catastrophe. Now we're stepping back to look at the nervous system connecting it all: communication itself.

Welcome to the Internet: humanity's largest accidental construction project. A planet-wide web of machines duct-taped together by optimism, mutual faith, and the unshakeable belief that someone else knows what they're doing. You tap a screen in Berlin, and a server in California dutifully responds with cat memes or stock prices. It feels seamless. Beneath that illusion lies a structure so delicate it occasionally folds under its own genius.

At the heart of this fragile harmony are protocols—the choreography that lets machines "speak" to one another. Imagine a country-line dance in a roadside bar: if everyone knows the steps, it looks graceful. The moment one cowboy turns left when everyone else turns right, you get chaos, bruised egos, and spilled beer. Networking is exactly that—only the bar never closes, and nobody really knows who started the music.

These acronyms might sound like alphabet soup, but they're the backbone of how the Internet somehow holds together. BGP tells your data which path to take across the planet—and occasionally sends it on unscheduled intercontinental detours. DNS translates human-friendly names into machine numbers—until it forgets, and half the Internet becomes unfindable. TLS keeps your secrets sealed during transit—assuming everyone remembers who to trust and why. Load balancers distribute incoming traffic across multiple servers so no single machine collapses under the weight—or at least, that's the theory.

In practice, they're middlemen who occasionally become the bottleneck, amplify failures, or route requests in perfect circles until everything chokes. And hovering above this organized chaos are the cloud providers—the self-proclaimed demigods of reliability—promising to make everything "simple" while their engineers pray to uptime gods and prepare for the inevitable moment lightning hits a datacenter or someone mistypes a single character into a live console.

On paper, it's elegant: a global relay race where packets fly seamlessly between continents. In practice, it's a relay race where every runner is blindfolded, hoping the baton somehow lands in their hand. Sometimes it does. Sometimes it flies straight into the audience.

If the first part showed what happens when systems stumble in isolation, this one listens to the slurred conversation between them—the misunderstandings, routing loops, trust failures, and cascading collapses that turn minor hiccups into global migraines.

The Internet isn't a pyramid of perfection. It's a sprawling Jenga tower held together by duct tape, faith, and the miracle of low latency. And somehow, against all odds, it mostly works.

Until it doesn't.

Before we begin:

To all network engineers, sysadmins, and protocol purists: take a deep breath. Unclench your Ethernet cable. The simplifications ahead may induce mild nausea, spontaneous RFC quoting, or an uncontrollable urge to send me diagrams. Resist it. This isn't a certification exam —it's a guided tour through chaos.

Yes, BGP is messier than this, DNS has more exceptions than Catholic doctrine, and TLS handshakes could make even a priest doubt the concept of trust. But if we paused to explain every packet header, this book would be longer than the IPv6 address space. So let's agree on a truce: I'll simplify mercifully, you'll forgive generously, and together we'll keep the ping times low.

CHAPTER 6:
BGP - HOW THE INTERNET FINDS ITSELF

Before we can talk about what breaks, we have to understand what holds it all together. The Internet isn't just a pile of blinking boxes and buried cables—it's a living, breathing map that keeps redrawing itself. Every piece of information has to decide which way to go, and yet there's no central GPS, no all-knowing dispatcher pointing the way. Instead, thousands of networks whisper directions to each other like overly confident tourists arguing over who's got the better map. That exchange of directions, promises, and occasional lies is called BGP—the Border Gateway Protocol—and it's the system that lets the Internet quite literally find itself. Remarkably more effectively than Karen on her six-month meditation retreat in India.

Before we dive into the disasters, let's take a closer look at how this self-discovery process actually works. Because if you've ever wondered how a few lines of text can reroute the world, you're about to find out.

 **Explainer:**
The Internet's Honor System

The Internet isn't one massive machine; it's a patchwork quilt of millions of smaller networks scattered around the planet. Each of these "autonomous systems" owns a piece of cyberspace, routing traffic for its users. The tricky bit is making sure that information from your laptop in Berlin finds its way to a random server in Singapore, even though neither side has a clue where the other is. That's where BGP, the Border Gateway Protocol, enters the picture. It's the system where networks announce to their neighbors: "Hey, I know how to reach these addresses, send that stuff my way." The neighbors nod, pass the message along, and forward the data to whoever seems slightly closer to the goal. No GPS, no central command — just the digital equivalent of "I've heard a guy down the road knows a guy who might know."

Now, about those routes. This logic is often called hot-potato routing, because routers try to toss traffic away as quickly as possible, not necessarily wisely. (Yes, there's also "cold-potato routing." No, you don't need to know it unless your paycheck depends on it.)

Imagine working in a postal hub in Berlin. You don't need a map of the whole planet, just enough to guess whether a letter should go north, south, east, or west. Letter to Cologne? West. Done. Letter to Munich? South. Forward. Letter to Frankfurt? Hmm... southwest? Close enough — just hand it to whichever neighbor claims they know the way.

Note: real postal services don't work like this. The Internet kind of does.

Here's one more thing most people never think about: in the Internet (and any computer network, really), data isn't sent as a single blob. It's broken into *packets*, tiny parcels that travel independently and reunite at the destination. Think of it like ordering a big armchair online. The backrest might take the highway through Cologne, the seat could fly via Munich, and the armrests detour through Zurich because someone's logistics algorithm had a moment — and yes, sometimes the people (and routers) running these sorting centers make equally ridiculous decisions. In the end, all parts (hopefully) arrive and fit together. Usually.

Of course, routers aren't literally flipping coins; they follow a cocktail of tables, rules, and priorities, but they still rely heavily on trust. And that's where the comedy begins.

Picture a tiny post office in Wansdorf, a real village near Berlin, population as for the time of writing this 874. One morning, its postmaster, Hans, proudly declares, "I can deliver every letter in Germany. Trust me." And somehow, the entire country believes him. Within minutes, convoys of mail trucks reroute everything to Hans, a man whose main worries until now were counting the days to retirement and feeding the local stray cats. Predictably, disaster follows.

That's what can happen in BGP. If one network, through typo, hubris, or sheer chaos, starts shouting "I know how to reach everywhere," and nobody checks, the Internet takes it at face value. Suddenly, global traffic funnels through a place that was never meant to handle it. The result: outages, slowdowns, confusion, and one metaphorical Hans quietly losing his mind.

<hr>

**MINI-LESSONS TO REMEMBER
BEFORE THE NEXT ROUTING APOCALYPSE:**

- BGP is built on trust, not verification. That's fine until someone sneezes near a config file.
- There's no built-in sanity check. If a random village claims it can reach Amazon, someone will probably believe it.
- "I know the way" does not mean "I should be routing your traffic."

<hr>

Think that sounds too ridiculous to be true? Let's move on to the real stories.

——— Verizon BGP Leak ———
The Day A Small Pa Company Helped Break The Internet

Date: June 24, 2019

Impact: Massive slowdowns and outages across Amazon, Facebook, Cloudflare, Google, and more

Root cause: A small regional network accidentally told the world it could deliver traffic for half the Internet — and Verizon believed it.

DQE Communications was a modest Internet provider in Pennsylvania, mostly serving local businesses. Nothing fancy — just a quiet, regional ISP (the kind of company whose employees you yell at when your Wi-Fi dies) doing its job.

But the trouble didn't start with DQE; it started with one of their clients. Allegheny Technologies was trying to speed up their connection using software from a vendor called Noction. It was the kind of corporate nesting doll that makes you miss the days when tech was simple: a steel company running niche routing code, talking to a regional ISP, talking to a global telecom. Think of the software as a digital travel agent for data: shaving milliseconds here and there by finding quicker roads for packets to take. But one morning, that software went rogue. Instead of announcing a few improved routes, it shouted to the world, 'I can handle 20,000 destinations!'

Those "destinations," called prefixes, are essentially neighborhoods of IP addresses — the digital equivalent of ZIP codes. Each one represents a block of online real estate. Suddenly, this small network in Pennsylvania was claiming responsibility for neighborhoods that belonged to giants like Google, Facebook, and Amazon.

Normally, a larger network (called an *upstream provider*) is supposed to sanity-check what its smaller clients tell it. Verizon was that upstream. In theory, it should've said, "Hold up, you're a small town — why are you suddenly claiming to host half the planet?" Instead, Verizon simply nodded and passed the message along to everyone else. And since BGP is built on trust, the rest of the Internet said, "Cool, Pennsylvania it is."

Within minutes, global traffic started rerouting through DQE's modest infrastructure. Imagine every highway in America suddenly being redirected through one sleepy town with a single gas station. Servers strained, packets piled up, and the whole system began to choke.

For a few surreal hours, DQE became the digital equivalent of Hans — our overconfident postmaster from Wansdorf — suddenly in charge of delivering every letter in Germany. And just like Hans, they were never built for it. The result: massive slowdowns, outages, and one very confused operations team wondering why their quiet Tuesday had turned into an international incident.

LESSON LEARNED

- Route optimizers are like toddlers with matches: helpful until they're not.
- Prefixes may look harmless on paper, but twenty thousand of them can topple global giants.
Upstream providers are supposed to be the adults in the room — filter what you accept from your clients.
- "Trust, but verify" isn't just a proverb. In BGP, it's survival.

The moral of this story is simple: if your neighbor tells you they can reach everywhere, maybe — just maybe — take a quick look at the map first.

Facebook Outage
How To Bgp Yourself Out Of Existence

Date: October 4, 2021

Impact: Facebook, Instagram, WhatsApp, and Messenger all vanished from the Internet for nearly six hours — along with every internal tool the company relied on to fix it.

Root cause: A misconfigured BGP update accidentally withdrew every route to Facebook's own infrastructure, effectively erasing the company's presence from the Internet.

At around 16:00 UTC, Facebook performed what was supposed to be a routine update to its BGP configuration — the part of its infrastructure that told the rest of the Internet how to find it. The update went catastrophically wrong. Instead of announcing routes, it withdrew them. In plain English: Facebook told the world, "We don't exist." It was a bit like the mayor of New York deciding to replace the entire city on world maps with a drawing of a sea monster — and everyone else just nodding and saying, "Fair enough."

The chain reaction was immediate. Systems across the Internet tried to look up where Facebook lived, failed, and gave up. Every one of Facebook's services — Messenger, Instagram, WhatsApp — fell off the grid. For users, it looked like a global outage. For engineers inside the company, it was far worse: they couldn't even reach their own network to fix it.

In the process, Facebook didn't just erase directions to its public-facing services. It also erased the directions to the cartographer. Or, more technically speaking, they wiped from the Internet the very routes to the internal tools needed to fix the mess. When the Internet forgot where Facebook was, Facebook also forgot how to reach itself.

And then came the real punchline. With all internal tools wiped off the map, Facebook's engineers had to do the unthinkable: drive to the data centers in person, like it was 1997, and fix things manually.

But the irony didn't stop there. When they finally arrived, they discovered that Facebook had done such a thorough job erasing itself that the door systems no longer recognized anyone. The smart locks and badge readers couldn't confirm whether the people outside were employees or just an especially persistent crowd demanding their memes back.

Eventually, engineers managed to gain physical access and manually reset systems — the kind of "turn it off and on again" exercise that hadn't been needed at this scale since the 1990s. By the time routes were restored and traffic began to flow again, the damage was already legendary: roughly $100 million in lost ad revenue, global headlines, and a fresh meme for the ages.

LESSON LEARNED

- Don't centralize everything — especially your ability to fix things.
- BGP is not a toy. Handle it like nitroglycerin.
- Redundancy is worthless if it all depends on the same fragile system.
- If your network engineers need bolt cutters to resolve a config issue, it's time to rethink your architecture.

Facebook: the company that accidentally unfriended itself from the Internet.

Rogers Communications Outage
The Day Canada Got Unplugged

Date: July 8, 2022

Impact: Over 12 million customers offline; emergency services disrupted; ATMs and debit cards useless; airports paralyzed.

Root cause: A misconfigured core routing update triggered a cascading failure that crippled the country's network backbone.

Rogers Communications is one of Canada's telecom giants, controlling a massive slice of the country's digital life: mobile networks, home internet, payment systems, and even parts of government communications. On a quiet Friday morning, because nothing says "high-risk change" like doing it right before the weekend, engineers rolled out what was meant to be a simple configuration update in the company's core routing infrastructure. What followed was one of the largest communications meltdowns in Canadian history.

The update deleted a critical filter, triggering not a loop, but a massive routing flood.

Instead of a polite exchange, distribution routers suddenly unloaded every single path and prefix they knew onto the core network all at once. The central routers, overwhelmed by the sheer volume of screaming data, capitulated and crashed. And because the system was now choking on its own traffic, the recovery efforts backfired. As routers tried to come back online, they just broadcasted the same torrent of information again. Each attempt to fix the problem only made it worse, like trying to calm a crowd by shouting *"Nobody panic!"* through a megaphone.

Within minutes, Rogers' core systems collapsed under the load. The backbone, the internal superhighway that kept data flowing, tore itself apart. Vast portions of Canada's digital infrastructure went dark. It wasn't just people unable to stream Netflix or refresh Instagram; it was hospitals losing access to internal networks, airports reverting to paper check-ins, and 911 emergency calls failing outright. Payment services like Interac, used for debit card transactions across the country, went offline, meaning millions couldn't pay for groceries or gas.

For nearly 19 hours, Canada got a glimpse of what a pre-Internet world looks like. Except this time there was no dial-up tone, no patience, and no backup plan.

When Rogers finally restored service, the country's collective blood pressure dropped, but public outrage shot through the roof. Parliament demanded answers. Competitors expressed public sympathy and offers of assistance.

In corporate standards, that meant Bell and Telus offered to temporarily reroute Rogers' traffic — an offer Rogers declined for "technical reasons," and we can only speculate how much those so-called "technical" reasons had to do with Rogers' accounting books. Meanwhile, rival marketing departments wasted no time launching promotions like "Switch to Our Network That Won't Leave You Hanging," complete with $100 discounts for new customers.

Rogers issued a statement promising to "invest in resilience." According to best big-tech practices, that probably meant more meetings, external consultants, and plenty of PowerPoint. Not to mention higher prices, which conveniently arrived in February/March 2023.

LESSON LEARNED

- If your infrastructure can take down hospitals and banking at the same time, test your configuration changes twice, and then once more just to be sure.
- Feedback loops aren't just theoretical; they can take down entire nations when left unchecked.
- Monoculture in infrastructure equals national vulnerability.
- Redundancy that all runs through the same company isn't redundancy.
- One router config. Twelve million people. Zero Internet.

For nineteen hours, Canada didn't need a sophisticated firewall to block the internet. One bad config file did it for free.

CHAPTER 7:
DNS - HOW NAMES REPLACE NUMBERS

You can't navigate a world built on coordinates alone. Sure, BGP gives us the map — a tangled atlas of digital highways — but even the best GPS is useless if every city is just a number. That's where DNS comes in: the Internet's naming bureau, the friendly cartographer who writes "Paris" instead of "48.8566N, 2.3522E," and occasionally mislabels Australia as Austria.

It's the system that turns human-friendly names into machine-friendly destinations — a planetary phonebook disguised as a geography lesson. But before we watch the map burn, we need to see how it's drawn.

 **Explainer:**
The Internet's Phonebook

The Big Idea

When you type facebook.com into your browser, your computer stares back blankly. It has no idea what that means. It needs an IP address — something like 157.240.20.35 — a real, numeric location it can talk to.

So how does it find that number? Enter **DNS**, the *Domain Name System*: a gigantic, planet-wide directory that turns human-friendly names into machine-friendly numbers. Think of it as the contact list in your smartphone — except instead of friends, it lists servers that may or may not currently be on fire.

You look up *Alice*, you get *+49 123 456 789*.

Here it's *facebook.com → 157.240.20.35*.

And just like your phone might list "Alice (home), Alice (work), Alice (fax – for reasons no one remembers)", DNS stores multiple record types — A, AAAA, MX, TXT, CNAME

— each doing its own obscure job. Don't worry, we're not here to train sysadmins. We're here to understand why, when DNS sneezes, the rest of the Internet collapses in sympathy.

Where Do Domains Come From?

At the top of the hierarchy sits **IANA** (Internet Assigned Numbers Authority). It hands out **TLDs** — top-level domains — to organizations worldwide:

- **.pl** – Poland (NASK)

- **.it** – Italy (famous for wordplay like *do.it*, *make.it*, or the Polish *szkolenia.it* — literally "IT trainings")

- **.com** – Verisign, the corporate landlord of the Internet

- **.ai** – Anguilla, a tiny Caribbean island that accidentally won the AI lottery. In 2023, .ai domains brought in about **20% of the country's Government's Revenue.** That's right — artificial intelligence is literally paying someone's rent in paradise.

These authorities then *sell* second-level domains like *facebook.com* or *gov.pl* to whoever's got a credit card and a dream. Each buyer configures their DNS however they please — a glorious combination of freedom, bureaucracy, and infinite opportunities to screw up.

How Dns Actually Works

Imagine your computer as that one overly polite friend who doesn't know an address but insists on finding it for you. It starts small:

"Hey, router — where's *maps.google.fr*?"

Router: "No clue, but let me ask my friend at the ISP."

ISP: "I don't know either, but I know someone handling *.fr*. Hold on."

.fr server: "I can't help, but I know who's responsible for *google.fr.*"

google.fr nameserver: "Mais bien sûr! It's 142.250.186.174."

And the answer travels all the way back — friend to friend — until it reaches your browser.

Like any good gossip chain, each participant quietly jots the answer down for next time — that's **caching**. And like any respectable gossip, none of them bothers to verify it later. As long as the story feels fresh enough, they'll happily repeat it without checking. Efficiency, not accuracy, is the name of the game.

The Root Servers – Oracles Of The Internet

At the top of this whisper network sit the **root servers** — 13 coordinated constellations (labeled A through M) comprising almost 2000 servers in more than 400 locations worldwide as of October 2025. These numbers shift slightly over time, but the structure remains the same: a handful of trusted organizations quietly keeping the Internet's compass aligned. They don't know where *facebook.com* lives, but they know who runs *.com*. Think of them as the Internet's wise elders, humming quietly in fortified data centers, making sure everyone starts their gossip in the right direction.

If that sounds a bit too centralized for comfort, congratulations — you've grasped the existential problem of the modern Internet.

Bonus Weirdness

Even something as mundane as DNS has its shadow side. One of the lesser-known quirks is the concept of **private zones** — internal-only DNS records used inside organizations or home networks. Think of them as office phone extensions: useful internally, invisible to outsiders. Unless, of course, someone misconfigures them — then they become a public map of your internal infrastructure, freely accessible to anyone curious enough to look.

LESSON LEARNED

- DNS is the Internet's contact list — ancient, elegant, and slightly cursed.
- Root servers are the closest thing the Internet has to a priesthood. Be nice to them.
- Your browser reaching google.com is less "direct lookup" and more "global gossip that somehow works."
- The Internet pretends to be decentralized, but deep down, it's a well-governed anarchy held together by trust, caffeine, and a collective prayer that nobody fat-fingers a config file.

Now that we've got a rough idea of how DNS actually works, let's take a look at what happens when it doesn't — when a single misstep in this delicate choreography sends half the Internet stumbling.

Dyn DNS Attack
When Your Toaster DDoSes The Internet

Date: October 21, 2016

Impact: Massive outages across the US and parts of Europe — Twitter, Reddit, Spotify, Netflix, GitHub and many others went dark.

Root cause: A massive, distributed DDoS attack targeting Dyn, a major DNS provider, powered by a botnet of hacked IoT devices.

Since this entire incident revolves around a DDoS, let's clarify what that actually is.

Imagine you're trying to finish a report, and one coworker keeps interrupting you every five seconds with random nonsense. That's a Denial of Service (DoS) — annoying, but manageable. You can ignore them, tell them to shut up, or — in the most extreme case — tie them to a chair and gag them (not recommended unless you enjoy long conversations with HR).

Now imagine instead that it's not one coworker, but the entire open-plan office. Everyone's shouting questions, demanding your attention, and blocking every escape route. It's chaos. That's a Distributed Denial of Service (DDoS) — the same principle, but multiplied across thousands of participants.

Or picture a press conference where dozens of journalists scream questions at once and you're expected to answer every single one. Eventually, you just shut down. That's exactly what happens to a server under a DDoS: the flood of incoming requests overwhelms its ability to respond, and it collapses under the noise.

Dyn was one of the backbone providers of DNS, handling a significant portion of name resolution for major websites. When the attack began early that Friday morning, engineers initially thought it was a routine service hiccup — DNS providers deal with constant background noise of smaller attacks. But within minutes, traffic patterns became unmistakably apocalyptic.

The Mirai botnet wasn't just big — it was ingenious in its simplicity. It didn't rely on sophisticated malware or zero-day exploits. Instead, it roamed the Internet searching for simple household and office devices — IP cameras, baby monitors, printers, probably even smart toasters. Mirai simply cycled through a hardcoded list of over sixty of the most common username-password pairs like `admin:password`, `root:12345`, and `user:user`, looking for devices whose owners never bothered to change them. Each infected device quietly joined the growing zombie army.

When Dyn's infrastructure was hit, the sheer flood of requests overwhelmed even its massive capacity — a tidal wave of nonsense queries from every corner of the planet. Within minutes, large parts of the Internet simply stopped being reachable.

Now, the inability to tweet or stream *"Love Yourself"* by Justin Bieber on Spotify (yes, that was the biggest hit of 2016 — don't ask me why; I understand technology, not music taste) might sound like a mild inconvenience. But this was bigger than pop culture downtime: major financial exchanges, payment gateways, and government systems also relied on Dyn's DNS services. For several hours, some of them became unreachable or unstable — a reminder that even the supposedly solid parts of our infrastructure still hinge on surprisingly fragile foundations.

By mid-morning, users on the US East Coast started noticing something was off: Twitter wouldn't load, GitHub returned errors, Spotify hung on startup. As Dyn engineers scrambled to re-route DNS traffic and isolate affected zones, attackers changed tactics and launched a second wave. Then a third.

For hours, the Internet felt... fragile. Not broken, but visibly shaking. It wasn't until late in the day that Dyn, with help from other providers and ISPs, managed to absorb and deflect enough traffic for services to recover. In total, the siege lasted most of the day and showed just how dangerous it was to have a few DNS providers serving as the Internet's keystones.

LESSON LEARNED

- DNS is invisible until it breaks — and when it does, everything breaks.
- A botnet doesn't need GPUs; it just needs enough cheap, unsecured junk connected to the Internet.
- The defense against DDoS is part skill, part luck, and mostly bandwidth.
- If you can `ping google.com` but your browser won't load it, now you know why.
- The "Internet of Things" has a funny way of turning into the Internet of Broken Things.

Dyn recovered, but the lesson stuck: the 'S' in IoT stands for Security.

Explainer:
DNSSEC – The Notary Who Burned the Library

To understand a few next ones, we need to talk about DNSSEC — the Internet's paranoid notary who checks every signature twice, panics when they don't match, and sets the library on fire just to be safe. Its job is to verify that every DNS response is legit and hasn't been tampered with.

Think of it as a bureaucratic control freak with a love for cryptography. Don't worry — we'll unpack the crypto part in the next chapter. For now, picture a notary holding a magnifying glass over every domain name, muttering "trust, but verify" until the ink burns through the paper.

Normally, DNS is built on trust—one server tells another 'here's the address you asked for,' and everyone politely believes it. But that leaves room for mischief: an attacker could redirect your bank's login page to a fake server and steal your credentials. Or worse—redirect `www.sweet-kitties-pictures.com` to a site serving puppies. For cat lovers, that's unforgivable.

DNSSEC (Domain Name System Security Extensions) fixes that by adding a kind of digital stamp to DNS responses. When you ask where a domain lives, your resolver not only gets an answer but also checks that the "stamp" matches the one on file. In theory, it prevents impostors from faking responses. In practice... it adds yet another layer of complexity where things can go spectacularly wrong.

Now that the acronym finally makes sense, let's look at what happens when DNSSEC *actually* causes an outage.

——————— **The Swedish Fuckup** ———————
When A Missing Dot Unplugged A Nation

Date: October 12, 2009

Impact: Entire .se top-level domain offline for ~1 hour; degraded resolution well into the next day

Root Cause: A routine zone-file update pushed invalid DNSSEC signatures due to a missing trailing dot

Let's kick off our *Tour de DNSSEC* with a breakaway move nobody expected: an entire country dropping out of the Internet peloton because of automation, DNSSEC, and... a missing dot.

Yes. A dot. The tiny punctuation mark at the end of a Fully Qualified Domain Name — the one most humans never see and most DNS engineers fear forgetting — was all it took to send the entire Swedish namespace off a cliff.

On October 12, the .se registry ran a routine update of their zone. Routine, in DNS terms, is the same as "hold my beer" in human terms — with equally spectacular results. A script responsible for generating DNSSEC-signed records failed to append the trailing dot to certain entries. Without it, the signatures didn't match. And because DNSSEC is basically DNS with trust issues, any mismatched signature is treated as a crime against the natural order.

Validators across the world took one look at the new .se zone and collectively rejected it like a bad Tinder bio. As far as they were concerned, Sweden had become a forged document — an untrusted namespace. So they did what DNSSEC resolvers do best: they blocked everything.

For roughly an hour, anything ending in .se simply ceased to exist. Banks? Gone. Newspapers? Gone. Government portals? Gone. Entire businesses? Also gone. Around 900,000 domains disappeared in an instant.

Users who tried to load their favorite Swedish sites stared at browser errors that might as well have said: "Sweden? Never heard of it."

To their credit, engineers at IIS (the .se registry) found the bug quickly, corrected the zone, re-signed it, and pushed it out. Job done, right? Except the Internet doesn't heal instantly — it sulks. DNS caches across ISPs, CDNs, and resolvers happily kept serving the old, broken signatures until TTLs expired. For many Swedes, the outage lasted far longer than the official timeline.

What makes this case timeless is not the technical detail — you already learned how DNS and DNSSEC work earlier in the chapter — but the sheer asymmetry of the failure. No hackers. No DDoS. No state-sponsored cyberwarfare. Just a script missing a dot and a global security system that did exactly what it was supposed to do: protect users from untrusted data. Even when the "attacker" was a sleepy sysadmin.

It also served as a quiet reminder that .uk was not alone in nearly yeeting itself into the digital void. Different cause, similar effect: a country wiped off the Internet because DNS really, really hates being misconfigured.

LESSON LEARNED

- DNSSEC enforces trust brilliantly — even when the only villain is a typo.
- A missing trailing dot can do more damage than most cyberattacks.
- Caches turn brief outages into lingering hauntings.
- "Routine maintenance" is never routine when DNS is involved.

> • National connectivity should not depend on the punctuation habits of a single script.

Sweden didn't get hacked — it got punctuated. One missing dot, and an entire country got temporarily unpublished from the Internet.

——— Slack's "Rollback from Hell" ———
When Security Locked The Doors From The Inside

Date: September 30, 2021

Impact: Global Slack outage for ~24 hours; millions of users unable to connect

Root Cause: DNSSEC rollback performed without removing the DS record from the parent zone (.com), triggering global validation failures

DNSSEC had already proven itself capable of catastrophic outcomes — Sweden learned that the hard way with a missing dot. Slack, however, discovered an even more exquisite failure mode: doing everything "by the book" and still locking the entire world out. This wasn't an attack, a misconfiguration in the traditional sense, or even a typo. It was pure procedural correctness weaponized against its own operator.

It all began with good intentions. Slack wanted to increase security, and enabling DNSSEC seemed like the natural, responsible step forward. Publish signatures, advertise them to the world, and enjoy the comfort of cryptographic authenticity. For a short while, that's exactly what happened. Slack's domain became properly signed, resolvers validated its responses, and the rollout appeared smooth.

Then the cracks formed — quietly at first. A handful of DNS resolvers, including Google's widely-used 8.8.8.8, began rejecting Slack's newly signed records. To an experienced engineer, this is usually the kind of transient anomaly you wait out. Except this one refused to go away. The errors grew. User reports spiked. The anomaly was now a pattern.

Under growing pressure, the team made a decision that would have been perfectly correct in any non-DNSSEC world: roll back. Remove the signatures. Return to the unsigned state that had been working fine just minutes earlier. In ordinary DNS, this is a trivial, instant recovery.

But DNSSEC does not live in ordinary reality.

Slack removed their signatures, fully expecting resolvers to treat the domain as unsigned again. But DNS, as explained earlier, behaves like a global gossip network. And the gossip that mattered most — the signal from the **.com** servers — hadn't changed.

Those servers still held the DS record: the tiny but authoritative flag telling the entire Internet, *"Slack is DNSSEC-signed. Expect signatures. Reject anything unsigned."* Slack had changed their story. The parent zone had not.

At that moment, two contradictory truths existed. And DNSSEC resolvers always side with the parent zone.

Slack had effectively told the world, "I'm no longer signed," but the .com zone continued shouting, "Yes you are!" The resolvers, acting as strict cryptographic librarians, followed protocol: if a domain claims to be signed but cannot produce signatures, it must be a counterfeit. No warnings. No fallback. Just a hard, absolute block.

That is exactly what unfolded.

Resolvers worldwide checked the .com DS record, queried Slack, found no signatures, and — following DNSSEC rules to the letter — declared Slack invalid. Millions of users were abruptly locked out, not by attackers, not by malware, but by DNSSEC protecting them from the *real* Slack.

And the cruelty didn't end there.

Even once Slack restored a consistent configuration, they were still trapped. The DS record in the .com zone carries a **24-hour TTL**. Meaning: the mistaken trust signal would persist across global resolvers for an entire day. Nothing Slack did could accelerate this. No patch, no mitigation, no engineering heroics.

They simply had to wait.

For roughly 24 hours, Slack's availability was governed not by engineering effort, but by the slow, indifferent ticking of global cache expiry.

It was the DNS equivalent of locking yourself out of your house, calling a locksmith, and being told: *"We can't help you. Come back tomorrow."*

LESSON LEARNED

- DNSSEC failure modes are sharp, instant, and merciless.
- Rolling back DNSSEC requires removing the DS record first, or everything explodes.
- Parent-zone TTLs can trap a service in purgatory for 24 hours.
- DNSSEC is not "just a switch" — it's a commitment.
- Debug first, panic later.

Slack tried to increase security. DNSSEC replied: "Cool, I'll just increase your downtime instead."

The Most Ironic Example: Comcast Blocks Nasa

Date: January 18, 2012

Impact: Comcast customers across the US unable to reach nasa.gov during a globally watched political moment

Root Cause: NASA performed a DNSSEC key rollover but failed to correctly update the parent-level trust anchor (DS record), causing resolvers to reject nasa.gov as invalid

Coming off Slack's DNSSEC disaster, you might think we've covered the major failure modes already. But DNSSEC has one more trick up its sleeve — the kind where security works *so well* it ends up protecting users from the actual website owner. We'll dig into the mechanics of trust, signatures, and the broader security model in the next chapter. For now, all you need to know is this: DNSSEC keys must be rotated periodically. And rotated **correctly**.

NASA did not rotate theirs correctly.

On January 18th, 2012 — the exact day the Internet was engulfed in protests against SOPA, the Stop Online Piracy Act — nasa.gov suddenly became unreachable for millions of Comcast customers. Timing could not have been worse. People immediately assumed the blackout was political: that Comcast, one of the largest ISPs in the US and a known supporter of various lobbying efforts, had begun censoring government websites in solidarity with anti-piracy legislation.

The truth was far funnier.

NASA had attempted a DNSSEC key rollover but botched the update of the DS record — the parent-level signature that tells resolvers which public key to expect. Their own zone used the new key. The parent zone still advertised the old key. And DNSSEC resolvers, including Comcast's (which were among the first major ISP resolvers to enforce strict validation), did the only correct thing they could: they assumed nasa.gov was being spoofed by an attacker.

They blocked it entirely.

This was not a political statement. It wasn't censorship. It wasn't sabotage. It was security functioning flawlessly — and NASA accidentally locking itself outside the airlock.

As memes spread and confusion escalated, the irony only deepened: in a moment where millions feared private corporations controlling access to knowledge, Comcast was actually doing the **right** thing by the book, protecting users from what appeared to be a spoofed government domain.

NASA fixed the configuration within hours, but caches held on to the mismatched trust signal, delaying full recovery for many users. The SOPA conspiracy theories outlived the outage itself.

LESSON LEARNED

- Key rollovers must be exact. Even NASA doesn't get a grace period.
- DNSSEC protects users from attackers — and from the domain owner if they screw up.
- ISPs enforcing strict validation can amplify mistakes dramatically.
- Outages during politically sensitive moments spawn conspiracy theories instantly.

> • Sometimes the most secure outcome is indistinguishable from sabotage.

In 2012, DNSSEC didn't protect NASA from hackers — it protected users from NASA.

——— Akamai DNS Software Blunder ———
When The Internet's Memory Lost Its Mind

Date: July 22, 2021

Impact: ~1 hour of outages for major websites: Amazon, Delta, Capital One, Costco, and more (~15-20% of entire Internet traffic)

Root cause: Faulty software update in Akamai's authoritative Edge DNS platform

It was a routine update—those famous last words of the internet.

Akamai's gig is being the internet's invisible bodyguard—caching content, routing traffic, and resolving DNS so you don't have to think about it. So when they fart and the web wheezes, it's comedy gold. On July 22, 2021, around 11 AM ET, the outage hit like a stealth ninja: no dramatic DDoS fanfare, just sites vanishing faster than a bad Tinder date.

Users trying to shop at Costco? Nada. Booking Delta flights? Error city. Logging into Capital One? Laughable. Browsers spun helplessly, then declared defeat. For millions of users, checkout pages died mid-purchase, flight bookings hung mid-air, and the digital equivalent of tumbleweed rolled across the web.

Picture the internet's recursive resolvers (run by your ISP) as frantic librarians. They run around trying to find where websites live. Akamai's role is to be the Master Reference Book—the Authoritative DNS—that holds the actual answers. The update wasn't supposed to fix the librarians; it was supposed to organize the library. Instead, it effectively set the reference section on fire.

It introduced a bug that made resolvers spit out error codes from hell and buckle under normal traffic. One bad loop in the code, and boom: cascading failures rippled from Akamai's edge servers worldwide. Millions of queries hit a wall, turning the web into a ghost town.

Traffic didn't "reroute" so much as panic. It ran to the so-called healthy nodes—and killed them too, like lemmings with a death wish. Within minutes, Akamai's backbone was choking on its own DNS vomit, as queries piled up like bad traffic in rush hour hell.

Engineers at Akamai spotted the red flags (spiking errors, fried CPUs) and yanked the update like ripping off a Band-Aid. Rollback took about an hour—eternity in internet time—before resolvers caught their breath and the sites flickered back. Akamai's postmortem was refreshingly blunt: "We triggered a bug in our DNS system. It sucked. We're fixing it." No excuses, just accountability in a sea of corporate spin.

The takeaway? The internet's dependencies are so intertwined that a single provider's hiccup can ripple into global e-commerce paralysis. In this case, a few bad DNS packets managed to simulate the effect of an asteroid strike on online shopping.

LESSON LEARNED

- "Routine update" is tech's most dangerous phrase.
- Recursive doesn't mean immortal—DNS can crash itself if you let it.
- Test in staging, not prod—unless you want millions rage-tweeting your downtime.
- Never assume resilience when your entire stack depends on one provider.
- Postmortems save face: own the fuckup fast, or let memes do it for you.

For one surreal hour in 2021, DNS—the Internet's phonebook—forgot how to read. And once again, the web learned the hard way that when the map fails, nobody knows where anything lives.

CHAPTER 8:
HOW THE INTERNET LEARNED TO TRUST ITSELF (SSL/TLS)

By now, the attentive reader has probably noticed a pattern: the Internet is basically a chain of polite strangers passing notes to each other and hoping nobody reads them on the way.

Packets hop between random computers, cables, and routers — a cheerful relay race with zero background checks.

And that's fine, until you realize that at any step, someone could quietly copy, read, or even swap those notes for something else. Every email, every cat meme, every online purchase — all of it rides across a public highway where anyone with the right screwdriver and a bad attitude could set up a listening post.

We built a global communication network first... and only later remembered that maybe, just maybe, we should think about privacy and trust.

Someone could impersonate a website, steal data, or redirect traffic entirely. The possibilities were endless, and none of them good. So we needed a way to tell who's who, and to make sure nobody tampers with the conversation along the way.

That's where SSL (Secure Sockets Layer) — and its slightly more grown-up successor, TLS (Transport Layer Security) — entered the story. Think of them as the Internet's awkward handshake ritual, born out of mutual distrust.

Properly explaining how cryptographic trust works requires more math than anyone deserves on a weekday evening, so I'll spare you the formulas and focus on two questions that actually matter:

1. How can two computers that have never met agree to trust each other?

2. How do you know the server you're talking to is really *the* one you wanted? Or, more simply: what's behind that little padlock icon in your browser — or the big red "Not secure" warning when it's missing?

We'll skip the fine print and focus on the bigger picture: how trust is built, delegated, and occasionally spectacularly broken.

Because while the Internet absolutely runs on mathematics, it only works because people built the systems that make those equations count — and convinced the rest of us to believe in them.

 **Explainer:**
How Two Computers Can Learn to Trust Each Other

Let's dive into how computers build trust to share secrets securely, using the clever Diffie-Hellman key exchange. No math needed—just picture a vivid story about paint! Alice and Bob want a shared secret to chat privately, safe from Eve, the nosy eavesdropper. Their process unfolds in three simple stages.

Stage 1: Agreeing On A Public Starting Point

Alice and Bob need a common cipher to begin. They openly discuss their options: Alice says, "I can do A, B, or C." Bob replies, "I know B, C, and D." After a quick chat, they settle on C because it's got a cooler name (okay, in practice, the criteria are a bit different). This choice is public—Eve can overhear it all, no problem. They've picked a shared base color, like bright yellow, visible to everyone. No secrets here, just a starting point for all to see.

Stage 2: Creating A Shared Secret With Asymmetric Magic

Now, they need a secret key only they share, without sending it publicly. This is where Diffie-Hellman's asymmetric trick comes in. Alice secretly picks her private color, red, and Bob chooses his blue. They keep these hidden from everyone, including each other. They mix their private colors with the public yellow: Alice's mix turns orange, Bob's turns green. They swap these mixtures openly, so Eve sees yellow, orange, and green—but not the secret red or blue. Then, Alice adds her secret red to Bob's green, and Bob adds his secret blue to Alice's orange. Magically, both end up with the same brown shade —a shared secret key. Eve can't recreate it, no matter how hard she stares. The beauty of asymmetric encryption? Mixing colors is a breeze, but unmixing that brown blob to find the original red or blue? Nearly impossible.

Stage 3: Chatting Securely With Symmetric Encryption

With their secret brown key, Alice and Bob can now chat privately using symmetric encryption. If Alice wants to send Bob a message like "Meet me at the Tate Modern," she smears it with their brown paint, turning it into an unreadable, muddy mess. Eve, snooping as always, sees only gibberish. But Bob, with the same brown key, uses a magic brush to wipe away the paint and reveal the message. Symmetric encryption is like a lock and key: Alice locks the message, and only Bob's identical key unlocks it. They must guard that brown key fiercely—if Eve snags it, she can unlock their entire conversation.

In computer terms, this 'smearing' is called *encryption* and the magic brush is *decryption*. Because IT nerds like to sound smart and latin derived terminology definitely screams "pro" better than "scramble/unscramble."

How This Works On The Internet

In practice, computers follow the same three steps, choosing separate algorithms for Stage 2 (mixing paints to create the secret key) and Stage 3 (smearing messages with that key). Instead of paints, though, they use massive prime numbers. No math class here! Just know that untangling those mixed-up numbers to find the original components is like wrestling with the factorial growth I mentioned in Part I. You'll need a lot of free time to do that... compared to this, the age of the entire universe is quite short. Hope you prepared enough snacks!

This system relies on mixing being easy, but unmixing being a nightmare. Still, a word of caution: quantum computers, those futuristic machines in the news, could one day unravel this whole setup. Good news: people much smarter than me (thankfully!) are already working on new tricks for the post-quantum era.

So, Alice and Bob can plan their Tate Modern date in peace. But one question remains: how do they know they're really talking to each other, and not Eve pulling a sneaky impersonation? That's where the Internet's chain of trust comes in—stay tuned!

Explainer:
How the Internet Decides Who to Trust

Now that Alice and Bob can safely exchange secrets, another question appears: how do they know *who* they're actually talking to before they even start? In the digital world, identity is proven through certificates.

A certificate is basically a monstrously long, encrypted message that says, "I am who I claim to be — trust me." The fun part? Anyone can create one. You could issue yourself a certificate right now declaring you're the Emperor of the Internet, and your computer would politely nod — but no one else would believe it.

Here's the trick: certificates must be signed by someone else. That signature says, "I've checked this person — they're legit." And that signer has their own certificate, which (you guessed it) is signed by someone else. The result is a chain of trust, where each link vouches for the next.

It's like paperwork in the real world: your signature on a document isn't enough, so a notary adds theirs to confirm it's valid. But that notary also needs a license — proof that someone higher up recognizes them as official. The same hierarchy exists online.

At the top of this digital pyramid are Certificate Authorities (CAs)—big shots like DigiCert, Amazon, TrustAsia, and a few others you've never heard of but your browser swears by. They're the "nice neighbors" who always say good morning and help carry your grocery bags, trusted by default by everyone in town because their self-signed root certificates are pre-installed in every browser and device—like the Internet's starter pack for belief. And it works... until it doesn't. But let's not get ahead of ourselves.

Your browser checks a website's certificate, follows the signature chain up to one of these trusted roots, and if it all adds up, you get that shiny padlock in the address bar.

But nothing stops you from declaring yourself a CA. You could decide that your cousin Frank is the supreme authority on all things secure and tell your computer to trust any certificate he signs. It'll work — just for you. The rest of the Internet, however, will treat Frank's seal of approval the same way a police officer on the highway would react if you handed over a crayon-drawn driving licence.

So yes, anyone can claim authority. But only those on the global trust list actually get believed. And that's how the web decides who's trustworthy enough to start mixing those digital paints in the first place.

And just like real-world IDs, all these certificates come with expiration dates. They need to be renewed periodically to ensure the information is still valid and the signatures are still trustworthy. Forget to renew, and your website's "identity card" suddenly expires — browsers will start flashing warnings like overzealous airport security.

In fact, this isn't just a hypothetical issue. Remember the .se DNSSEC fiasco from the previous chapter? The whole mess started because the digital equivalent of new ID templates was introduced, but nobody told the rest of the world that the design had changed. Computers take that sort of thing personally.

After that slightly overlong foreplay of trust mechanics, let's finally see what happens when the machinery of trust decides to take a day off.

Cloudbleed
When The Buffer Overflow Came Back Wearing A Tie

Date: February 17–February 18, 2017

Impact: Private data from millions of HTTPS requests leaked into public cache across the Internet, exposing cookies, passwords, and private messages from sites like Uber, Fitbit, and OKCupid.

Root cause: A memory leak in Cloudflare's HTML parser caused fragments of HTTPS traffic to bleed into unrelated pages.

For a company whose entire business model revolved around keeping the Internet safe, Cloudflare managed to pull off something spectacularly ironic: they accidentally leaked everyone's secrets while trying to protect them. The bug, later nicknamed *Cloudbleed* in a grim nod to the infamous Heartbleed, wasn't a hack but a logic error in how Cloudflare's servers handled HTML. (And yes, we'll talk about *Heartbleed* itself in Part V — it deserves its own bloody spotlight.)

Let's pause for a second. An HTML parser is like a software librarian that reads and rearranges the code behind web pages to make them look nice on your screen. Cloudflare had built a faster, shinier one using Ragel, a mature and reliable parser generator, to speed up features like automatic HTTPS rewriting and email obfuscation. Ragel is a tool that creates efficient parsers by letting developers define rules for processing data, like a blueprint for a machine that interprets HTML. HTTPS, for the uninitiated, is HTTP with encryption added—the "S" stands for Secure, painting your data with the cryptographic voodoo mixed by Alice and Bob.

Everything worked like a charm, until it didn't. Under very specific conditions, the parser had what engineers call a *buffer overflow*, which we met back in Part I: when a team of digital football players shoves data around so aggressively that it knocks the neighbor's boxes right out into the street. In Cloudflare's case, those boxes contained private user data — cookies, tokens, and chat messages — and the street was the open web.

Think of it like a law firm that diligently gathers all the confidential documents after a big meeting, only to neatly stack them at the photocopy shop across the street. Not stolen, not hacked — just sitting there, ready for anyone to make copies.

And one of those copy-happy passersby? Our old friend Google, the Internet's most enthusiastic collector of everything that isn't nailed down. It's nice of them to preserve the world's knowledge from the darkness of dead servers, but it's slightly less charming when what they preserve are your bank passwords or private dating-site messages. And let's be honest, not all those conversations are about dinner plans.

The fallout was instant. Cloudflare engineers scrambled to disable the affected features, patch the bug, and beg search engines to flush their caches. The exposure window was only a few days, but the data came from months of traffic. The Internet had sprung a leak right in the middle of its own security company.

Now, here's the kicker: TLS (and its friendly public face, HTTPS) encrypts data **in transit**, meaning while it's moving between your browser and a server. But once the data arrives, the encryption layer comes off so the server can actually read it. That's called data **at rest**, what's stored in memory or on disk. Cloudflare's servers temporarily held decrypted data in memory so they could filter and re-encrypt it before forwarding. The encryption worked perfectly; the momentary handling didn't. A tiny bug turned those microseconds of plaintext into a global embarrassment.

TLS protects data *on the road*, not *in the office*. Once decrypted, it's as vulnerable as any other file, and Cloudflare's HTML parser tripped over its own paperwork. The cryptography was bulletproof; the janitor spilled the coffee..

LESSON LEARNED

- Encryption ends where the software begins. The math was flawless; the parser wasn't.
- Middlemen multiply risk. Every extra hop that handles your traffic adds a new opportunity for chaos.
  Performance tweaks are booby traps. Chasing milliseconds sometimes opens wormholes.
- Old sins echo forever. Buffer overflows never die — they just get promoted to management.
- Transparency beats denial. Cloudflare's fast, honest disclosure turned a scandal into a case study in crisis control.

It was the enterprise version of a sticky note: strong crypto means nothing if the server simply decides to read the secrets out loud.

FREAK
When Politics Weakened Math

Date: March 2015

Impact: Over 35% of HTTPS websites and millions of connections vulnerable to downgrade attacks, forcing browsers and servers to use weak 1990s-era encryption. Affected major players like Apple, Android, and OpenSSL.

Root Cause: Legacy export-grade RSA ciphers, mandated by outdated U.S. laws, allowed attackers to trick systems into using crackable encryption.

Back in the 1990s, the U.S. government treated strong encryption like it was the recipe for a nuke. Export laws basically said, "If you want to sell your software overseas, make your crypto as tough as wet tissue paper." The folks in charge didn't understand the math—they just figured, "If foreigners can't have strong encryption, they can't plot in secret." Spoiler: that logic was dumber than a bag of hammers. So, every major product shipped with two modes: a solid one for the U.S. and a pathetic, export-friendly one that screamed, "Hack me, I'm easy!"

The star of this mess was RSA (Rivest–Shamir–Adleman), the granddaddy of mathematical paint-mixing. It was a brilliant way for strangers to create a shared secret without spilling it. But its strength hinged on key size—and those export rules forced tiny, laughably weak keys. These outdated ciphers got baked into software and lingered like forgotten relics. Crypto ages like milk, not wine.

Here's the kicker: cryptography is the most open-book game in tech. The algorithms are public—everyone knows how the paint gets mixed. The security comes from the secret ingredients, not the recipe itself. That's by design;

the math is supposed to be so hard to crack that hiding the method would be pointless.

But when you leave the recipe out for the world to see, you get people with way too much free time—officially we call them "researchers" so they don't feel bad—poking at it like it's a Sudoku puzzle on steroids. And you know what? That's a *good* thing. These nerds aren't (usually) out to ruin your day; they're just solving the world's most annoying jigsaw puzzle. Finding a hole doesn't mean they dug it—it was already there, waiting for some creep to exploit it, like what happened with DigiNotar... but that's a story for another case. Ethical researchers shout their findings from the rooftops so the good guys can patch things up before the bad guys throw a party.

Returning to our case, by 2015 those export-grade RSA ciphers were still lounging in the codebase like forgotten relics. Researchers realized that browsers and servers could still be tricked into using them. They dubbed the bug FREAK — short for *Factoring RSA Export Keys*. The exploit was simple but devastating: a hacker sitting in the middle could intercept the connection and whisper, "Let's use that 90s junk," and both sides would politely agree, downgrading their shiny modern encryption to something a kid with a calculator could crack before lunch. (Researchers managed it in about seven hours on a modest computer — that's not encryption, that's a coffee break.)

If you prefer a simpler image: imagine a scene in a school classroom. Alice wants to pass a note to Bob at the other end of the room, inviting him to meet after class. She writes a list of secure options — A, B, and C — and asks a classmate to pass it along. But halfway through the room sits Eve, who's not just curious but a little jealous. She swaps the note for her own version that lists only the weakest option, B. Bob sees it, thinks it came from Alice, and agrees. Alice and Bob believe they're talking privately, but Eve is now the one choosing the rules. That's a *man-in-the-middle attack* in a nutshell.

Tying this to our paint-mixing story: FREAK attacked Stage 2, where Alice and Bob create their shared secret key. If that key is weak, it doesn't matter how securely they smear messages in Stage 3—it's like locking a paper door. A weak key exchange makes the whole system collapse.

The irony was delicious. The export ciphers designed to protect national interests ended up endangering the global Internet. Apple, Google, and OpenSSL scrambled to patch their systems, finally throwing export-grade crypto into the digital dumpster. The industry learned a painful truth: "weakened for your safety" is the most dangerous oxymoron in cybersecurity.

TLS has since evolved with stronger key exchanges and forward secrecy, but the FREAK debacle remains a reminder that bad political compromises age even worse than bad math — and both age catastrophically.

LESSON LEARNED

- Don't legislate math. Physics doesn't care about your export laws.
- Backdoors rot like garbage. Designed for control, they're catnip for attackers.
- Legacy code is a zombie. It doesn't retire—it lurks until someone digs it up.
- Security theater lingers. Political compromises outlive their excuses.

- Freedom wins eventually. FREAK killed export-grade ciphers, proving encryption isn't a privilege—it's a must.

Perhaps politicians should stick to messing up tax codes. They don't understand the math there either, but at least society has accepted that the tax system is supposed to be a disaster.

DigiNotar
When Trust Got Hacked

Date: June–September 2011

Impact: Hundreds of fraudulent SSL certificates issued for domains like google.com, yahoo.com, and cia.gov. Around 300,000 Iranian users were spied on. DigiNotar, once a respected Dutch Certificate Authority, collapsed within weeks.

Root cause: Compromise of the internal signing infrastructure and inadequate security controls at DigiNotar allowed attackers to issue valid certificates for any domain.

If you remember the explainer about Certificate Authorities — those "nice neighbors" the Internet collectively trusts — here's where the story takes a darker turn. It's all fun and digital groceries until one of those neighbors gets drunk, blackmailed, or just leaves the keys to the trust vault under the doormat. That's roughly what happened with DigiNotar.

It started as a small, well-intentioned CA trying to make the Internet safer. For years, DigiNotar quietly printed those cryptographic "I swear I'm real" badges for websites, each one a tiny handshake of faith. Then someone broke in and turned their badge printer into a black-market certificate factory.

Hackers compromised DigiNotar's systems and began minting fake certificates for some of the biggest domains on the planet: Google, Yahoo, even the CIA. These forgeries were convincing enough to fool browsers and users alike because they were made using the same trusted materials — the digital equivalent of someone stealing the paper, ink, and presses from a national mint, churning out dollars so legit even the Treasury would cash them.

Practically no one could tell the difference between a genuine certificate and one produced in the hackers' secret workshop. That created perfect conditions for man-in-the-middle surveillance. TLS relies on certificates to prove a server's identity, but a fake one turns that security into a handshake with a liar. The scheme went unnoticed from at least June to September.

Most of the fraudulent traffic was traced to Iran, where the certificates were used to spy on hundreds of thousands of users. Entire inboxes, searches, and private messages were laid bare because one trusted neighbor left their windows unlocked.

When the breach finally became public, the Internet collectively freaked out. Browsers like Chrome and Firefox immediately blacklisted DigiNotar's root certificate, effectively deleting the company from the global trust chain. Dutch authorities stepped in, hoping to contain the damage, only to find that nearly every system inside had been compromised — including those signing official government sites. Within a month, DigiNotar filed for bankruptcy, because nothing says 'we're done' like being erased from every browser's trust list.

The incident was a slap in the face to the entire idea of Certificate Authorities. If one hacked company could impersonate Google, what did "secure connection" even mean? The web's security model depends on a small circle of CAs acting perfectly, forever. DigiNotar proved that "forever" can last right up until someone forgets to patch a server.

Of course, the official response included big words and bigger promises. The industry vowed to rebuild trust: Certificate Transparency logs, multi-party validation, stricter audits, and other shiny acronyms followed. All good ideas — but mostly the digital equivalent of installing more locks after the burglars have already sold your TV.

In practice, the real outcome was more psychological than technical. Users realized that the Internet's trust wasn't enforced by math or magic — it was a gentlemen's agreement with a side of hope. The CA model didn't collapse that day, but it definitely lost its innocence.

LESSON LEARNED

- Like every chain, the trust chain is only as strong as its weakest link — except here, we call them certificates.
- Compromise one CA, and the whole Internet catches a cold.
- Transparency isn't optional; it's survival.
- Never confuse good intentions with good security.
- Once trust breaks, there's no patch for reputation.

No wonder DigiNotar folded. It turns out you can't run a business selling trust when you have absolutely zero inventory.

Symantec CA
Too Big To Be Trusted

Date: March 2017 – October 2018

Impact: Chrome, Firefox, and other major browsers removed trust for all Symantec-issued certificates, affecting more than 30% of the global HTTPS ecosystem.

Root cause: Years of misissued and poorly validated certificates eroded industry confidence in Symantec's ability to act as a responsible Certificate Authority.

If DigiNotar was the story of a good neighbor gone rogue, Symantec was the tale of the neighborhood landlord who simply stopped caring. At its peak, Symantec controlled a third of all SSL/TLS certificates on the Internet. Their certificates vouched for banks, hospitals, government portals — basically the adult supervision of the web. And then it turned out the adults had been signing permission slips in crayon.

Between 2015 and 2017, researchers uncovered a growing number of misissued certificates from Symantec and its subordinate CAs. Some were test certificates issued for high-profile domains like google.com and opera.com; others were handed out with missing or incorrect validation data. It wasn't one spectacular breach — it was death by paperwork, a thousand little clerical sins that collectively said: "We have no idea what's going on."

Google eventually got fed up. In 2017, Chrome's security team published a brutal post outlining Symantec's repeated failures and announced that trust in its certificates would be gradually revoked. Mozilla, Apple, and Microsoft soon followed, leaving companies scrambling to replace certificates overnight. It was the corporate equivalent of being excommunicated from the Church of Trust.

Symantec tried to fix the mess, promising new oversight, audits, and procedures. But reputation doesn't grow back, especially when your entire business model is based on being trustworthy. So in 2018, Symantec sold its CA division to DigiCert, a company with a cleaner record and a less ironic name, hoping to wipe the slate clean.

The incident was a reminder that incompetence can be just as destructive as malice. TLS depends on CAs to anchor trust, but Symantec proved even giants can fumble the chain. DigiNotar showed what happens when a CA gets hacked; Symantec showed what happens when a CA just stops paying attention. Trust doesn't always explode in flames — sometimes it quietly dissolves in bureaucracy.

LESSON LEARNED

- Even giants can lose their trust badge.
- Audits aren't optional; they're oxygen.
- A 30% market share doesn't make you immune to consequences.
- Trust is binary — once it's gone, it's gone.
- The Internet never forgets arrogance.

It was the ultimate backyard sale. Symantec cleared out the inventory, and DigiCert paid for the empty boxes where the credibility used to be.

AddTrust
When The Clock Ran Out On Trust

Date: May 30, 2020

Impact: Expired root certificate caused connection failures across legacy systems, blocking access to thousands of sites, mail servers, and APIs. Services like Shopify, Roku, and Heroku were among those hit, leaving some services offline for hours or even days.

Root cause: The AddTrust External CA root certificate expired, and many older systems failed to recognize the newer replacements.

As you already know from our earlier explainer, digital certificates behave a lot like real-world IDs — they come with expiration dates and need regular renewal to stay valid. Passports expire, driver's licenses expire, even milk cartons expire — and yet, somehow, we still act surprised when computers do the same. Every few years, the "official stamp" of a Certificate Authority has to be renewed or replaced. It's not glamorous, it doesn't get a press release, and it certainly doesn't make for a flashy keynote slide — but it's essential. Forget to update the template, and suddenly half the Internet can't prove who it is.

That's exactly what happened with AddTrust. On May 30, 2020, the root certificate that underpinned a massive number of intermediate certificates quietly expired. Newer systems had already learned to trust its successor, but plenty of older devices — embedded systems, industrial controllers, dusty enterprise servers — still relied on the old one. When the clock hit zero, they simply stopped believing.

It's a bit like a government office updating its seal design and forgetting to tell anyone. The new documents are perfectly valid, but everyone still holding the old stamp suddenly looks like a fraud. To make matters worse, this wasn't the first time the industry had seen it happen — but, like most maintenance tasks, nobody remembered until it was too late.

The result was a wave of random outages: payment gateways, IoT services, email providers — all choking on expired trust chains. Engineers scrambled to patch systems while muttering 'who forgot to check the damn calendar?', replace certificates, and reassure customers that nothing was hacked, just... expired.

For a brief moment, the Internet's obsession with "cutting-edge innovation" met its least glamorous enemy: calendar math that, for a while, turned AddTrust into SubtractTrust — a wonderfully literal ending for a company built on arithmetic trust.

LESSON LEARNED

- Trust has a shelf life.
- Certificate maintenance isn't sexy, but neglect is fatal.
- Backward compatibility is a polite way of saying "we'll regret this later."
- Automation only helps if someone sets a reminder.
- Sometimes the scariest vulnerability is a date field.

Ultimately, AddTrust proved that forgetting your spouse's birthday is only the *second* most dangerous date you can miss.

CHAPTER 9:
HOW WE LEARNED TO SHARE THE LOAD

We've already covered the basics of how machines find each other, how names replace numbers, and how trust somehow became a protocol. Now it's time to look at the narrow doorway through which all that traffic must squeeze before it reaches anything useful — the point where "the world" meets a specific system, whether that's an autonomous system from the BGP chapter, a corporate data center, or a single application humming away in the cloud.

Enter load balancers: the digital receptionists smiling politely as they direct traffic to the right place, projecting calm even when the corridors behind them are on fire. On the surface, it all seems straightforward — just distribute requests evenly, avoid overload, keep things flowing. But here's the twist: they are the ones that decide whether a system holds the line and behaves in a civilized, orderly manner, or whether it panics, staggers, and collapses into a beautifully synchronized disaster.

But before we can properly appreciate the spectacular ways load balancers fail — and oh, they do fail spectacularly — we need to establish some terminology and understand how they actually work when things are going right. Because the difference between "distributed load" and "distributed catastrophe" often comes down to a single misconfigured parameter, a subtle timing issue, or an algorithm that seemed brilliant in theory but collapses the moment reality shows up uninvited.

 **Explainer:**
OSI Model – The Seven-Layer Cake of
Networking

Let me warn you upfront: this may be the driest and most abstract explainer in the entire series. But it's worth getting a surface-level grip on the idea — it makes the rest of the networking world far less mysterious.

Think of computer networks as a pyramid made of seven layers. Each layer builds on the one below it, adding a bit more meaning, structure, or intention. The lower layers move bits. The upper layers decide what those bits *mean*. Together, they form the OSI model (Open Systems Interconnection) — a tidy abstraction for a very messy reality.

Here are the seven layers in the classic model — in plain, human language:

1. **Physical** – the "wires and waves" layer. It's the part where signals physically travel: electricity in cables, light in fibre, radio in the air.

2. **Data Link** – neighbours talking to neighbours. Devices on the same local network saying "hey, this message is for you."

3. **Network** – finding paths. Figuring out how to get a message from one place in the world to another.

4. **Transport** – deciding *how* the message should travel: in one piece or many, carefully or quickly, with or without double-checking.

5. **Session** – keeping a conversation going. Making sure two sides can talk for a while without losing track of where they are.

6.Presentation – making the data understandable. Turning raw bytes into something meaningful — like decoding text or preparing something to be shown.

7.Application – the part you actually use. Websites, apps, messages — anything that looks like a feature instead of plumbing.

Now, the good news: **you do not need to memorize this.** Even people who work with networking professionally rarely remember all seven layers. Most engineers (myself included) only keep layers **4** and **7** in active memory — and even that depends on caffeine levels.

What matters is the concept: in this pyramid, higher layers can always peek *down* to see what's happening underneath, but lower layers have no idea what lives above them. A conversation between two apps can examine how the connection behaves, but the connection itself has no clue whether it's carrying a movie, a map, or your latest attempt at creative emoji usage.

Treat the OSI model as a map, not a law. Real-world networking bends these rules constantly. TLS/SSL? Technically layer 6 — there's no wiggle room there. DNS is *officially* layer 7, but depending on implementation details it can slip into layer 6 or even behave like layer 4. And BGP... BGP is chaos wearing a protocol badge. On paper it's layer 7, yet it decides how layers 3 and 4 behave, which is why some engineers jokingly call it layer 3.5 — or layer 8 (politics). In practice, the OSI stack is less a strict hierarchy and more a polite suggestion that reality cheerfully ignores whenever convenient.

And one last note: in my previous book (*IT Dictionary*) I mentioned that basement-dwelling IT folks sometimes talk about a "Layer 8 issue." That's a direct reference to this model — and it's basically a polite way of saying "the user messed up."

Explainer:
What a Load Balancer Really Is — The Checkout Line Analogy (and Then Some)

Time to get to the point: what *is* a load balancer? Well, a load balancer is a system that... balances load. Distributes work. The end.

Ok, let's dig a bit deeper because the idea matters. It may surprise you, but Netflix or Google are *not* powered by one gigantic super-server sitting in a bunker under a volcano. They run on thousands upon thousands of machines.

To picture why this matters, imagine doing your weekly shopping. You fill your cart and head towards the checkout area. There isn't one cashier — there are many. You walk along the row of tills, pick one that's open, and join the queue... only to watch every other line move faster, for reasons known only to the gods of retail. It's simple, but it has one big flaw: *you*, the customer, must figure out which cashier will serve you.

That's basically what the internet *would* look like if you had to pick a server manually. Typing `google.com` would require also choosing `google1328.com` or `google7623.com` and hoping you picked the faster one.

Some supermarkets solve this with a single, unified queue that assigns you to the next available cashier. The system knows which tills are open, which ones just finished serving someone, and where to send you so the line keeps moving. *That* is a load balancer.

But let's crank this analogy into Monty Python absurdity. Imagine each cashier can scan **only one item at a time**. You step up, hand over your milk, it gets scanned... and then you go back to the queue. Then you return with your bread. Then your tomatoes. Then your pasta. Every item is its own tiny interaction. And you know what? That's how the internet works.

So let's move on and look at the different kinds of load balancers, how they make decisions, and how each of them can either save your system... or ruin your day.

Two Challenges Hiding In Our Supermarket Analogy

Before we classify load balancers, we need to stay in our supermarket fantasy for just a moment longer. It turns out this silly image helps explain two very real challenges.

1. Knowing which checkouts are actually open

As a shopper, you'd prefer the system to send you only to a cashier who's *actually there*. That means continuously checking whether a cashier has gone on break and whether a new one has just opened. In tech, these two responsibilities are called *health checks* and *service discovery*.

Oh, and just in case it slips: the digital equivalents of "open checkouts" are often called *backends* or *upstreams* —

there are more terms, but we'll spare ourselves the glossary.

2. Remembering who you are (or pretending to)

Now for the fun part: in our absurd Monty Python supermarket, the cashiers don't talk to each other and don't remember you. Every time you return with one more item, you're treated as a completely new customer with a fresh receipt. Buying alcohol? They'll ask for your ID every single time.

Many internet protocols work exactly like that — including HTTP. They forget you instantly unless the software running the place (our metaphorical supermarket manager... or, in reality, the developer) adds extra logic. One workaround is *sticky sessions*: the assistant remembers which cashier handled you before and keeps sending you back there. Sure, you still have to queue again, but at least someone vaguely recognises your face.

Of course, if that cashier closes mid-shopping, your entire adventure restarts from zero.

The Four Species Of Load Balancers
(At Least The Ones People Admit Exist)

I'll confess: when I first sat down to outline this section, I confidently remembered only two types — Layer 4 and Layer 7. If someone had put a gun to my head, I might have guessed there must be something lurking below them... and I would've been right, mostly by luck.

In practice there are **at least four** commonly discussed types. They differ not just in how smart they are, but in *what* they look at when making decisions.

L2 — The "Switch With Ambition"

This one barely qualifies as a load balancer. It forwards traffic based on physical addresses, making decisions that are fast, simple, and almost aggressively unintelligent. Think of it as a switch that woke up one day and said, "I, too, want responsibility," and everyone politely let it try.

In fact, the industry isn't even fully convinced this deserves to be called a load balancer at all — it usually goes by *Link Aggregation (LACP)* or *NIC Teaming*. But for completeness, we'll acknowledge its ambitions.

L3 — "Routing Roulette"

Layer 3 balancing happens at the IP level. Packets are forwarded based on routes, and which backend receives which request can depend on the whims of routing tables. It's structured, logical... and occasionally feels like watching a roulette wheel spin.

L4 — The "Connection Bouncer"

This is where most real load balancing begins. L4 systems look at connection metadata — a term we'll properly unpack in Chapter 13 of the next part; for now just remember it means the basics: who's sending, who's receiving, and through which "door" (the port — yes, the very same door analogy from Chapter 5) — and decide who should handle each connection. They don't understand *what* you're doing, only that you want in. Like a nightclub bouncer: they check your ID, not your life story.

L7 — The "Overworked Receptionist With Mood Swings

The smartest — and sometimes the most temperamental — of the bunch. An L7 balancer doesn't just see that a request exists; it tries to understand *what the request is trying to do*. It can peek at the shape and intent of the message, make decisions based on what the user is asking for, and steer traffic in ways that feel almost personal. It's like a receptionist who doesn't merely say "next please," but listens just long enough to decide where you should really go — and occasionally sends you to the wrong room out of sheer stress.

One last thing: load balancers exist everywhere in modern systems, not just at the front door. Inside applications, between microservices, within clusters — anywhere traffic moves, something's deciding where it goes. You'll see exactly why this matters when we look at how Slack's entire platform collapsed — not because their visible, public-facing load balancers failed, but because the internal ones nobody admits are load balancers did.

And yes, purists will insist these aren't "real" load balancers. They'll invent elaborate names to avoid the association. Ignore them. If it decides where traffic goes, it's load balancing — regardless of what engineers call it to feel special.

With those four characters introduced, we can finally start exploring how they behave, why they fail, and why choosing the wrong type can turn a smooth architecture into a Greek tragedy.

Cloudflare
The Regex That Broke The Internet

Date: July 2, 2019

Impact: 80% drop in global traffic; widespread 502 errors; Cloudflare edge CPUs pinned at 100%; outage lasted ~30 minutes

Root Cause: Catastrophic backtracking (ReDoS) in a newly deployed WAF rule intended to stop XSS attacks

In theory, a Web Application Firewall should protect the Internet from bad actors. In practice, on July 2nd, 2019, Cloudflare's WAF protected precisely no one — unless you count stopping the entire Internet as a security feature.

The disaster began innocently. An engineer deployed a new rule meant to block XSS attacks — short for Cross-Site Scripting, a class of vulnerabilities where an attacker injects malicious code into a website so they can steal data or impersonate users. Blocking XSS is good. Blocking the Internet is less good.

No hackers, no DDoS botnet of rogue toasters, no alien EMP. The culprit? A single, cursed regex rule in their Web Application Firewall (WAF).

Think of a WAF as the airport security of the Internet: it doesn't just check if your suitcase has the right label (like a normal firewall), it opens it up to make sure you're not smuggling something dangerous. Regex — short for regular expression — is the instruction manual for that inspection. It tells the system what to look for: "Hey, anything that looks sharp, suspicious, or smells like SQL injection — stop it."

The problem? Regex can be a bit too literal. Describe "scissors" the wrong way, and suddenly grandma's rolled-up recipe for apple pie gets flagged for secondary inspection. In computing terms, if the pattern is too vague or too complex, the firewall ends up exhaustively searching every possible interpretation of incoming text. It's like hiring an over-zealous security guard who performs a full-body search on every traveler for "suspicious vibes" — or worse, letting a dude with dynamite stroll through because you misspelled "bomb."

Yes, one regular expression — those compact, arcane patterns programmers use to match text — brought Cloudflare to its knees. Someone had deployed a new WAF rule meant to detect malicious payloads. The intention was noble: stop the bad guys. The result: stop everyone. This is your CPU going from "hello world" to "I am become death, destroyer of cycles."

Cloudflare propagates WAF rules globally within seconds. Normally that's a strength. This time, it meant the faulty regex was deployed to every edge server on the planet before anyone had time to say "did you test that?" And because the WAF is part of Cloudflare's Layer 7 load-balancing path, every HTTP request had to pass through the hungry regex first.

It didn't go well.

Within moments of rollout, edge servers worldwide began chewing through CPU like a toddler discovering sugar. The regex examined incoming traffic, hit its pathological pattern, and triggered a backtracking explosion that consumed all available compute. On each machine, WAF workers slammed to 100% CPU, leaving no cycles for anything else — including answering requests, performing health checks, or even emitting telemetry.

From the outside, users saw a wall of **502 Bad Gateway** responses. From the inside, Cloudflare engineers saw... nothing. Their dashboards were also down, because those dashboards were behind Cloudflare. Dogfooding: great for culture, terrible for visibility during global meltdowns.

To make matters worse, the underlying L3/L4 load balancers were still technically alive — packets could reach the servers — but the L7 logic that actually processed requests had been starved to death. The Internet was trying to talk to Cloudflare, and Cloudflare was too busy running an out-of-control regex to respond.

Rolling back sounds simple: just hit 'undo.' But the servers were too busy dying to listen. Each one was so deep in its regex spiral it barely had cycles left to receive commands, let alone process them. Engineers pushed the rollback globally. Some data centers snapped back immediately. Others sat there overwhelmed, with the rollback command waiting politely in a queue while the server continued its death march through infinite pattern matching. A few were so far gone they needed a hard restart—the digital equivalent of smelling salts. The recovery took nearly as long as the initial deployment, except this time millions of users were watching their browsers spin, wondering if the Internet had given up.

After roughly 30 minutes of chaos, Cloudflare managed to restore stability. In their postmortem, they dryly referred to the issue as a "CPU exhaustion bug triggered by a WAF rule." In the same way that a meteor smacking into a city is a "minor structural integrity event."

LESSON LEARNED

- Smart load balancers create smart failures — simple checks can prevent global tears.
- Never deploy regex-based security rules without timeouts, guards, and a strong drink.
- Global propagation is a force multiplier for both protection and disaster.
- Observability must not depend on the same systems that are melting.
- A single bad pattern can take down a planet's worth of servers.

Cloudflare set out to block malicious scripts — and succeeded, by briefly treating the entire Internet as one.

Slack Outage
The Load Balancer Ate Its Own Routing Table

Date: January 4, 2021

Impact: Global outage during peak US morning; millions unable to connect; even the status page went down

Root Cause: Retry storm + amplification loops + AWS Transit Gateway (TGW) saturation

Slack began 2021 the way most of us began that particular year: with good intentions, brittle infrastructure, and an immediate nervous breakdown.

Before we go further, here's the crucial architectural backdrop. Modern applications — Slack included — are not one big monolithic program. They're closer to a bustling town made of hundreds of tiny specialised shops, each responsible for exactly one thing: storing messages, delivering notifications, handling files, tracking presence, and so on. These mini-programs, called **microservices**, rely on each other constantly. If one gets confused, the rest usually follow.

And whenever microservices need to talk to each other, guess who stands in the middle? The protagonists of this chapter: **load balancers**[17].

On the morning of January 4th, just as the US workforce was returning from the holiday coma, Slack's systems collectively decided that work was overrated. A small

---

[17] Pedants will note that the component that actually failed here was the AWS Transit Gateway — technically a high-availability cloud router, not a traditional Load Balancer. Fair enough. However, since it sits in the middle of the traffic flow, distributes packets across network segments, and has the power to ruin your day by dropping everything when overloaded, it earns its place in this chapter. If it quacks like a bottleneck and walks like a bottleneck, I'm calling it a Load Balancer.

upstream service began misbehaving — nothing dramatic at first, just a bit slow, a bit flaky, like a hungover intern on their first day back. Clients, being polite and helpful creatures, did what polite distributed systems are taught them to do: **retry.**

Unfortunately, retries in distributed systems behave like cute, fluffy rabbits — adorable until you remember that rabbits don't multiply additively, they multiply *exponentially*. One retry becomes two, then four, then eight, then sixteen... and suddenly your entire system looks like the petting-zoo version of Chapter 5's exponential growth nightmare. This was no different. Each Slack client, upon not hearing back fast enough, sent more requests. Each request that timed out spawned more retries. And because Slack is used by millions of people at the same time, this blossomed into a well-intented DDoS.

The load balancers were the first casualties — not because they lost their routing maps, but because they ran head-first into the physical packet-per-second limits of the AWS Transit Gateway. Think of a nightclub bouncer suddenly confronted with 10,000 people trying to get through one door: he doesn't organize a queue, he just locks the entrance. The TGW did the same — hit the ceiling, bolted the digital doors shut, and everything behind it started panicking. Microservices, convinced the silence meant "try harder," fired off more retries, forming a perfect thundering herd and turning a traffic spike into a self-sustaining meltdown.

That pressure didn't stay localized. Each overwhelmed component did what polite software often does: it tried to "help" by retrying even more. Amplification loops kicked in: every retry spawned more retries, which spawned even more retries, until the entire platform resembled a crowd stuck in a revolving door, all pushing in the wrong direction.

By the time engineers intervened, Slack was mostly down — clients couldn't connect, messages didn't load, calls failed instantly, and the status page, hosted on the same infrastructure (because of course it was), politely reminded visitors that it, too, was having a bad day.

The fix wasn't glamorous. Engineers essentially walked into the room, clapped loudly, and told every component to calm the hell down. They limited how many times things were allowed to "try again," added mechanisms that say "stop, this is getting stupid," and gave the traffic directors (our heroic load balancers) sturdier clipboards so they wouldn't lose track of who goes where. Sometimes the correct response to failure isn't to push harder — it's to take a breath, slow down, and stop making the problem worse.

LESSON LEARNED

- Retries need budgets — unlimited politeness becomes collective suicide.
- Load balancers can become the weakest link when overwhelmed.
- Microservices tend to die together, beautifully and in perfect synchrony.
- Amplification loops don't require malice — just enthusiasm and no guardrails.
- Status pages should not live on the same failing infrastructure.

It was January 4th — the universal "oh God, work again" day. Maybe Slack was just trying to give everyone one more unofficial holiday.

Roblox
73 Hours Of Silence And The Consensus Trap

Date: October 28–31, 2021

Impact: 73-hour global outage; 50+ million daily players locked out; internal systems including monitoring taken down

Root Cause: Consul service discovery meltdown — BoltDB write amplification, leader-election loops, and cluster starvation

Roblox's 2021 outage is what happens when a system built for children's games accidentally reenacts an academic paper on distributed-systems failure modes. It lasted **73 hours**, which in Internet time is roughly equivalent to the Bronze Age.

It all started with an innocent-looking configuration change. Roblox relies on Consul, a service-discovery system that tells microservices where other microservices live. Think of it as a phonebook for an absurdly complicated city. When Consul works, everything knows where everything else is. When Consul fails, the city turns into a crowd of people wandering the streets, yelling each other's names — all while wearing earplugs, just to make sure nobody can actually hear the answers.

The root of the disaster was BoltDB, the embedded database Consul uses to store its internal state. During the rollout, Consul hit a nasty corner case: a configuration change caused its internal state to grow into a massive, ever-expanding list that BoltDB had to rewrite to disk on every update. BoltDB works like a notebook where you can't erase—every change means copying the entire page. When Consul's state list grew massive, BoltDB had to rewrite gigabytes of data for every tiny update. What should have taken microseconds ballooned into multiple-second write operations.

That slowdown was fatal. Consul's coordination logic relies on a steady rhythm of "I'm alive" signals between nodes. When BoltDB was busy shovelling gigabytes of state around, Consul couldn't keep up. Leaders stopped responding in time, followers assumed they had died, and from the cluster's perspective the leadership chair remained cursed — every new leader would immediately freeze trying to write state to BoltDB, prompting yet another election.

And so began the Leader Election Loop, a distributed version of musical chairs where the music never stops and nobody ever wins. Each time a new leader was elected, it immediately froze while trying to catch up on the enormous backlog the previous leader had left behind. From the cluster's perspective, this looked exactly like another failure — so it would elect yet another leader, who would stall in the same way. And so on. For hours.

With Consul constantly rebooting its own leadership, the service-discovery database was in a perpetual state of amnesia. No microservice could know where any other microservice lived. Roblox's internal traffic collapsed into a tangle of failed requests, timeouts, and existential confusion.

The outage should have been visible instantly — but here's the twist: Roblox's observability systems also relied on Consul. All of them needed Consul to find their own backends. When Consul fell, monitoring fell. Engineers were effectively blind. Imagine trying to diagnose a burst water pipe with the lights off and the floor quickly becoming a swimming pool.

Meanwhile, in a moment of completely understandable panic—the kind that happens when your monitoring is blind, your platform is dead, and 50 million kids are screaming at their screens—engineers did what stressed humans do: they threw hardware at the problem, 128-core monsters to be exact. "Unfortunately, BoltDB is not a fan of overwhelming concurrency. More CPU meant more threads hammering the database, which increased internal contention and made the situation *worse*. The cluster was now failing faster, harder, and with more enthusiasm.

Recovery took 73 hours of careful, terrifying work. Engineers couldn't just restart Consul—that would trigger another election loop. They had to rebuild the cluster from scratch, restore internal connectivity piece by piece, and pray each step didn't cascade into a new disaster.

LESSON LEARNED

- Service discovery is a dependency you only notice when it dies — and then it's all you notice.
- Consensus algorithms are powerful, but they fail in spectacular, self-reinforcing ways.
- Monitoring systems must not rely on the same infrastructure they are monitoring.
- Scaling up hardware doesn't fix architectural bottlenecks; sometimes it just lets you fail faster.
- Strong consistency (CP) is great — until instability makes your system choose "C" over "A" and stop serving entirely.

Roblox promised an immersive world powered by imagination — which finally came in handy, because for three days players had no choice but to imagine the game working at all.

—————————— **Google Cloud** ——————————

When Automation Took Down The Internet's Backbone

Date: June 2, 2019 & August 2020

Impact: Hours-long outages affecting YouTube, Gmail, Google Cloud services, and global customer workloads

Root Cause: Two distinct automation failures — GFE crash loops (2020) and control-plane descheduling triggering BGP route withdrawals (2019)

Google Cloud likes to describe its infrastructure as self-healing, self-optimizing, and generally self-sufficient — an intelligent mesh of global systems that can route around failures before humans even notice. Unfortunately, on two separate occasions, the automation got a bit *too* self-confident and helpfully took down large chunks of the Internet.

Both outages — one in 2019, one in 2020 — share the same moral: if you let automation run the asylum, don't be surprised when the inmates vote to evict themselves.

2019: The Day The Control Plane Went On Vacation

In 2019 Google got a painful reminder that even "self-healing" infrastructures sometimes heal themselves straight into a coma.

A faulty automation job descheduled the services running Google's global control plane — basically firing the air-traffic controllers *mid-flight*. One minute everything was humming; the next, the layer that updates routes and keeps the planetary network aligned had vanished for a spa weekend.

The packet-moving underlayers kept going, but the brains of the operation went silent. Google's safety mechanisms saw the void and did what any panicked watchdog would do: withdraw BGP routes for whole regions. Translation: "These data centers? Never heard of them."

Traffic instantly flooded into regions that were never meant to handle it. Gmail, YouTube, GCE — all wobbling. The global load balancers, normally the adults in the room, started improvising badly, shoving traffic into whichever region was still whispering "I exist." Think evacuating a stadium through the janitor's closet because it's the only unlocked door.

Once engineers revived the control plane and re-announced routes, the network reconverged at its usual glacial, planetary pace.

The outage lasted over four hours — long enough for everyone to take notes and pretend they weren't one automation job away from the same fate.

2020: The GFE That Forgot How To Exist

If you think Google learned its lesson in 2019, I have bad news. They mostly learned how to fail in a completely new way.

In August 2020, Google pushed a configuration change to GFE (Google Front End), the global entry point for Google's L7 load balancer. GFE is the place that:

- "unsmears the brown paint" from Chapter 8 (decrypting TLS so Google can read what you *meant* to say), and

- parses HTTP, basically the bouncer checking IDs at the front door of Google.

The new software contained a bug that sent GFEs into crash loops. Each instance tried to process certain requests, hit the faulty code path, and immediately collapsed. Supervisors dutifully restarted it because nothing says "robust automation" like slamming into the same wall over and over. At global scale, this produced a perfectly synchronized percussion of GFEs face-planting in unison.

The result: widespread 502 errors, broken connections, and major services, including YouTube, blinking out. Since the GFE layer *is* the front door, the impact was instant and loud: when your receptionist keeps fainting, nobody gets checked in, pizza deliveries get lost, and everyone starts yelling.

Engineers rolled back the change, resurrected the previous stable version, and gently reminded GFE how to exist. The disruption lasted long enough for people to rediscover hobbies they didn't realize required an Internet connection, like staring at walls or talking to family.

LESSON LEARNED

- Automation is a powerful tool — until it blindly trusts its own assumptions.
- Control planes must degrade gracefully; silence should not equal "withdraw from the Internet."
- Global load balancers amplify even tiny bugs into planetary-scale incidents.
- Canarying (gradual rollout to catch bugs early) isn't optional for L7 edge software; it's oxygen.

> • The cloud may be global, but failures still propagate at the speed of configuration.

Google's self-managing systems worked exactly as designed—they managed to take themselves down twice, globally, without requiring any human intervention whatsoever.

Azure Front Door
The Empty Array That Silenced The World

Date: October 29, 2025

Impact: 8-hour global outage across Azure Front Door and Microsoft 365; millions unable to access services; cascading failures in airlines, gaming, and enterprise workloads

Root Cause: A configuration change containing incompatible metadata propagated globally—interpreted by the system not as "no change," but as "block everything"

Note: At the time of writing, only Microsoft's Preliminary Post-Incident Review was available, along with a promise that the final version would land within 14 days. It didn't. Instead of the promised document, Microsoft dropped a YouTube retrospective — so this case is based on the preliminary PIR plus whatever they were willing to say on camera.

If software disasters had a sense of humor, this one would qualify as performance art.

On October 29th, 2025, Azure Front Door—Microsoft's global entryway for web traffic—deployed what should have been a routine configuration update. The change was meant to update backend origin mappings: essentially telling Front Door which servers should handle which requests. Simple stuff. Happens all the time.

Except this particular update contained metadata that two different versions of the control plane couldn't agree on. When processed, it created what Microsoft engineers call a "reference count mismatch"—essentially telling the system that certain backend configurations existed when they actually didn't. It was the digital equivalent of submitting a change-of-address form claiming your house still exists at an address that's been demolished.

The configuration passed through deployment safety checks. The system loaded it, reported everything healthy, and gave the thumbs up. It was the digital equivalent of a pilot checking the flaps, seeing them fall off, and giving a thumbs-up because the checklist didn't explicitly ask 'are they still attached to the wings?'. Five minutes later, when background processing tried to access those non-existent references, the data plane crashed.

Front Door sits in front of thousands of services: Microsoft 365, Teams, Xbox Live, Minecraft, the Azure Portal itself, and countless third-party platforms. When the data plane concluded there were no valid backends to route to, the effect was planet-wide. Requests arrived, Front Door checked for origins, found corrupted metadata pointing to nothing, and dropped everything on the floor.

Xbox players couldn't log in. Airline passengers at Alaska and Hawaiian Airlines couldn't check in—kiosks went manual. Office workers stared at spinning cursors where their email used to be. And Microsoft's own diagnostic tools? They also flowed through Front Door. When the edge collapsed, observability collapsed with it. Engineers were locked outside their own building, staring at alarms they couldn't reach.

The recovery became an eight-hour war of attrition.

Microsoft's incident commander faced an ugly choice. The system snapshots "last known good" configurations every 15 minutes. But the poisoned metadata had passed validation checks and made it into the last four snapshots. Rolling back risked either reintroducing the bug or—if they went further back—overloading the few healthy nodes still serving traffic.

Instead, engineers manually edited the latest snapshot to remove the corrupted configurations, then deployed it globally. But loading configurations for 750,000 customer applications took over four hours, even after connectivity was restored. Edge nodes that had been running in a broken state were reluctant to trust new instructions—like someone who's been lied to all day suddenly being asked to believe one more thing.

By 11:20 PM UTC—over seven hours in—Microsoft reported 98% availability. The last stragglers limped across the finish line shortly after midnight. Eight hours total.

In short: incompatible metadata between two control plane versions had achieved what nation-state attackers dream of—silencing enormous portions of Microsoft's cloud by convincing the front door that there was nowhere left to send anyone.

LESSON LEARNED

- Asynchronous processing can turn "validation passed" into a time bomb with a five-minute fuse.
- Global configuration systems must validate not just "healthy now" but "will stay healthy after background tasks complete."

- When your observability pipeline depends on the same entry point that just failed, recovery becomes archaeology without tools.
- Loading 750,000 application profiles takes four hours; there is no "quick" recovery at hyperscale.
- If your last-known-good snapshot is poisoned, "rollback" becomes "creative surgery with a deadline."

When you tell a global content delivery network that nothing exists, it takes you very, very literally—for eight hours.

CHAPTER 10:
WHEN THE CLOUD RAINS

By now, we've toured the Internet's plumbing: the maps (BGP), the names (DNS), and the trust glue (SSL/TLS). Each layer kept the illusion alive that your cat photos and bank transfers move through a rational, well-ordered world. Now it's time to talk about the last foundation stone of our digital empire — the thing that promised to make all that chaos someone else's problem: the cloud.

The word *cloud* is one of tech's greatest linguistic scams. It sounds gentle, almost poetic, like something that drifts lazily across the sky. In reality, it's "other people's computers" sealed inside fortified warehouses that consume as much electricity as small nations. Most of the Internet lives there now: in humming data fortresses guarded more tightly than some military bases, glowing under a billion-dollar promise of reliability, scalability, and simplicity. Three words that sound reassuring until you've seen what happens when one line of code goes wrong.

Before we talk about what breaks, let's agree on what "the cloud" even means — because the term is tossed around like confetti at a startup launch party. Depending on who you ask, it means at least three different things.

First, there's cloud-native, the architectural religion of breaking your app into bite-sized, independently scalable microservices. It's a mindset, not a location. You could, in theory, run a cloud-native app from your basement if your patience (and power grid) can handle it. We'll politely ignore this flavor here; this isn't a textbook on software architecture.

Second, there's the everyday version — where "the cloud" simply means "my stuff is on the Internet somewhere." Upload a photo, sync your contacts, and voilà, you've joined the cult. Except sometimes, that "cloud" is a single dusty server sitting under someone's desk with decent marketing. We'll mercifully ignore this version too — it's not much of a cloud, more like a faint puff of breath on a cold evening, barely enough vapor to fog a mirror.

And finally, there's the one we actually care about: the cloud as infrastructure, those global computing behemoths like AWS, Google Cloud, and Azure. They are the landlords of the digital world, renting out slices of their machine farms to everyone else. Think of them as the Internet's stage crew: mostly invisible, occasionally heroic, and occasionally the reason the show gets canceled.

To grasp why this chapter treats them as a foundational layer of the Internet, just follow the money and the cables. Amazon may be best known for selling kitchen gadgets and cat toys, but its real powerhouse is **Amazon Web Services**, running roughly 30% of the Internet and generating about half of Amazon's total profit. Microsoft, famous for PowerPoint misery and the occasional Blue Screen of Death, runs **Azure**, which powers about 20% of the Internet and accounts for 31% of its corporate profit. And Google — yes, the one that helps you find cat videos — operates **Google Cloud Platform (GCP)**, hosting roughly 12% of the Internet and contributing about 9% of its revenue. Altogether, the top five companies control about 75% of the world's online infrastructure. When they sneeze, the rest of the Internet catches pneumonia.

These aren't mere providers; they're digital utilities — the pipes of civilization. When they falter, it's not just memes that vanish, but banks, hospitals, governments, and all the dull but vital parts of modern life.

That's the cloud we're dissecting here: the physical side of the digital dream. The cables, switches, and air-conditioned chaos behind the glossy dashboards. The part where one misplaced keystroke in Virginia can black out half the planet, and where "redundant system" sometimes translates to "everything failed at once, but in stereo."

Cloud providers strike a deal: they handle the machinery, you manage yours. But when that machinery stumbles, boundaries dissolve. This chapter probes their foundation — the part meant to hold firm.

Spoiler: when that foundation shakes, the tremor ripples worldwide.

AWS US-East-1 Outage

Date: February 28, 2017

Impact: A single command typo in Amazon's largest data center region disrupted major online services worldwide for roughly four hours.

Root Cause: A mistyped parameter during routine maintenance on S3's billing subsystem shut down critical index and placement servers, crippling S3's ability to locate and route stored data.

Every empire has its capital, and for Amazon Web Services, that capital is US-East-1 — the oldest and most interdependent region, located in Virginia. Behind the friendly talk of "availability zones" and "global redundancy," this region quietly acts as the *central control hub* for many of AWS's internal systems, including key authorization and routing components. In simpler terms: it's the brainstem of the world's biggest cloud.

On February 28, 2017, an AWS engineer was performing what should have been routine maintenance on S3, Amazon's service for storing files with effectively infinite capacity. (Technically the limit obviously exists, but Amazon has enough hard drives and optimism to ensure you'll run out of money long before they run out of space.)

The engineer was debugging a slowdown in S3's billing system and ran a command to remove a small subset of servers from that subsystem. A typo in one parameter escalated it, shutting down far more — including critical index and placement subsystems that managed S3's metadata and object routing. In human terms: someone meant to reboot a few lights, and instead cut power to the control room.

Within minutes, S3-dependent services began collapsing. Photos on Dropbox stalled. News sites like *The New York Times* froze. Slack went offline. Financial dashboards and even NASA's satellite data feeds blinked out. And just to complete the irony, Amazon's own service status dashboard went dark — because it was hosted on S3.

For roughly four hours, large chunks of the modern web simply didn't work. It wasn't the whole Internet, but it was enough to expose how deeply so many systems relied on a single AWS region. Major companies, media outlets, and startups learned the same uncomfortable truth: "cloud-native" didn't mean invincible.

When services finally recovered, the damage ran into millions of dollars and countless apologies. During the incident, AWS engineers provided updates through alternative channels like Twitter and developer forums — since their primary dashboard was out of commission.

Afterward, Amazon published one of the most candid post-mortems in its history. They detailed the sequence of events, acknowledged the root cause, and outlined fixes. Unlike many corporations, they followed through: redistributing key internal systems across multiple regions, adding guardrails to internal tools that now block operations risking critical capacity drops, and auditing other operational utilities for similar single points of failure.

In their official statement, AWS wrote: "We will do everything we can to learn from this event and make Amazon S3 even better."

And to their credit — unlike Rogers in 2022 — they followed through, earning back trust without a price hike.

LESSON LEARNED

- The cloud is powerful, but not mystical — it's still software running on hardware run by humans.
- If one person with a command line can take down critical global services, your redundancy plan is fiction.
- "Highly available" doesn't mean "typo-proof."
- And for the love of uptime, don't host your status page in the same region you're reporting on.

US-East-1: The single point of failure disguised as an entire cloud region.

AWS US-East-1 Outage
When A Race Condition Broke The Beating Heart Of The Cloud

Date: October 20, 2025

Impact: ~15-hour outage affecting DynamoDB, EC2, Lambda, IAM, and major global platforms (Snapchat, Fortnite, Slack, Atlassian, Ring, banking & retail apps)

Root Cause: Race condition in AWS's DNS automation layer for DynamoDB, which deleted the primary regional endpoint and triggered a cascading failure across AWS control planes

AWS loves to describe its cloud as self-healing and self-managing — a benevolent automated caretaker humming along while engineers sleep. On October 20, 2025, that caretaker quietly removed DynamoDB's main DNS record and spent the next 15 hours learning why self-confidence is not a substitute for supervision.

The outage began shortly after 3:11 AM Eastern Time, when `dynamodb.us-east-1.amazonaws.com` simply stopped existing from the Internet's point of view. The servers behind it were healthy, but in distributed systems existence is not about hardware — it's about *being findable*. And with the DNS entry gone, DynamoDB became the world's most overprovisioned Schrödinger's database: alive, running, and unreachable.

The root cause was a race condition — the same old friend from Chapter 4 — playing out inside AWS's automated DNS machinery. Two enactors, acting on slightly different timelines, collided: one tried to apply an outdated configuration file at the exact moment another deleted it to make room for a new one. The result was a silent, clean deletion of the *live* DNS record. Nothing malfunctioned. The automation simply followed instructions in an unlucky order.

The blast radius was immediate. DynamoDB sits at the center of so many AWS control-plane rituals that when it vanished, the rest of the cloud reacted like a group project where the one responsible adult suddenly stops answering messages. Services that normally behave with calm professionalism began pacing in circles. Some waited politely for instructions that never came. Others froze mid-sentence like actors forgetting their lines. A few, realizing they had no idea what to do without DynamoDB whispering state updates into their ears, simply lay down and refused to participate. It wasn't one subsystem failing — it was the collective moment when AWS tried to remember how to tie its shoes without the part of the brain responsible for shoelaces.

When AWS restored the DNS entry, the second disaster began: a perfectly synchronized global **retry storm**. Every microservice, script, IoT doodad, mobile app, cronjob, and enterprise backend that had been failing for hours instantly retried. It was a textbook self-inflicted DDoS — millions of well-behaved clients stampeding through a freshly reopened door.

AWS spent the afternoon throttling and shaping traffic until the control plane could breathe again, while customers around the world kept refreshing the status page and updating their internal war rooms — the author was in one of those. The lesson was painfully clear: automation didn't fail because it was wrong — it failed because it was fast, literal, and absolutely sure of itself.

LESSON LEARNED

- Automation can execute correct steps in a catastrophically incorrect order.
- Race conditions don't disappear with scale — they scale with you.
- DNS failures are never "just DNS"; they're entry-point failures for entire ecosystems.
- Retry logic can turn resilience patterns into synchronized self-DDoS events.
- Multi-region architecture is not a luxury — it's the parachute you hope you never need.

AWS will undoubtedly harden this corner of the system so this particular stumble doesn't happen again. Still, there's an uneasy metaphor at play — building the airplane mid-flight. The infrastructure keeps evolving while serving billions of requests, and when turbulence hits, it's the passengers (everyone else on the internet) who feel it first.

Fastly Outage

Date: June 8, 2021

Impact: Major global websites and platforms — including Reddit, GitHub, Twitch, Amazon, PayPal, Spotify, Stack Overflow, and *The Guardian* — went offline within seconds.

Root Cause: A customer's configuration change, deployed via Fastly's self-service tools, triggered a software bug introduced during a May 12 update. Within seconds, the bug cascaded and disabled about 85% of Fastly's global network.

At 10:47 a.m. UTC, the Internet briefly forgot how to Internet. Fastly, one of the world's leading edge network providers accidentally demonstrated what happens when the system designed to make websites faster suddenly stops working everywhere at once.

If the main data centers of cloud providers are like massive fortified bases, edge locations are their forward observation posts — smaller, distributed outposts placed all over the world. They don't have the full firepower of a central hub, but they respond far more quickly. In the digital world, that means shorter travel distances for data. Since light itself has a speed limit and humans hate waiting even half a second for their cat photos, these outposts make everything feel instantaneous.

This type of network, called a Content Delivery Network (CDN), doesn't process your data — it simply delivers it faster by caching frequently requested content such as images, videos, and music. When it works, everything feels smooth and effortless. When it breaks, even the simplest website can vanish.

On that day, a customer's configuration change — deployed through Fastly's self-service interface — triggered the dormant bug introduced weeks earlier. Within seconds, servers across continents began to fail in sync. News sites froze, payment portals stalled, shopping carts emptied, and entire sections of the web went dark.

The fallout was spectacular. Reddit, Twitch, PayPal, GitHub, Spotify, *The Guardian*, *Financial Times*, and countless others went down. Even Amazon and sections of the UK government's online services were hit. For millions of users, it was a vivid reminder of how fragile the supposedly "distributed" web really is.

Yet amidst the digital chaos, one site remained gloriously online: **Pornhub.** Their engineers had designed for precisely this scenario — redundant DNS providers, diversified CDNs, and no single dependency on Fastly. While the rest of the web panicked, Pornhub quietly served as the most reliable content platform on Earth.

Somewhere, a hypothetical sysadmin lit a cigarette and whispered, "I told you we needed a fallback."
And for once, nobody could argue.

The Internet collectively exhaled when Fastly rolled back the change 49 minutes after the outage began, with full recovery within an hour. In their post-mortem, the company acknowledged that a dormant bug had been triggered by a routine customer configuration update and promised to improve validation, testing, and isolation procedures to prevent similar cascades.

LESSON LEARNED

- Even the edge can have a bad day — decentralization without isolation is still fragility.
- Caching can't save you if configuration syncs spread failure faster than data.
- Always plan for the edge case where the edge collapses.
- And yes, redundancy may not be sexy — but apparently, that's the only thing that still works when the Internet breaks.

Cultural Footnote:
The meme that dominated the day came straight from Broadway: *"The Internet Is for Porn."* The song, originally from the Tony Award–winning musical *Avenue Q*, became an anthem of dark irony.

On June 8, 2021, it wasn't just funny. It was empirically true.

Google Global Outage

Date: December 14, 2020

Impact: Gmail, YouTube, Google Drive, Docs, Calendar, and even Nest devices went offline worldwide for nearly an hour.

Root Cause: A misconfigured internal quota system disabled Google's identity services, locking out both users and automated systems.

On a chilly Monday morning, the Internet experienced a brief existential crisis: Google forgot who everyone was. For 47 surreal minutes, one of the most sophisticated digital ecosystems in history stopped recognizing its own users.

It started around 3:40 a.m. PST, when people across continents began reporting that Gmail refused to load, YouTube videos wouldn't play, and Google Docs stared blankly back like an amnesiac assistant. Even smart home owners found themselves locked out of their own houses — Nest devices went offline, turning "smart home" into "expensive hostage situation."

The issue traced back to Google's internal authentication infrastructure — the brain responsible for verifying who's allowed to access what. Every service, from email to YouTube to cloud storage, checks in with this system to confirm identities and permissions. When that brain malfunctioned, everything else followed.

In this case, a routine maintenance update to the User ID quota management system — an internal tool that controls how many authentication requests Google's identity servers can handle — went spectacularly wrong. The configuration accidentally set global authentication quotas to zero. In effect, Google told its own network: *"Nobody is allowed to log in."* Not users, not admins, not even the automated recovery tools that were supposed to fix such things.

The result? A company worth over a trillion dollars spent nearly an hour locked out of itself.

And it wasn't just Google's own empire that went silent. The outage rippled outward, breaking login systems for hundreds of third-party services including Slack, Spotify, Snapchat, Discord, and even Pokémon GO. Thousands of people found themselves wandering parks and streets in confusion, unable to chase digital monsters or message their friends about it. For a brief, disorienting moment, humanity was forced to experience fresh air without the aid of Charizards or playlists.

Engineers eventually rolled back the configuration and restored services after approximately 47 minutes. Google later confirmed that the incident wasn't caused by an attack but by "an internal storage quota issue." They promised improvements to validation systems and better isolation between quota changes and production authentication services.

LESSON LEARNED

- Centralized identity is a single point of failure wearing a friendly face.

- "Zero trust" takes on new meaning when your systems literally trust no one.

- If your smart home stops working during a cloud outage, congratulations — you just learned what vendor lock-in feels like.

- Always have a backup plan that doesn't require logging in to the system that's broken.

> • Never allow quota changes to hit zero — it's rarely the right answer to "how many people should be able to use our service?"

December 14th started chilly in California. By 3:41 a.m., someone in Mountain View was learning that setting a quota to zero generates its own kind of heat

Azure AD Outage

Date: March 15–16, 2021

Impact: Microsoft 365, Teams, Outlook, and OneDrive went down for up to 14 hours, mainly affecting the Americas and Australia. Thousands of enterprises, including AT&T and Walmart, lost access to internal tools and communication platforms.

Root Cause: A bug in Azure AD's cryptographic key rotation process broke token trust verification, blocking logins worldwide until the fix propagated about 14 hours later.

On March 15, 2021, Microsoft's single sign-on dream became everyone's shared nightmare. Around 19:00 UTC, users worldwide discovered that logging into Microsoft services was suddenly impossible. Teams wouldn't connect, Outlook refused credentials, and IT departments collectively held their breath — which, given the timing, was about the only thing still working in sync.

The failure originated in Azure Active Directory (AD), Microsoft's identity doorman for both consumer and enterprise users. It acts as the master key to Microsoft's cloud kingdom: verifying credentials, issuing tokens, and maintaining sessions for everything from Office 365 to Xbox Live. When that key falters, every door stays locked.

Azure AD also serves as the silent ticket controller for thousands of organizations worldwide, including industry heavyweights like AT&T and Walmart. Unlike Google's identity layer, which governs public-facing apps, Azure AD often underpins a company's internal machinery — email systems, reports, HR portals, and those endless "collaboration tools" designed to keep everyone productive, or at least looking busy.

The culprit was a failure in cryptographic key rotation — a bug introduced during a routine update of signing keys used to verify login tokens. When the new keys propagated, applications stopped trusting issued tokens, effectively revoking access across Microsoft's global network. It was the digital equivalent of the earlier "document template" analogy: a small mismatch in how something is signed or linked, and suddenly nothing seems valid anymore.

During the incident, engineers attempted a configuration change to the token issuance service — the component responsible for generating access tokens — which compounded the issue. Authentication requests failed globally. In plain terms, Azure AD decided that no one, anywhere, should be allowed in.

Microsoft engineers initiated a rollback, but propagation across the vast identity network took time. Recovery began about six hours in, with full restoration achieved near the 14-hour mark. Microsoft later confirmed that the outage stemmed from cryptographic key rotation logic and that its automated rollback mechanism had failed due to circular authentication dependencies — the fix needed to log in before it could start fixing logins.

To their credit, Microsoft released a thorough post-incident report and made architectural improvements. They enhanced validation pipelines, isolated rollback mechanisms, and refined key rotation workflows. As a result, the *Service Level Agreement (SLA)* for Azure AD was raised to 99.99% uptime in April 2021 — the corporate equivalent of a blood oath stating that someone, somewhere, will be sacrificed if the service dips below target. In practical terms, "four nines" means a maximum downtime of just **52 minutes and 34 seconds** of downtime per year — impressive, unless you lived through those 14 hours.

LESSON LEARNED

- Centralized identity systems offer convenience — and perfectly centralized points of failure.
- Automation is great until it needs permission to fix itself.
- Never tie your recovery tools to the same login system that just collapsed.
- Many companies adopted backup authentication systems (like Okta) afterward — because redundancy isn't paranoia, it's survival.
- When people start rediscovering pen and paper, your "digital transformation" has gone too far in the wrong direction.

Single Sign-On was supposed to simplify life. On March 15th, it certainly did—locating the point of failure across hundreds of enterprises became trivially easy. Success?

PART II: SUMMARY
THE INTERNET'S HOUSE OF CARDS

We've now walked through the foundations of the modern Internet — and it turns out, many of them are built less on granite and more on sticks, hope, and chewing gum. Beneath the sleek interfaces and glossy cloud dashboards lies an ecosystem so complex and interdependent that a typo, expired certificate, misconfigured load balancer, or botched key rotation can shake the whole digital world.

If the first part of this book explored how individual systems learned to fail spectacularly, this part examined how we managed to industrialize those failures at global scale. We've seen routing protocols send traffic on intercontinental detours, watched DNS forget the names that hold the Internet together, discovered that trust itself can expire when certificates age out, learned that load balancers can amplify chaos instead of distributing it, and witnessed cloud providers — the supposed paragons of reliability — take down vast swaths of the web with configuration errors or cascading failures.

The Internet, in theory, is the pinnacle of human achievement — a global nervous system linking billions of minds and machines. In practice, it's more like a precarious tower of systems that keep standing mostly because everyone's too scared to touch them. It's not built on sand. But it sure behaves that way when someone sneezes in Virginia, forgets to renew a certificate, or adds one too many retry loops to a load balancer.

Yet the point of this part isn't to mock the engineers behind these disasters. Quite the opposite. Each story is a reminder of how impossibly difficult it is to maintain systems of this scale — where milliseconds matter, layers multiply, and a single configuration mistake can cascade into millions of dollars in losses. These failures aren't proof of incompetence; they're proof of complexity.

Every incident revealed another invisible dependency, another single point of failure hiding behind buzzwords like "redundancy," "resilience," or "high availability." Each one also pushed the industry forward: routing protocols gained better validation, certificate authorities improved their monitoring, load balancers learned to fail more gracefully, and cloud providers hardened their blast radius containment.

If there's a pattern emerging, it's that the Internet's strength comes not from perfection, but from iteration. Systems fail, engineers learn, and slowly — painfully — the web becomes a little more stable. That's the paradox at the heart of modern infrastructure: progress through failure. The question isn't whether systems will fail — it's whether we'll be smart enough to learn from them when they do.

In the next part, we'll shift our focus from how machines talk to each other to how they remember — or fail to remember. Because while the Internet's communication layer may wobble, it's nothing compared to what happens when the systems storing our data decide to forget, corrupt, or simply lose track of what they were supposed to preserve.

III. THE FRAGILITY OF DATA

PART III:
WHEN DATA FIGHTS BACK
— WHY STORAGE FAILURES HURT THE MOST

After exploring how computers **think** (compute) and how they **talk** (networking), we now arrive at the third and final pillar of everything digital systems do: they **store**. They remember. They accumulate context. They preserve the past so the present can make decisions. And when this pillar fails, it isn't just inconvenient — it's irreversible. A crashed CPU can be restarted, a dropped packet can be retransmitted, but lost data vanishes in a way no amount of engineering can undo.

A brief disclaimer before we proceed. Data storage and data processing have always been close to my heart professionally. I've spent enough years staring into databases, distributed systems, and recovery pipelines to develop both deep respect and deep paranoia toward how fragile our digital memory truly is. So yes — I may be biased. But the bias comes from experience rather than abstraction — and from a particular philosophy about information that I'll briefly sketch out here.

Because the truth is simple: compute and network failures cause disruption; data failures cause amputation. Downtime hurts — financially, operationally, emotionally — but downtime ends. Even in the previous chapters, where outages triggered spectacular financial losses, the impact was, at its core, a setback rather than an ending. A rocket destroyed on launch can be rebuilt. A trading glitch that wipes billions off a stock index is, in the long arc of markets, a fluctuation that will eventually be absorbed. Systems recover, capital regenerates, markets heal, and infrastructure can be reconstructed. There is one irreversible exception in compute and network failures: human life. And as we'll see across the entire series, that exception appears everywhere — far beyond storage. Systems come back. Queues drain. Services recover.

Data, however, does not grow back. Once corrupted or deleted beyond reach, it is gone. History has already erased countless works of art, scientific records, manuscripts, and archives through accidents, neglect, cost-cutting, or pure entropy[18]. Modern systems simply repeat ancient failures at digital speed.

And this matters not only for culture or memory. Data increasingly forms the substrate of our future. It is what trains our algorithms, calibrates our models, directs our automation, and shapes the decisions of the systems we rely on. But the consequences of that — both good and catastrophic — belong to Volume II.

Here, in Volume I, we focus on something more elemental: the fragility of stored information itself. In the chapters ahead, we'll look at the core ways data can slip away — through physical loss, through the loss of our ability to interpret it, through accidental deletion or overwriting, or through the simple illusion that a safe backup exists when it never did.

Data loss is not one phenomenon but a constellation of them — mechanical, logical, organizational, and human.

---

[18] **Entropy** – a fancy term coined in 1865 by German physicist Rudolf Clausius from the Greek words ἐν- (en-, "in") and τροπή (tropé, "transformation"). In practice, it simply means chaos and disorder. The second law of thermodynamics states that entropy in the universe can only increase – which boils down to the fact that order requires energy, but mess is free.

Yes, as a teenager I used this argument when my mom told me to clean my room.

The universe was on my side. My mom was not.

What they share is permanence. And that is why this entire part of the book exists: to show how quickly, quietly, and creatively information can disappear, and why protecting it is among the most important (and most underestimated) responsibilities in modern computing.

Note: this section will feel a little different from the rest of the series. Many data-loss catastrophes are not single events at all, but slow-moving processes — failures that unfold quietly over months or years, only revealing themselves when recovery is no longer possible.

Alright, that got a bit philosophical... but don't worry, that tone doesn't come naturally to me, so let's get back to my usual voice. Before we continue our journey, we need to clarify two basic data characteristics that will matter throughout this part.

 **Explainer:**
Availability vs Durability — The Forgetful Friend Problem

When it comes to data and IT systems, there are two terms that sound almost interchangeable — *availability* and *durability.*

For most people, that difference barely matters. The app either works or it doesn't.

But in engineering, those two ideas live on opposite ends of the survival spectrum — and mixing them up has caused more late-night panic than caffeine shortages.

Availability measures how often your friend answers the phone when you need them.

Durability measures how often that same friend remembers who you are.

Those two aren't the same thing:

• A *durable* friend remembers the Friday beer you agreed on last week — even if they don't pick up when you call to confirm.

• An *available* friend, on the other hand, answers right away but might react with *"What Friday beer?"*

The same logic applies to data:

• A system can be *available but not durable* — happily serving corrupted or outdated bits with a smile.

• It can also be *durable but not available* — all your data still exists somewhere, but you'll need an archaeology degree to retrieve it.

Both sound comforting in PowerPoint slides — until they don't.

There's also *reliability*, and an entire zoo of metrics pretending to measure it. And just like working in an actual zoo, it comes with a long list of rituals, certifications, and questionable practices that people swear make everything safer.

That, however, is a story for Part V. For now, that's enough.

CHAPTER 11:
DATA – DEATH BY NATURAL CAUSES

When we talk about losing data, most people picture cinematic disasters: hackers in hoodies, catastrophic system failures, maybe even a few blinking red lights for dramatic effect. In reality, the vast majority of data loss is far less theatrical. Information doesn't usually vanish in an explosion—it fades away quietly, the digital equivalent of paint peeling off a wall.

The irony is brutal: we built computers because they were supposed to remember perfectly. And yet, everything conspires against that promise. Physics erodes stored charge. Bits flip. Materials fatigue. Time gnaws at everything we encode. None of it is loud, or sudden, or even particularly noticeable. It's mundane—and relentless.

Worse still, even when the bits survive, their meaning often doesn't. Software becomes un-runnable. Formats turn obsolete. Documentation disappears into the void. You're left with immaculate, untouched bytes whose context has evaporated so thoroughly they might as well be ancient tablets in a language no one remembers. The data exists, but the story it once told is gone.

This chapter is dedicated to those quiet failures—the ones without headlines or drama—where nothing breaks spectacularly, yet entire archives drift toward oblivion. And here's the twist that makes this chapter unusual: we'll focus on cases of data loss that *didn't* happen. Or rather, didn't happen completely. These are near-misses, close calls, slow-motion dissolutions that were halted only because someone, somewhere, noticed the quiet warning signs and acted.

They're stories of engineers doing unglamorous, meticulous work to keep entropy at bay. No hero shots, no last-minute explosions—just people refusing to let decades of information disappear on their watch.

To appreciate the complexity of those rescues, we need to ground ourselves in two concepts that define everything that follows: what bit rot actually is, and why data decay is a different—yet equally treacherous—beast.

Explainer:
Bit Rot vs Data Decay

When we talk about the natural loss of information, it helps to distinguish two closely related but fundamentally different failure modes: **bit rot** and **data decay**.

Bit rot is what happens when physics and chemistry quietly reclaim your storage. No information carrier is eternal. Magnetic media slowly lose magnetization. SSD cells leak charge over time (pro-tip: if you store important data on an unplugged SSD, plug it in every few weeks). Optical discs degrade under UV light—or simply because time exists (chemistry does its thing: the materials themselves slowly break down). The mechanism varies, but the outcome is painfully consistent: bits flip, fade, or—

in the case of some analog-adjacent media—drift into absurd in-between states like 0.5.

It's like taking handwritten notes only to discover, months later, that the ink has faded so badly you can't read a single word. Physical degradation erases the medium itself; nothing is left to interpret, because the information has literally disappeared.

Data decay, on the other hand, occurs when the information is still *there*, but we no longer know how to interpret it. Old applications get uninstalled, formats become orphaned, documentation disappears, and we're left with byte sequences that might as well be ancient runes. It's the digital equivalent of a dead language: the symbols still exist, but we have no idea what they mean.

Or, returning to our earlier analogy, it's like rediscovering your own handwritten notes months later—first struggling to decipher the letters, and then, if you finally manage to read them, wondering what on earth you meant by writing something like "bananas, cat, cinema."

In short: bit rot destroys the data, while data decay destroys the ability to understand it.

In theory, data decay is reversible—just as 19th-century linguists eventually cracked Egyptian hieroglyphs. In practice, the effort and cost required are often, to put it politely, prohibitive.

———— SSD Bit Rot & Flash Amnesia ————

Date: 2010–Present

Impact: Silent corruption of cold SSD archives; large-scale data loss; costly re-migration efforts

Root Cause: Charge leakage in NAND cells when unpowered; heat-accelerated retention decay

Let's start with clearing up the pro-tip from the explainer: why you actually need to plug in an SSD from time to time. This isn't folklore or a one-off failure — it's a pattern backed by research, lab tests, and hard operational lessons. Starting around 2010, engineers began openly acknowledging an uncomfortable truth: solid-state drives stay reliable only as long as they're powered. The moment you unplug them, the countdown to amnesia quietly begins.

NAND flash stores data as trapped electrons inside floating-gate transistors — basically tiny charge buckets pretending to be long-term memory. That sounds reassuringly high-tech until you remember that electrons are tiny, lazy escape artists — and the hotter it gets, the faster they tunnel out. At room temperature, an unplugged consumer SSD may retain data for a year or two. Raise the temperature to 40°C (a warm cupboard, a sunny shelf, a server room corner) and retention time can drop below twelve months. TLC and QLC drives? Even worse. Their per-cell charge states are packed so tightly that they forget faster than a goldfish with commitment issues.

While specific numbers are often trade secrets, a 2015 study by Facebook and Carnegie Mellon revealed that **up to 34% of flash drives** in their fleet developed uncorrectable errors. Meanwhile, the JEDEC industry standards explicitly warn that enterprise SSDs stored in a warm room (40°C / 104°F) may lose data in as little as

three months. At 55°C (131°F) data retention drops to **weeks**.

SMART logs? They catch issues late. Scrubbing jobs? Too infrequent to stop the rot. By the time anyone notices, the only reliable fix is expensive: power on the drive and rewrite everything, or migrate the archives back to HDDs or cloud systems that don't evaporate in warm storage — or at least not quite as fast.

Hyperscalers have collectively spent billions re-migrating "cold" flash archives they once believed were the future. The new rule of thumb is painfully clear: flash is fantastic for active workloads and a terrible choice for anything resembling long-term, unplugged preservation.

LESSON LEARNED

- Flash isn't forever; it's barely patient.
- Unpowered SSD = countdown timer.
- Heat is a rot accelerator.
- Silent corruption is still corruption.
- Backups aren't safe just because you're proud you made them.

Physics and electrons don't care that your drive is called "solid state" — they'll leave the moment you stop looking.

The Google "Lightning Strike" (2015)

Date: August 2015

Impact: Permanent loss of a slice of persistent disk data across multiple nodes

Root Cause: Repeated lightning-induced power disturbances bypassing battery-backed write protection

Google likes to think it has defeated the laws of physics. And to be fair, if anyone could, it would be them. Their data centers are the Fort Knox of information: multiple layers of redundancy, power conditioning that could shame a nuclear plant, and enough engineering ego to declare themselves effectively invincible. But in August 2015, the sky over Belgium decided to conduct a live audit.

The St. Ghislain data center was struck by lightning. Not once. Not twice. Four times. In rapid, mocking succession. Imagine Zeus repeatedly mashing the "smite" button because someone on the ground said, "Don't worry, redundancy will save us."

Now, to be clear: the lightning didn't hit the servers directly. That would at least make for better storytelling. Instead, the strikes created violent power fluctuations that rippled through the electrical infrastructure. Most of the time, Google's battery backup systems catch these anomalies instantly, absorbing spikes and smoothing out dips. But on that particular weekend, for a very specific cluster of persistent-disk servers, the system blinked.

And that was enough.

Some machines lost power mid-write. Not in a clean, polite, "we shall now shut down" sort of way, but in the catastrophic, "your bytes are halfway through a sentence and the pen explodes" sort of way. Anyone who has ever yanked a drive out mid-write knows what comes next:

corruption. But this wasn't ordinary corruption. These writes didn't fail—they evaporated. Entire chunks of data simply stopped existing.

Google later quantified the loss as 0.000001% of data. A number so small it looks like marketing spin, until you remember who we're talking about. At Google scale, one-millionth of persistent-disk storage is not a rounding error —it's a crater. The cloud, we were assured, was supposed to be immortal. The whole sales pitch is "your data is safer with us than anywhere else on Earth." Yet here we were, watching the universe casually poke a hole in that narrative with a well-placed lightning storm.

Engineers pored over logs, checked redundancy states, reconstructed what they could, and published one of the rare Google post-mortems that quietly admitted permanent data loss. No heroic last-minute restore. No miraculous recovery. Just gone. If you wanted philosophical closure, you had to imagine Zeus shrugging.

What made this incident so memorable wasn't the scope —it was the symbolism. If even Google, with its cathedral-grade infrastructure, can lose data to a perfectly ordinary atmospheric tantrum, what hope does anyone else have? The "cloud" begins to look a lot less like a reliable utility and a lot more like a weather-dependent gamble.

LESSON LEARNED

- Redundancy is impressive until physics decides otherwise.
- Battery backups are great—except for the times they aren't.
- "Tiny percentage lost" is still a funeral when your infrastructure spans continents.

> - The cloud is not invincible; it's just very confident.
> - Nature doesn't read SLAs.

Sure, 0.000001% may not *sound* scary—until you realise that at Google scale, that could easily have been the contents of your Google Drive... a few hundred times over.

— The Facebook "Indoor Rainstorm" (2011) —

Date: 2011

Impact: Widespread hardware failure; moisture-induced outages across multiple racks

Root Cause: Faulty evaporative-cooling control logic causing extreme humidity and in-room condensation

Facebook built its early data centers with a certain swagger. Why rely on traditional, boring, expensive cooling systems when you can invent something greener, sleeker, and more efficient? Thus Prineville, Oregon became the testbed for Facebook's ambitious evaporative-cooling design — a system that used outside air and massive swamp coolers to keep thousands of servers comfortably chilled.

Nature, however, has never been impressed by tech swagger.

One day in 2011, the Prineville cooling system decided to stop following the script. A control bug allowed humidity to spike to rainforest levels — 95% — while warm air continued to pour into the server halls. Combine heat with that much moisture and you get a predictable, yet somehow still unbelievable, outcome: a literal rain cloud formed inside the data center.

Not metaphorical "rain" — actual water droplets suspended in the air, condensing, gathering weight, and finally falling. Indoors. Onto the racks. Engineers walking the aisles could hear the quiet patter of precipitation hitting steel and plastic. Some reportedly just stood there, staring upward, contemplating their life choices. .

Then came the sound no one in a data center ever wants to hear: *pop... fzzzt... pop.* Power supplies began to short as moisture beaded on metal surfaces. Servers flickered, rebooted, or died outright. The evaporative-cooling system, meant to save energy, had reinvented itself as an indoor weather generator.

To Facebook's credit, they avoided data loss — triple replication and distributed storage likely saved the day — but hardware? That took a beating. Entire racks had to be powered down and replaced. The incident became legendary not because it brought Facebook to its knees, but because it perfectly captured a universal truth: whenever engineers try to bend nature to their will, nature responds with a slapstick counterexample.

Even now, the story circulates inside the industry like a fable: "Remember that time Facebook made it rain indoors?" It's the perfect reminder that humidity, temperature, and physics don't negotiate with software patches.

LESSON LEARNED

- Humidity is just water doing stealth mode.
- If your cooling system can create weather, it will.
- Nature doesn't care about your efficiency goals.
- Triple redundancy saves data, not dignity.

> • Always check the humidity controls — unless you enjoy indoor precipitation.

In the end, Facebook tried to save energy and ended up inventing seasonal weather patterns. Somewhere, a meteorologist is still laughing.

The Wrocław University of Science and Technology "Dust Bowl"

Date: May 30, 2023
Impact: Full outage of university systems; widespread hardware contamination; multi-day recovery
Root Cause: Accidental activation of aerosol-based fire suppression while servers were running at load

Let's step away from hyperscalers and global tech giants for a moment. Failure is democratic. It does not discriminate by budget, scale, or international reputation. So instead of looking at Google or Facebook, let's turn our attention to a university in Poland — specifically, Wrocław University of Science and Technology. It may not be MIT or Oxford, but it *is* one of the top technical universities in Poland and in Central Europe. In other words: the people working there absolutely know what they're doing — which makes what happened next even more spectacular.

In 2023, the university delivered one of the most unintentionally slapstick data-center incidents in recent memory.

On May 30th, during what should have been a routine fire drill, something went very wrong. Instead of switching the suppression system into test mode — the mode where nothing actually fires — someone left it live. And so, when the drill commenced, the fire suppression system did exactly what it was designed to do in a real emergency.

It discharged.

Before we continue, it's worth noting one thing that every firefighter, safety engineer, and facilities designer learns early on: extinguishers and suppression systems are built for *specific* types of fires. Standards differ across continents (as usual), but there is one bit of global consensus:

- **Class A** — solid combustibles
- **Class B** — flammable liquids
- **Class C** — flammable gases

There are more nuances — temperatures, voltages, chemical compositions — but this isn't a "junior firefighter manual." What matters is this: powder-based extinguishers are considered the most universal. They can put out almost anything.

Electronics are the exception.

For data centers, the correct choice is almost always **gas-based suppression**, which starves a fire of oxygen without dumping material into circuits. The system at Wrocław, however, used a **pressurised aerosol powder** — excellent for warehouses, workshops, and industrial halls... catastrophic for server rooms.

Unfortunately, that's exactly what was discharged.

Servers in the room were running at full power. Their cooling fans, doing what cooling fans do, immediately inhaled the airborne powder. The result was catastrophic and instantaneous. Motherboards were coated. Contacts were bridged. Heatsinks clogged. Short circuits began popping across the racks like a string of firecrackers.

Within minutes, the university's digital infrastructure collapsed. The main website went down. Core internal systems failed with it. For tens of thousands of students and staff, the university effectively disappeared from the internet.

Then came the cleanup.

This was not a situation where you run scripts, restore from backups, and go home. This was a full physical dig-out. IT staff had to open every server, every chassis, every power supply, and painstakingly vacuum, brush, clean, and dry components. Racks had to be inspected one by one. It took days just to bring core services back and much longer for full recovery.

The bitter irony? A safety system designed to *protect* the data center became the sole cause of its destruction. The drill worked beautifully — it proved the system was ready. Too ready.

The unofficial summary circulating among students captured it perfectly: "Administrators scheduled a fire drill to ensure the safety of their data. They succeeded in proving that the fire suppression system worked — by spraying the running servers with aerosol powder. The fans inhaled the dust, and the university's digital brain choked to death on its own safety equipment. Restoring the data required vacuum cleaners, not code."

LESSON LEARNED

- If your suppression system uses powdered chemicals, never test it in live mode.
- Cooling fans will inhale anything — including your IT career.
- Safety equipment can be the biggest threat in the room.

> - Not all disasters require clouds, hyperscalers, or lightning — sometimes it's just Tuesday at a university.
> - Always verify test mode. Always.

People imagine scientists in lab coats surrounded by microscopes, precision instruments, and high-tech gear — not someone sprinting around a server room with a broom and a vacuum cleaner, trying to undo the world's most enthusiastic fire drill.

——— Voyager 1 Bit Rot in Deep Space ———

Date: 1977–Present

Impact: Corrupted telemetry, command glitches, mission-threatening misfires

Root Cause: Cosmic-ray-induced bit flips (SEUs) in 1970s radiation-hardened memory

Remember when we said bit rot can happen anywhere? Voyager 1 took that personally. Launched in 1977, built with ~70 KB of radiation-hardened RAM, and currently transmitting from over 24 billion kilometers away, it is the most extreme example of "your environment hates your data." There are no backups. No redundancy. No second chance. Just a 48-year-old spacecraft, a stream of cosmic rays, and a very patient team at NASA.

Out there, far beyond the heliosphere, physics stops pretending to be subtle. High-energy particles slam through Voyager's electronics and flip bits in its memory every few months. These are single-event upsets (SEUs):

cosmic-ray dice rolls that turn a **1** into a **0**, or vice versa, with all the grace of a toddler rewriting your tax return.

Sometimes the effect is harmless. Sometimes it's corrupted science data. And sometimes — like the 2010 X-band anomaly — it causes command misfires that nearly silence the spacecraft. The only debugging technique available? A 38-hour round-trip uplink of hand-crafted assembly patches, aimed at a machine running hardware older than most countries' constitutions.

NASA mitigates what it can. Triple-voted memory. Checksums. ECC. Ritualistic caution. At this point the procedures manual probably has more patches than the original codebase — when your RAM lives in deep space, every workaround eventually becomes a chapter. You don't stop bit rot — you negotiate with it.

Voyager 1 survives today not because it is immune to decay, but because engineers keep painstakingly repairing the rot faster than space can introduce it. In a very literal sense, bit rot is now Voyager's fuel — the limiting factor of a mission that has already outlived its power reserves.

LESSON LEARNED

- In space, bit rot isn't a metaphor — it's weather.
- Redundancy doesn't matter when cosmic rays roll higher than your ECC.
- Every bit flipped is a reminder that "failure modes" don't disappear; they just get farther away.
- Longevity in deep space = engineers with infinite patience.
- Beating bit rot is possible - it just requires resources most of us don't have.

In deep space, even your RAM experiences cosmic mood swings — and there's no one around to hard reboot it.

BBC Domesday Project
When "Digital Forever" Lasted 15 Years

Date: 1986–2002

Impact: Near-total loss of a national digital archive; £1M+ rescue effort

Root Cause: Hardware-locked format, no migration plan, extreme data decay

In case your 11th-century British tax law is a little rusty: **the original Domesday Book (1086)** was a handwritten land survey commissioned by William the Conqueror. It survived **939 years** of invasions, fires, wars, monarchs, revolutions, and the English weather. You can still read it today with nothing more than eyes and patience.

In 1986, for the 900th anniversary, the BBC set out to create a modern equivalent — a digital snapshot of life in the UK. It became one of the largest crowdsourcing projects in history: **250,000 people** (schools, clubs, local groups) contributed photos, essays, maps, recordings, and videos. The goal was noble and ambitious: *"Preserve the present for the next thousand years."*

The technology... was less ambitious.

The project was stored on **two 12-inch LaserDisc LV-ROMs**, an analog–digital hybrid format only a Philips VP415 player could read. It required a **BBC Master 128** computer with a custom SCSI controller, a bespoke OS, and a hypertext interface that predated the Web. Total cost: **~£2.5M** (≈ £10M today). For 1986, it was futuristic. For 2002, it was dead.

It didn't take a catastrophe, a fire, or a grand archival scandal. All it took was time. By 2002, just sixteen years after launch, the Domesday system had quietly drifted into extinction. The Philips VP415 player required to read the discs hadn't been manufactured since 1990. The last functional unit anyone could find sat behind glass in a museum exhibition, more artifact than tool. The LV-ROM format, once sold as the future of multimedia, was now a linguistic dead end — understood by no modern machine, translator, or adaptor.

The BBC's entire digital Domesday archive effectively existed in a single usable copy: two discs, one player, zero replacement parts, and an operating environment that had dissolved around it. It was a masterpiece trapped in amber.

The punchline writes itself:

The 1086 Domesday Book survived 939 years. The 1986 version lasted 15.

Rescuing the archive required something between archaeology and necromancy. The CAMiLEON team — a joint effort between the University of Michigan, Leeds, and the BBC — began by hunting for surviving hardware. They eventually unearthed three VP415 players, including one abandoned in the basement of a school. From there, they reverse-engineered the entire Domesday stack: the player, the BBC Master computer, the custom SCSI interface, and the bespoke hypertext system.

They didn't rebuild it physically — they emulated it. Piece by piece, they recreated the machine in software, then extracted the LV-ROM data bit by bit until it could be migrated onto modern storage. In 2004, the resurrected archive appeared online as domesday1986.com: a digital ghost finally released from its obsolete shell.

The rescue cost over £1M — a substantial fraction of the original £2.5M project — a tidy demonstration that "doing it right later" is always more expensive than "planning for later now.""

One BBC archivist summarised it perfectly:

"We planned an archive for a thousand years. We got fifteen."

"Parchment survived invasions, fires, and wars. LaserDisc died for lack of spare parts."

LESSON LEARNED

- Migration isn't optional — it's rent you pay to the future.
- "Working once" is not the same as "lasting forever."
- Proprietary hardware is time-bomb-as-a-service.
- Digital preservation is not a one-time cost — it's a subscription.
- The most durable archives are the ones someone bothers to copy.

If you want something preserved for a thousand years, use parchment — or at least a format that doesn't require archaeological hardware to boot.

Adobe Flash
The Internet's Biggest Mass Extinction Event

Date: 1996–2020

Impact: Millions of interactive works rendered unplayable; large-scale cultural erasure

Root Cause: Proprietary plugin dependency; browser-level execution bans; no forward-compatible runtime

Before we begin: *Flash* here has nothing to do with SSD flash memory or electrons misbehaving. This Flash was Adobe's (originally Macromedia's) multimedia runtime — the format that powered almost a quarter-century of creativity on the Web. And while most people remember the endless ocean of minigames, Flash was far more than that: interactive art, experimental animation, political satire, educational tools, early machinima, even entire micro-communities.

For a generation, Flash *was* the interactive Web — the beating, jittery, occasionally malware-ridden heart of online culture.

And then, in December 2020, it simply... died. Not gradually. Not dramatically. Adobe ended support and every major browser — Chrome, Firefox, Safari, Edge — simultaneously blocked Flash at the executable level. One browser update and an entire ecosystem went the way of the dinosaurs, but with worse documentation. The Web didn't break; it amputated a limb.

Flash's death wasn't sudden. Years of mounting security vulnerabilities turned the plugin into a liability. Browsers began restricting execution, then hiding it behind warnings, then disabling it entirely. HTML5 was the promised successor, but parity never fully materialised. Flash was a bespoke ecosystem with its own language (ActionScript), graphics model, timing quirks, and —

crucially — no complete emulator when the final shutdown came.

The result was a digital extinction event. Millions of websites and creations — from Newgrounds animations to Homestar Runner episodes to early educational software — went dark overnight. Roughly 80–90% of all Flash content vanished, not because it was deleted, but because nothing could run it anymore.

Preservation efforts emerged, heroic but incomplete. Ruffle, a Rust-based emulator, can run many simpler SWF files. BlueMaxima's Flashpoint project has archived tens of thousands of games and animations — a monumental community effort. But dynamic content, server-side integrations, and complex ActionScript 3 projects remain effectively unplayable. The early Web's creative frontier is now partly a museum, partly a graveyard.

The tragedy is not just technical — it's cultural. Domesday decayed because no one tended it; Flash's demise was a sudden meteor strike delivered by Chrome, Firefox, and Safari — because everyone actively pulled the plug.

What makes this case particularly striking in the context of this chapter is the brutal asymmetry of the outcome: despite extraordinary volunteer efforts — emulators, archives, rescue projects — most of Flash's creative universe could not be saved. Millions of works didn't just become inconvenient to access; they effectively ceased to exist. A generation's worth of expression evaporated almost overnight, leaving behind only scattered fragments to prove it ever happened.

LESSON LEARNED

- Plugins are extinction events waiting for a browser update.
- A format without emulation is a memory with an expiration date.
- "The Web never forgets" — unless your work needed a plugin.
- Preserve or perish.

The end of Flash proved that the internet is permanent — right up until the day the browser says otherwise.

CHAPTER 12:
ACCOUNTANT'S REVENGE

Many data catastrophes aren't accidents — they're cost-cutting dressed as strategy. Organizations discover too late that "savings" and "priorities" rarely point in the same direction.

Fair warning: the tone here will sharpen. These failures don't come from physics or cosmic rays — they come from spreadsheets and the persistent illusion that cutting corners equals efficiency. If the previous chapter made you think "well, entropy happens," this one should make you think "what the fuck were they thinking?"

I won't pretend to be neutral. About this topic, I'm not.

One more thing: this chapter doesn't introduce any terminology needed later — it stands on its own. If a more cynical, aggressive tone isn't your thing, feel free to skip straight to Chapter 13. I won't mind.

But it is an essential part of the story. Without understanding how easily cost-cutting mutates into self-inflicted amputation, the rest of this book would feel incomplete. The choice is yours.

 **Explainer:**
Why Storing Data Was (and Still Is) a Problem

To understand why organizations kept overwriting irreplaceable data, you first need to understand the scale involved — how storage evolved from a luxury item to something we treat as disposable. Today, storage feels cheap. Your laptop has a terabyte. Your phone auto-uploads photos to the cloud. An entire decade of family pictures costs less than dinner. But this was not always the case.

In 1956, IBM released the first commercial hard drive: the **IBM 350**, part of the RAMAC system. It held **5 megabytes** and cost **$35,000 per year** to rent (about **$385,000 in today's money)**. That's roughly **$7,000 per megabyte** — about the price of a used car for a single photo in today's terms.

By comparison:

2025 typical SSD: 1 TB (1,000,000 MB) → $60 total → **$0.00006 per MB**.

Storage has become more than **100 million times cheaper** per unit. And yet... the problem didn't go away. It just changed shape.

Today, the world produces an absurd amount of data — roughly **181 zettabytes per year** (for reference: **1 zettabyte = 1,000 exabytes**, which is why these prefixes lose all intuitive meaning). For scale: the entire informational output of humanity up to the year 2000 — estimated at **5–10 exabytes** — now materializes in **less than two days.** Most of this isn't "knowledge" in any meaningful sense. It's CCTV footage, IoT chatter, infinite social-media video, server logs, telemetry, and digital exhaust.

The challenge is no longer the cost of a megabyte — it's deciding which megabytes matter.

The global data-storage market in 2025 weighs in at $250–260 billion annually, covering disks, SSDs, NAS/SAN systems, cloud storage, and software to wrangle the flood. Even with modern economies of scale, storage still consumes 10–15% of all data-center spending, because the tsunami never stops.

And that's the point: even when storage becomes cheap, *important* storage never does. The cost of keeping data is trivial; the cost of identifying, migrating, preserving, and securing the right data is enormous.

And yes — the stories in this part frustrate me. But at least the broad economic context is understandable. What's less understandable is how tiny the so-called "savings" often were. As you'll see, some of the worst losses weren't the result of grand strategy, but of saving amounts so small they barely made sense even back then.

NASA
The Lost Moon Tapes

Date: 1969–2006

Impact: Loss of original Apollo 11 telemetry and high-quality footage; costly reconstruction

Root Cause: Tape reuse driven by cost-cutting; no archival policy

The story of the Lost Moon Tapes reads like satire written by an accountant. In 1969, humanity took its most iconic step — Neil Armstrong planting a boot on another world — and NASA captured it on high-quality telemetry tapes far sharper than the grainy broadcast we all know. These were the master records, the raw data streamed directly from the lunar surface.

And then, in the 1970s, NASA recorded over them.

Not because of sabotage. Not because of negligence in the dramatic sense. Simply because the tapes were expensive — a little over a thousand dollars each — and new missions needed blank reels. In fact, the reels were most likely overwritten during the early 1980s **Landsat** program, a project with an annual budget of roughly **$90–100 million**. In other words: a nine-figure Earth-observation mission "saved" a four-figure tape — roughly the price the same facility was probably spending on toilet paper. Paraphrasing Armstrong's famous words: *"That's one small win for accountants, one giant fail for mankind."*

Four decades later, when NASA engineers finally went searching for the original recordings, the result was predictable in the most depressing way: the tapes were gone. Permanently. The only surviving versions of the Moon landing were TV rebroadcasts — degraded by transmission, re-scanning, and analog limitations. The very moment that proved what humanity was capable of had to be reconstructed from tapes that looked like they'd survived a washing machine.

And here's the cosmic joke: conspiracy theorists spent years claiming the Moon landing was faked... *because the footage looks terrible.* Meanwhile, somewhere in the 1970s, someone probably earned praise for "optimizing tape usage," unknowingly guaranteeing that the only record of Armstrong's first step would forever resemble a corrupted VHS.

The 2006–2009 restoration effort stitched together Australian TV copies, international rebroadcasts, and interpolation to approximate what had once existed in pristine clarity. It cost millions — and even then, it could never match the originals.

LESSON LEARNED

- History is only as durable as the budget allows.
- Reuse beats preservation — until it doesn't.
- Cultural memory can be overwritten as easily as telemetry.
- Even the Moon wasn't immune to budget cuts.

Humanity walked on the Moon, but the tapes didn't survive a budget review.

HBO Max / Warner Bros. Discovery
The Accountant's Cut

Date: 2022–2023

Impact: 87+ titles removed; $825M+ content value erased; massive user backlash; industry-wide panic about "streaming purges"

Root Cause: Tax write-offs disguised as strategic consolidation; secondary confusion from metadata/ID mismatches during the Max merger

When Warner Bros. Discovery announced it was "reassessing content strategy," most people assumed it meant trimming underperforming shows. They did not expect a biblical purge.

During the 2022–2023 merger of HBO Max and Discovery+, more than eighty titles vanished from the platform — including high-profile originals like *Westworld, Infinity Train, Generation, Minx,* and multiple animated productions. Viewers initially blamed the Max merger. Engineers blamed metadata. Creators blamed executives. And for once, everyone was partially right.

But the math told the real story.

Roughly 80–90% of the removals were tax write-offs, part of Warner Bros. Discovery's $3.5–4.3B restructuring charges. By design, underperforming titles were removed to let WBD claim $2–2.5B in impairments — including the now-infamous *Batgirl* write-off, where a nearly finished $90M movie was shelved permanently for tax reasons. No glitches, no merge bugs — just accounting.

The remaining 10–20%? HBO Max and Discovery+ also happened to be merging two entirely different catalog systems at the same time — a technical mess in its own right. But compared to the scale of the tax-driven purge, those issues were background noise. Chapter 14 will dig into the mechanics of migration failures like these — for now, just know that metadata mismatches can make content vanish even when nobody intended it to.

To make things worse, both events happened simultaneously. Shows were vanishing due to tax math *and* because the systems meant to preserve them couldn't agree on what they were. Users had no way to tell whether a disappearance was strategic, accidental, or both. Even industry press struggled to distinguish "intentionally removed for cost savings" from "lost during ingestion."

The result was confusion, outrage, and a trending #BringBackWestworld campaign. By mid-2023, WBD quietly re-added a handful of titles, stabilized metadata pipelines, and launched the unified Max platform — slimmer, tidier, and culturally poorer.

And while this chapter won't dive deep into the migration-mechanics angle (that's next section's job), it's worth highlighting the uncomfortable truth: mergers amplify entropy. When cost-cutting meets schema-chaos, culture is the first casualty.

LESSON LEARNED

- Tax math is the strongest deletion algorithm ever invented.
- Metadata defines existence — lose it, and the content dies.
- Mergers don't just merge libraries; they merge chaos multipliers.

> - Creative work can vanish not because it failed, but because it balanced a spreadsheet.
> - When accountants outrank archivists, preservation loses every time.

When WBD chose the name *Max*, they probably didn't mean "maximum tax benefit achieved via cultural annihilation" — but the balance sheet definitely heard it that way.

The Great Magnetic Purge

Date: 1950s–1980s

Impact: Global loss of television history across every major broadcasting system

Root Cause: Tape reuse culture driven by cost; archival budgets near zero

For over three decades, broadcasters around the world shared one elegant, bipartisan philosophy: *magnetic tape is expensive — art is replaceable.* Capitalist, socialist, public, private — it didn't matter. BBC in the UK, NBC in the U.S., ABC in Australia, NHK in Japan, TVP in Poland, ČST in Czechoslovakia, DFF in East Germany, Gosteleradio in the USSR — all different systems, budgets, ideologies, and censorship rules, yet united in one universal belief: *blank tape was more valuable than whatever was already recorded on it.*

Tape cost over a thousand dollars per reel in today's money. Archival policy was an afterthought. And so, beginning in the 1950s and accelerating into the 1970s, broadcasters simply recorded over anything that wasn't needed *right now*. Not because of politics (though politics had its moments), but because budgeting made creativity a temporary privilege.

The cultural casualties were staggering:

- **BBC / ITV (UK):** 97 episodes of *Doctor Who* vanished; early *Monty Python* sketches; countless *Top of the Pops* performances. Some episodes resurfaced only decades later in **Nigeria** and **New Zealand**, discovered in vaults that had better retention practices than the originating broadcaster.

- **NBC / CBS (USA):** The broadcast of **Super Bowl I** (1967) — gone. Most early *Tonight Show* episodes — gone. The networks needed the reels for "future use," and nothing said "future" like wiping history.

- **ABC Australia & CBC Canada:** Erased talk shows, concerts, documentaries; even early footage of **AC/DC** and the **Bee Gees** fell victim to the purge.

- **NHK Japan:** Lost recordings of classic **kabuki** performances and much of the original **Tokyo 1964 Olympics** broadcast.

- **TVP Poland:** Over **90%** of *Sonda*, a beloved science program, was overwritten. Only ~20 episodes survived.

- **ČST (Czechoslovakia) & DFF (East Germany):** Children's shows like *Magion* and *Studio Kamarád* largely disappeared, surviving today only as partial VHS recordings from private homes.

- **Soviet Union (Gosteleradio & CT USSR):** Thousands of hours of science, culture, and space-program footage were wiped or cannibalized for politically "current" newsreels.

This wasn't malice. This wasn't censorship (well, not *only* censorship). This was pure accounting. Tape was expensive; history was cheap.

The irony, of course, is that today national archives, private collectors, and broadcasters spend obscene amounts of money trying to recover whatever scraps remain. The BBC famously mounted global search efforts to find missing *Doctor Who* episodes — and ended up locating some of them in dusty overseas storage rooms, lovingly preserved by accident rather than intent.

The Great Magnetic Purge is a global reminder that cultural memory isn't destroyed by ideology — it's destroyed by budgets.

LESSON LEARNED

- History becomes optional when tape has a price tag.
- Reuse beats preservation — until the bill arrives 40 years later.
- Cultural extinction doesn't require a villain, only a cost-cutting policy.
- Ideology changes nothing; bean counters are eternal.

Humanity invented television — and then deleted it to save money.

The Gaming Purge
How An Entire Medium Keeps Deleting Itself

Date: 1970s–Present

Impact: Systemic, ongoing loss of video game history across every platform and era

Root Cause: Neglect, format obsolescence, rights issues, and an industry structurally hostile to preservation

Television at least had the decency to regret its mistakes. After the Great Magnetic Purge, broadcasters eventually admitted that maybe—just maybe—erasing half their cultural output wasn't ideal. The BBC now sends archivists across continents to recover lost episodes. National institutions preserve entire vaults. Everybody learned.

The games industry did not.

Video games are the only major cultural medium that is *still* deleting itself in real time. Not metaphorically. Not gradually. Actively.

From the start, the mindset was simple: *"games are toys."* Toys don't need archiving. Toys don't get cultural funding. Toys don't deserve preservation. And so the default policy became neglect—followed by obsolescence, corporate indifference, and an increasingly aggressive stance that treating games as heritage is somehow the same as piracy.

The Arcade Era (1970s–1990s): Lost by Design

Source code was routinely thrown away. Cabinets were scrapped for parts. Many classics survive only because enthusiasts dumped ROMs before the hardware died. These aren't preserved artifacts—they're forensic reconstructions.

Console Generations: Orphan Platforms Everywhere

Cartridges die. Discs rot. Backwards compatibility is optional at best. Publishers didn't keep master copies of their own games. Entire libraries are now stranded on hardware no one can repair.

Digital Distribution Era (2000s–Present): The Always-Deleting Future

Platform closures mean permanent deletion: Wii Shop, DSi, 3DS eShop, PSP, all gone. Delisted games evaporate—*Silent Hill P.T.*, Marvel titles, licensed music games, *Scott Pilgrim vs. The World* (2014–2020). Online-only games cease to exist the moment the servers shut down. Mobile stores flush thousands of titles annually.

And the scale? According to the Video Game History Foundation, **87% of classic games are commercially unavailable**. Not damaged. Not rare. *Gone.* And the list grows every year.

Unlike TV, Games Keep Choosing the Worst Timeline

Broadcasting eventually realised what it had destroyed and changed course.

- The BBC hunts for missing *Doctor Who* episodes.

- Archives are funded.

- Cultural institutions treat television as heritage.

Meanwhile, the games industry has doubled down:

- Preservation is framed as a legal threat, not a responsibility.

- Publishers lobby against preservation laws in the EU and US.

- Rights holders prefer deletion to licensing headaches.

- The UK government's position: *current consumer protection laws are enough* — a response so narrowly focused on buyer rights that it completely ignores the actual problem: cultural preservation.

And then came **Stop Killing Games (2024–2025)**—a movement born from watching companies remotely disable products people paid for. In the EU, the Citizens' Initiative hit the threshold, forcing Parliament to address it. The industry immediately mobilised to weaken or kill it. In the UK, regulators shrugged. In the US, the lobbying power is so overwhelming the topic barely reaches a hearing.

The Most Frustrating Part

What makes this even more absurd is the contrast. Other cultural sectors actively protect their heritage[19]: film, television, literature, music — all have institutional preservation strategies, legal obligations, and public funding. Games, now a larger global market than **film and music combined** (2024 figures), are the only major medium that treats its own past as disposable.

This isn't history. This is happening *now*. Every year, dozens more games vanish permanently—not because technology failed, but because no one in charge believes they're worth saving.

---

[19] Most countries enforce a legal deposit system: every published book or audiovisual work must be submitted to national libraries.

The copy you're reading will, by law, end up in Leipzig and Berlin (and voluntarily in Poland's National Library and the Jagiellonian Library).

No such obligation exists for games, so unless a studio feels generous, nothing is preserved.

LESSON LEARNED

- A medium without preservation isn't a culture—it's a subscription.
- Digital convenience hides digital impermanence.
- "Protecting IP" often means destroying the work itself.
- 87% gone is not a statistic—it's a warning.
- Unlike film or TV, gaming is erasing itself faster than we can document it.

The future keeps asking whether games are art. At this rate, we'll never have enough left to prove it.

——— NASA and NOAA[20] Climate Data Gaps ———

Date: 1980s–1990s

Impact: Decades-long holes in global climate records; irreversible scientific loss

Root Cause: Chronic cost-cutting, cheapest-available storage media, and zero long-term preservation planning

NASA and NOAA spent billions launching weather and climate-monitoring satellites to track Earth's atmosphere and oceans. They spent almost nothing preserving what those satellites recorded. to monitor Earth's atmosphere. They spent almost nothing preserving what those satellites recorded. False economy doesn't care whether

---

[20] **NOAA (National Oceanic and Atmospheric Administration)** — the U.S. agency tasked with watching the weather, oceans, and climate; essentially the people trying to keep the planet's memory intact while everyone else is busy "optimizing" budgets.

you're measuring sitcoms or stratospheric ozone—accountants treat both the same way.

Each satellite program bought whatever tape format was on sale that fiscal quarter. No standards, no compatibility, no long-term plan. Nimbus wrote to one format, GOES to another, TIROS to a third. When budget reviews came around, preservation didn't make the cut. New missions needed storage media, and buying fresh reels "wasn't cost-effective."

So they did what broadcasters did: **they reused the tapes**.

Decades of atmospheric temperature readings, ocean surface data, ozone measurements—overwritten to save the cost of blank media. Not corrupted by accident. Not lost to equipment failure. Deliberately erased because someone determined that last year's climate data was less valuable than this year's storage budget.

The tapes that survived weren't much better. Stored in university basements with no climate control (irony: infinite). Degraded by humidity, heat, and time. And even when tapes remained intact, the drives didn't. Entire datasets sat perfectly preserved in formats no surviving hardware could read—because the machines that could interpret them had been discontinued, scrapped, or "optimized away" years earlier.

By the 2000s, climate scientists faced a hard truth: entire programs suffered catastrophic data loss.

Examples of programs whose records were partially or fully lost:

- **Nimbus satellites** — early ocean temperature and ice-cover data

- **TIROS weather satellites** — atmospheric measurement series

- **Polar observation stations** (Antarctic & Arctic) — multi-year gaps in baseline readings

These weren't minor inconsistencies—they were missing decades of atmospheric data. Temperature series that simply stopped. Ozone records with years-long holes. Metadata lost, contradictory labels, tapes that produced only static.

NASA and NOAA eventually funded rescue missions. Engineers rebuilt extinct tape drives from scavenged parts, spent over $100 million recovering what still emitted a readable signal. They got some data back. Most was gone forever.

Here's the contrast that matters: BBC sends archivists to Nigeria searching for lost Doctor Who episodes—and finds them. Climate scientists would pay millions for 1967 ocean temperature data. It doesn't exist. Anywhere. You can recover entertainment from foreign TV vaults. You cannot recover atmospheric measurements from decades ago. The data is not hiding in someone's basement. It was erased to save perhaps a few hundred dollars in tape costs back then — and in doing so they destroyed the entire point of the mission.

In 2025, climate scientists publish papers explicitly about "*the gaps in our historical record*"—not gaps in what happened, but gaps in what we bothered to preserve. Climate models are less accurate because we have incomplete baselines. We can't fully validate long-term predictions without the ground truth we deleted.

LESSON LEARNED

- Entertainment is recoverable; atmospheric physics is not.

> - Cheap storage becomes expensive science—just decades later
> - "Irreplaceable" means nothing to procurement departments
> - A project's success is meaningless if, in the process of running it, you destroy the very results it was meant to produce
> - You can find Doctor Who in Nigeria; you can't find stratospheric readings anywhere

Penny wise, pound stupid: they saved hundreds during the mission and destroyed data worth millions.

CHAPTER 13:
DB BLUNDERS

Before now, we've looked at all the wonderfully creative ways humanity manages to lose data through carelessness: tapes abandoned in basements, formats no one can read anymore, and heroic acts of cost-cutting that turned archives into confetti. But this was only the warm-up. We've barely scratched the surface of how thoroughly we can sabotage our own information.

Because if physical decay and organisational neglect are slow killers, databases are the high-speed power tools of self-inflicted data loss. They're powerful, precise, and indispensable—yet the difference between brilliance and disaster comes down to whose hands are on the controls. Useful in the right hands, terrifying in the wrong ones.

Databases aren't magical vaults. They are opinionated machines with sharp edges—and, as you'll soon see, they punish misunderstandings with biblical enthusiasm.

By now, you know the drill. You want the explosions, but I'm going to make you eat your vegetables first. Yup, we need to clarify a few fundamentals.

 **Explainer:**
Metadata — When Simple Data Is Not Enough

In the world of data storage, the word "metadata" appears so often that it starts to sound like a corporate incantation. In reality, it's just a Greek prefix that means "beyond" or "about." Of course, nothing boosts an engineer's confidence like sprinkling in a dead language while talking about modern systems.

Put simply, metadata means "data about data." It's not the content itself — it's the information that tells you how to interpret that content. Think of any file on your computer. The essay, the report, the presentation, or the video you're about to upload to YouTube — that's the data. The file name, creation date, last-modified timestamp, and file permissions are metadata. (If you've ever tried editing something in `C:\Windows\System32` and been told you lack permission, congratulations — you've met metadata enforcement.)

Zoom out to large datasets and the stakes rise sharply. What does "Bob, 80, 180, 150" actually mean? Is Bob a sharp fellow of average build (80 kg, 180 cm, IQ 150), or a not-especially-bright bowling ball of a man you could hurdle over (IQ 80, 180 kg, 150 cm)[21]? Without metadata, you're just guessing.

Before we get there, it's worth a brief detour. Broadly speaking, datasets fall into three buckets: structured, unstructured, and the wonderfully confusing middle child known as semi-structured data.

---

[21] **Note for readers thinking in Imperial units:**
180 cm / 80 kg ≈ 5 ft 11 in / 176 lbs;
150 cm / 180 kg ≈ 4 ft 11 in / 397 lbs.

Structured data lives in rigid, predetermined formats. Think of it like a tax form: every field has a place, every number fits a specific box, and after reviewing a hundred of them you instinctively know where everything is. Classic relational SQL databases belong here—let's skip the lecture on what "relational" means; you won't need it in this book.

Unstructured data is the wild west. Imagine filing your taxes as a free-form essay. All the information *might* be there, but you won't find anything without reading the whole thing. In practice, this category includes scanned books, audio, video, and other formats where computers can't rely on predictable structure.

Semi-structured data sits awkwardly in between. It follows rules—just rules it invents for itself. It's as if every tax advisor in the country designed their own personal version of the same form. They understand their layout perfectly, but the tax office needs a catalog describing all those formats just to make sense of them. Odd as it sounds, a massive amount of modern data lives here: Excel spreadsheets, ad-hoc exports, custom domain-specific formats, and countless niche databases built for single applications.

Semi-structured data has many advantages, but it demands extreme care in how its metadata is recorded, stored, and interpreted. When that layer goes wrong, everything above it follows.

Now that we're back from the detour: regardless of whether data is structured, unstructured, or living in the semi-structured twilight zone, one thing never changes — metadata is the glue that makes any of it meaningful. And, as you'll see throughout this chapter, a surprising number of failures — perhaps even most of them — don't come from the data itself but from mangling the layer that describes it. Mislabel it, misinterpret it, or forget it altogether, and systems fall apart in spectacular ways.

MongoDB Duplicate ObjectIds
The Cluster That Forgot To Be Unique

Date: Early MongoDB ecosystem (pre-3.x)

Impact: Silent overwrites of individual documents; sporadic data loss in unlucky deployments

Root Cause: ObjectIds generated on the client based on machine characteristics (e.g., MAC address, process ID, counters) that weren't actually unique

MongoDB loved to present itself as the friendly database where documents flow freely, identifiers are always unique, and everything "just works." And for the most part, it did—right up until people realised their supposedly unique `_id` values were sometimes being generated in perfect, accidental pairs. Not because MongoDB the server messed up, but because the *applications* using MongoDB all thought they were running on the same machine.

Here's the twist that surprised many developers: MongoDB itself doesn't generate ObjectIds. Your application does. Before a document even reaches the database, the driver has already created its `_id`—based on a few details about the computer it's running on. Details like "what machine is this?" and "which process am I?"

And that's where things get interesting. This approach works beautifully *if each machine is truly its own machine.* But modern computing isn't like that. Programs rarely run on a physical computer anymore. Instead, they run inside layers of illusion.

First illusion: **virtual machines.** Imagine you have a powerful computer ("the host") that runs a program pretending to be another computer ("the guest"). It's basically the same trick as running a Super Nintendo emulator on Windows—Mario thinks he's inside a console, but he's actually inside a simulation. Cloud platforms rely heavily on this idea, because it lets them create and destroy "computers" on demand.

The catch? These virtual computers often share the same artificial machine characteristics. This ability to save and clone their entire state is normally a huge advantage—except here, where it also means you can accidentally create perfect twins with identical "machine" traits.

Second illusion: **containers.** Instead of pretending to be a whole computer, a container isolates one application from others. It lets you run dozens of identical copies of the same program side by side. In some cases, you can have only one application running at once (like a life partner). If you want to run another, you need to kill the previous one (do **not** try this with your life partner). In containers, however, you can spin up fifty identical instances (a bit like having several partners who don't know about each other). This is very useful in computing (very immoral in real life).

Both technologies are incredibly useful. But they create a small, crucial problem: if MongoDB's drivers base ObjectIds on "a few properties of the machine," and that machine is an illusion that exists in *identical copies*, then the generated IDs will also be identical.

Same pretend machine → same pretend properties → same ID.

When traffic gets heavy and multiple identical containers are running side by side, they all happily mint the same `_id` values at the same time. And when these duplicate documents hit the server, MongoDB simply performs the only logical action available: it overwrites the old one with the new one. No screams. No log entries. Just a polite, quiet replacement.

Most developers discovered the issue backwards: they saw "missing" documents, bizarre overwrites, or updates no one remembered writing. Debugging became a ghost hunt. Race conditions were suspected. Queues were blamed. Interns were interrogated. Few thought to question the one thing everyone trusted: the uniqueness of `_id`.

Eventually, enough people compared notes to realise the pattern. It wasn't the server. It wasn't sharding. It wasn't bad luck. It was the environment: identical virtual machines and identical containers producing identical identifiers because that was exactly what they were built to do.

MongoDB 3.x introduced safer defaults and stronger randomness, but without explicitly saying the quiet part out loud—that the system had always assumed a world where machines were, well... real.

LESSON LEARNED

- Unique identifiers only work when the environment itself is unique — cloning machines means cloning IDs.

- Generating IDs on the client works fine until the client turns out to be a perfect copy of another one.

- Silent overwrites are the most dangerous failures, because nothing screams while the data disappears.

- Distributed systems take everything literally — if every node claims to be the same machine, the database plays along.
- Assumptions about how software runs age quickly, especially in a world built on virtual copies.

MongoDB didn't lose your data. It just trusted your machines to be different. Unfortunately, your machines were identical triplets wearing matching outfits.

Salesforce "Permageddon"
When Everyone Became Admin

Date: 17 May 2019

Impact: 100+ production instances taken offline; mass unintended admin privileges

Root Cause: Faulty permission-fix script granting "Modify All Data" to regular user profiles

Salesforce is famous for two things: powering most of the world's sales teams, and having a permission system so strict it makes nuclear launch protocols look relaxed. On 17 May 2019, both reputations were put through a blender.

It began as a tiny fix in Pardot—a maintenance script meant to give users access to a new feature. A simple metadata tweak. The kind of thing an engineer normally ships before the coffee cools.

Except the script didn't touch one permission. It touched *all of them*. Instead of giving access to a single feature, it handed ordinary users the most powerful flag in the entire Salesforce universe: `Modify All Data`.

If you don't speak Salesforce, here's the translation: this is God Mode. It ignores role hierarchy. It ignores sharing rules. It ignores every guardrail the platform has. Anyone who gets this flag can read, edit, or delete *anything*.

Within seconds, companies saw what "anything" really meant. Interns and junior staff suddenly had access to:

- Executive salaries and pay slips

- Confidential contracts and VIP clients

- HR notes, evaluations, disciplinary records

- Automation systems suddenly processing data they were never meant to see

It was corporate omniscience by accident. And even if you believe radical transparency is cool, this kind of transparency is terrifying. Not just because creepy Joe from IT can suddenly see Kathy-from-Marketing's private phone number (which is illegal in most jurisdictions), but because a well-meaning intern could confuse the test catalogue with the production one and change TV prices to $0.01. Yes, that happens. No, malicious intent is not required.

Salesforce noticed almost immediately—but so did the replication layer, which diligently spread the wrong permission to more than a hundred production orgs. Rolling back was impossible without erasing legitimate business transactions.

So Salesforce did something unheard of in SaaS: they cut the hard line.

For affected customers, the CRM didn't slow down—it vanished. Sales teams opened their laptops and found black holes where their pipelines used to be.

Behind the scenes, engineers spent the weekend writing a "scrubber" script to crawl millions of profiles and strip away the accidental omnipotence. Some customers regained access within hours; others waited days.

This wasn't an outage in the classic sense. It was something rarer: a failure of *identity itself*. One flipped bit in metadata turned a planet-sized enterprise platform into a brief experiment in universal admin rights.

LESSON LEARNED

- Permission metadata is more explosive than the data it protects. One wrong bit rewrites reality.
- Replication will always spread misconfigurations faster than humans can fix them.
- Restoring from backup is not a magic button when business activity has continued.
- Sometimes the only safe move really is the nuclear one.
- Democracy is bad for databases. Hierarchies exist for a reason.

Salesforce didn't get hacked—they just accidentally declared democracy. Then spent a weekend trying to put the hierarchy back together.

—— Instapaper Storage Limit Meltdown —— When "Read Later" Became "Down for 31 Hours"

Date: February 9–10, 2017

Impact: Impact: ~31-hour full outage; Instapaper effectively down; no data was lost

Root Cause: `ext3` filesystem 2TB limit on AWS RDS — the database hit the maximum addressable size and MySQL stopped responding

Instapaper is the premier tool for digital procrastination: save an article now, feel good about it, and absolutely never read it. But in February 2017, the service involuntarily pivoted from "read later" to "read never-ish," when its Amazon RDS instance hit the ext3 filesystem's 2TB addressable limit.

This wasn't a schema issue or a quirky edge case. It was the oldest failure mode in storage engineering: the underlying filesystem reached the maximum file size it could handle. Once the database files approached the 2TB cap, MySQL simply stopped responding — not because it ran out of logical room, but because it had nowhere left to write data or even store its own logs.

The outage began on Wednesday, February 9 at 12:30 p.m. PT and lasted until Thursday, February 10 at 7:30 p.m. PT. For roughly 31 hours, the service was effectively down. Database effectively stopped responding at all — no reads, no writes, nothing.

And if you're thinking, *"hey, if they can't write, surely reads still work, right?"* then... no. Databases constantly generate operational metadata to keep your data consistent and your queries fast. Even a simple read often triggers tiny internal writes. When the filesystem says *"no space left,"* the storage engine throws up its hands, mutters *"screw this, I'm done,"* and shuts itself off so completely that even the admin struggles to get a coherent status out of it.

With MySQL folded into the fetal position, the engineering team had to perform a full migration of the primary database to a filesystem that could handle the required size. of the primary database to a filesystem that could handle the required size. No data was lost, but uptime evaporated.

The root cause traces back to early assumptions — but not the kind involving hard numbers. When ext3 became widespread in the 2000s, nobody sat down to calculate a precise upper bound or worry about a theoretical limit. The expectation was simply: "this filesystem will handle huge amounts of data." And for many years, it did.

But by the late 2010s, the combination of a growing user base and an ever-expanding mountain of saved articles, metadata, and internal tables turned that once-abstract 2TB ceiling into a very real constraint. It wasn't a limit anyone consciously chose — it was one they inherited, and eventually slammed into.

The fix, in theory, was obvious: move the database from `ext3` to `ext4` – a filesystem that wasn't stuck in the mid-2000s. In practice, this meant migrating a massive, live production RDS instance with no room left to write logs, buffers, or temporary tables. You can't resize ext3 in place. You can't conjure space from nowhere. And you definitely can't keep the site online while your database engine is suffocating.

So the team had to provision new storage, copy everything over, validate integrity, update configuration, and pray the old instance didn't corrupt itself further during the process. Moving terabytes of live data inside AWS is not instant — physics and bandwidth do not negotiate.

The irony wasn't lost on users. A product designed to store an endless queue of unread content wasn't killed by the size of its queue — it was killed by the fact that its filesystem literally ran out of space to store it.

LESSON LEARNED

- "We'll never hit that limit" is the oldest lie in software engineering.
- Databases cannot operate in read-only fairyland — even reads require writes (metadata, stats, bookkeeping). If there's no room for those, everything stops
- Technical debt is like financial debt: it compounds whether you pay attention to it or not.
- Infinite procrastination requires infinite integers.

Your procrastination might be infinite, but your database schema is not.

GitHub MySQL Outage
When The Map Breaks, The World Stops

Date: October 21, 2018

Impact: 24+ hours of degraded service; GitHub effectively became a read-only ghost town

Root Cause: Automated MySQL failover triggered by a 43-second network partition, leading to split-brain and corrupted topology metadata

GitHub has survived DDoS attacks, traffic tsunamis, and developer meltdowns, but nothing takes a platform down faster than its own metadata turning against it. In October 2018, a routine piece of maintenance took GitHub from "global collaboration hub" to "static website with delusions of grandeur."

It started harmlessly enough: engineers were performing routine hardware maintenance when a tiny 43-second network hiccup appeared between their US East primary databases and the US West replicas.

Forty-three seconds. Shorter than a microwave timer.

But long enough for the automation to panic. The system watching over the databases suddenly lost sight of the primary and did what it was programmed to do: assume the main database was dead and redirect traffic to the backup. Within seconds, the West Coast replicas were promoted to be the new primary.

Except the East Coast wasn't down. It was just taking a brief nap.

When the network healed, GitHub suddenly had two Masters alive and accepting writes. A classic split-brain scenario: two timelines, both believing they were the chosen one. It's the distributed-systems equivalent of an IT team in corporate setup: an engineering lead and a product lead both thinking they're in charge — nobody knows who to listen to, the team freezes, and everything quietly goes to hell.

But the real disaster wasn't the conflicting databases. It was the metadata layer, Consul—the service directory that tells every application server 'here's your current database Master, trust this one'—had corrupted maps. Some servers were told East was Master. Others heard West. The application layer was getting contradictory GPS coordinates to the same destination. During the failover chaos, Consul's internal maps diverged. Some servers believed East was the Master. Others believed West. Many weren't sure what to believe at all.

GitHub's application servers were effectively handed two contradictory maps of reality. And when the map doesn't match the territory, the only sane move is to stop driving.

Fixing the metadata wasn't simple. With two Masters alive at the same time, GitHub couldn't trust *any* of the information describing the cluster. Both sides had accepted new writes — and just like in the MongoDB ObjectId case, the moment two databases generate new records that share the same primary key, you no longer have two timelines you can reconcile. You have two timelines that can't both be true.

GitHub couldn't just "pick a winner." Choosing one Master meant discarding real user data written to the other. Merging them was even worse: conflicting IDs, divergent sequences, and tables that now described two incompatible realities.

To guarantee correctness, they had to do something deceptively simple on paper but brutal in practice. A database keeps a history of every operation it performs — a long, ordered log of all changes. So the recovery plan looked straightforward: stop everything, create a clean new cluster from the last healthy backups, and then replay history of what happened after, step by step until the new cluster reached the present.

Calling this "simple" is generous. Replaying years' worth of changes, in strict order, across a rebuilt system is less like pressing a button and more like reconstructing a city by retracing every brick ever laid. It works — eventually — but only at the speed reality allows.

Even with expert engineers and automation, physics imposed a hard limit. Restoring and indexing terabytes of data is like a pregnancy — you can't speed it up by adding more people to the effort. It takes as long as it takes, no matter how many managers are on the call.

For over twenty-four hours, GitHub limped along: users could browse, clone, and read code, but writes and critical operations were throttled or disabled. It was the world's most famous read-only filesystem.

LESSON LEARNED

- Automated failovers are only as good as the assumptions behind them. If the observer can't tell "network delay" from "datacenter death," disaster is inevitable.
- Split-brain isn't just a database problem—it's a metadata nightmare.
- Maps (topology metadata) must always match the territory (actual state), or recovery becomes guesswork.
- Sometimes the hardest part of incident response is waiting for terabytes to finish moving.
- A tiny network glitch can trigger days of chaos if automation reacts faster than reality.

Forty-three seconds of network hiccup. Twenty-four hours waiting for reality to rebuild itself.

CERN CASTOR
Tape Catalog Corruption

Date: 2008

Impact: Thousands of LHC tapes became unlocatable; weeks of manual reconstruction; analysis pipelines slowed during commissioning

Root Cause: Oracle database corruption wiped CASTOR's tape-location catalog, leaving data intact but unmapped

While the world's media obsessively tracked the LHC's physical startup—waiting for black holes or the Higgs boson—a much less telegenic but equally dangerous crisis was brewing in the background. The physics community was focused on the magnets; the IT department, however, was fighting a silent war to keep the experiment's memory from developing amnesia.

What happened to CASTOR—the tape-management system designed to keep decades of scientific treasure organized—was not a sudden, thunderous collapse. It was a creeping rot. Engineers had been battling sporadic "cross-talk" errors and silent corruption warnings for some time. It wasn't just a single bad day; it was a system slowly losing its grip on reality.

Then, the dam broke. Engineers discovered that a corruption in the Oracle backend—specifically in the database journals—had compromised the recovery mechanisms. When they tried to roll back to fix a minor issue, they found the safety net was full of holes. CASTOR, the only entity that knew where the petabytes of data lived, had achieved a state of partial lobotomy.

The tapes themselves were perfectly fine—petabytes of physics data sitting quietly in darkness. But without the catalog, CERN suddenly possessed a mountain of data and absolutely no idea where any specific part of it was.

Schrödinger's dataset: present, but only in theory.

Scientists trying to run calibration jobs or validate detector responses were greeted with errors that translated loosely to: "We know we have it, but we can't find it." Jobs stalled. Pipelines collapsed.

The recovery option was gloriously low-tech: rebuild the catalog by hand. Teams spent weeks scanning tapes, reading headers, cross-checking scraps of logs, and reconstructing metadata relationships one cartridge at a time. It was digital archaeology performed with all the glamour of watching paint dry—but it eventually worked.

LESSON LEARNED

- Metadata is data—losing it renders the payload meaningless.
- A storage system without a catalog is archaeology with better acronyms.
- Redundancy must include the lookup structures, not just the content.
- Critical catalogs deserve isolated backups and independent verification.
- Never assume a component is "too important to fail."

CERN's scientists study quantum realities that can be both there and not there—but they weren't hoping to experience that phenomenon in their storage catalog.

"THE PERFECT CRIME"

You might be wondering: "If CERN lost the index to petabytes of scientific data, why wasn't this on the evening news?"

Partly, it was timing. The massive physical failure of the LHC magnets in September 2008 sucked all the oxygen out of the room. Compared to a multi-billion dollar machine exploding, a database needing manual repair felt like a footnote.

But there is also a pragmatic reality to working in an international organization of this magnitude. "Solving it quietly" isn't always about deception; often, it's about avoiding the Inquisition. The staff likely understood that making the incident official—creating a paper trail—would trigger something far worse than data loss: an investigative committee.

Faced with the choice between weeks of ungrateful, manual reconstruction or years of hearings, reports, and political bureaucracy under the gaze of twenty member states, the team made the only sane choice. They fixed it, kept their heads down, and left no paper trail.

However, the digital exhaust remains. While there is no glossy press release, the "smoking gun" exists in the operational meeting logs of the Worldwide LHC Computing Grid (WLCG) from May 2008. Buried in the minutes are dry notes about "database journal corruption preventing recovery" and data gaps. I have included the links to these logs in the bibliography for the curious.

That said, I recommend treating the specific operational details of the recovery as an educated reconstruction. What you read here is my professional synthesis of what recovering from this class of corruption necessarily entails — cross-checking tapes, scanning headers, rebuilding relationships, rehydrating metadata structures, and validating consistency. The "smoking gun" is public; the stitching between the clues is my reconstruction.

Regardless of the exact scale, I included this story because it serves as a flawless illustration of the core lesson: if you lose your metadata, you lose your data.

Explainer:

Indexes — When Finding Things Fast Actually Matters

Let's take a break to explain one more detail.

Among all forms of metadata, indexes deserve special treatment. They are the cheat sheets your database creates so it can find what you need *now*, not after a full archaeological dig. Both structured and semi-structured databases rely on them, because without indexes, every query becomes a slow, painful march through the entire dataset.

If you've ever flipped to the back of a book for the index —say, to find a specific explainer without rereading 300 pages—you already know the idea. The book has its narrative order, but the index gives you a shortcut: a pre-computed map of where things live.

Imagine you run a directory of companies. Maybe it's sorted alphabetically by name. That's useful—until you want all companies in a specific industry, or every business founded by someone named John Smith. Without indexes, your only option is to read the entire directory from cover to cover. With indexes, those alternate views are created once, maintained as data changes, and available instantly.

Databases use the same trick. Say you store every customer who ever bought something from your online shop. When a new customer appears, you want to record their data and move on—not spend extra time reorganizing everything. Worse, how would you decide the order or grouping once and for all? One day you might want to find all customers from Texas to offer them a shiny new Stetson hat, and another day you'll want to target everyone born before 1975 with a well-timed rollator promotion. Indexes are what let the database maintain those fast lookups in the background while you keep working.

They're powerful tools—but, as you'll see soon enough, when indexes go wrong, entire systems can slow to a crawl, return nonsense, or simply fall over. In the hierarchy of data failures, index mishaps rank surprisingly high.

PostgreSQL VACUUM Bug

Date: 2009 and 2018
Impact: Disk bloat, corrupt indexes, ghost data, and incorrect query results
Root Cause: VACUUM failed to clean dead tuples correctly, leaving behind stale entries and broken index pointers

PostgreSQL has a reputation for being the grown-up in the database family: stable, reliable, boring in the best possible way. Which makes it all the more entertaining that two of its most memorable failures came not from exotic edge cases or obscure extensions, but from housekeeping. Specifically, VACUUM—the feature responsible for cleaning up after PostgreSQL's own mess.

To understand what went wrong, you need a quick primer on how PostgreSQL works. Unlike many databases, it doesn't overwrite data in place. When a row is updated or deleted, the old version isn't removed immediately. It's simply marked as "dead," left behind like a shed snakeskin. The database keeps running fast because it avoids expensive rewrites in the critical path. The cost is paid later during a scheduled spring-cleaning pass appropriately named **VACUUM**.

It's a clever design: user-facing operations stay quick, and the disk—well, as we established earlier, disks are cheap. But letting junk pile up only works if you eventually take the trash out.

In 2009, a nasty surprise arrived. A bug in VACUUM FULL meant that dead tuples weren't cleaned up properly. Instead of being removed, they lingered, inflating indexes and confusing the query planner. PostgreSQL began seeing rows that no longer existed, and missing rows that did. Think of it as database schizophrenia: hallucinations mixed with selective amnesia.

Things quieted down for a while—until 2018, when another VACUUM bug decided to make an appearance. This time, VACUUM skipped certain "frozen" tuples, leaving behind yet more immortal dead data. Again, indexes bloated, query plans derailed, and the engine returned results that didn't match reality. Administrators described encountering "ghost data"—rows that appeared in one query and vanished in another, depending on which index happened to be consulted.

The consequences were subtle but dangerous: slower queries, corrupt indexes, inconsistent reads, and silent data corruption creeping into long-running production systems. To make this a bit more tangible: imagine your bank suddenly insisting you never finished paying off a loan whose last instalment you cleared a year ago — all because its database saw a "dead" record rise from the grave and shout for attention. Many teams didn't detect the issue until performance collapsed or manual audits revealed that the database had developed an active imagination.

PostgreSQL fixed the issues in subsequent releases (9.0.5 and 11.2), improving VACUUM's logic and handling of frozen tuples. But the damage was already done. Years of deployments had quietly accumulated dead data that was never supposed to exist.

LESSON LEARNED

- Throwing junk into a corner works only if someone actually comes to pick it up.
- Dead data doesn't stay dead—it haunts performance, indexes, and query plans.
- Background maintenance is as critical as foreground correctness.
- Silent corruption is the most dangerous kind.
- Databases, like humans, sometimes need therapy to let go of the past.

PostgreSQL didn't lose your data—just kept everything you ever gave it, forever, like an emotionally unstable hoarder.

Discord "The Memory Wall" When RAM Becomes The Final Boss

Date: November 2015

Impact: Severe latency spikes, cluster-wide slowdowns, and a near-meltdown of the messaging infrastructure

Root Cause: Working set (active data + indexes) outgrew available RAM, triggering I/O thrashing in MongoDB

Discord in 2015 wasn't yet the cultural empire it is today, but it was already growing at a pace that politely ignored the laws of physics: hundreds of millions of new messages per day, billions total. They were using MongoDB, spread across sharded replica sets. And for a while, everything was fine.

Right up until they hit The Memory Wall.

Discord was growing fast. Their MongoDB cluster kept up just fine as long as all the active data and its indexes fit comfortably in RAM. The moment it didn't, the entire system stumbled.

Remember the explainer from Part I, where RAM was the kitchen counter and disk was the pantry down the hall? Discord hit the point where the counter was full.

Once the working set stopped fitting in memory, the database had to start shoving ingredients off the counter and into the pantry. And every time it needed one of those ingredients again, it had to pause cooking, walk over, fetch it, walk back, and continue.

In computers, that walk isn't a minor inconvenience — it's the difference between nanoseconds and milliseconds. A million-to-one slowdown. A bit of this is fine. Too much, and the entire kitchen grinds to a halt.

Discord's workload made it worse. Users don't politely stick to recent messages. They scroll back through weeks-old threads, jump to pinned posts, search for that one meme from three months ago. Every action forces random reads across the entire dataset—exactly the workload pattern that murders performance once indexes leave RAM.

One day, Discord's working set simply grew larger than the RAM available across their MongoDB shards. And once the indexes spilled out of memory, the servers fell into **I/O thrashing**: nonstop disk churn, as the database desperately paged things in and out.

Latency didn't just rise—it exploded. Writes queued up behind stalled reads. Nodes locked up. The cluster began to stall.

Discord's engineers eventually realised the uncomfortable truth: MongoDB's architecture wasn't the issue. Their workload was. They needed a database designed for high-write, time-ordered operations without requiring massive indexes to sit fully in RAM.

The solution wasn't choosing a "better" database—it was choosing one that matched Discord's actual behavior. MongoDB excels at flexible queries across complex data. But Discord's workload was simpler: accept an endless stream of messages, write them in chronological order, and retrieve them later without keeping massive indexes in memory.

Cassandra fit that pattern naturally. Instead of maintaining giant indexes to find anything anywhere, it stores messages in time-ordered sequences. When you want messages from a channel, you know exactly where to look —no index archaeology required.

It wasn't a matter of clever tricks. It was picking the tool that matched the shape of the problem: "people send messages forever, and they want to read all of them."

LESSON LEARNED

- RAM is the hardest limit in database engineering; once you exceed it, performance doesn't degrade—it collapses.
- Random-access workloads punish systems that depend on large in-memory indexes.
- A database can be excellent and still completely wrong for your access patterns.
- Latency isn't a curve; at the memory wall, it's a cliff.
- If your users insist on reading everything, build for a system that can handle everything.

RAM is finite. User expectations aren't. Discord learned this the hard way: once your working set exceeds memory, performance doesn't degrade gracefully—it falls off a cliff.

Explainer:

OLTP vs OLAP — The Waffle House Edition

This chapter is already long, but I need to sneak in one more idea about how databases are classified. If you've made it this far, congratulations — you're entering the advanced tier of database nerdery. If that wasn't your plan... my sincere apologies.

Behind the two acronyms OLTP and OLAP hide:

- **Online Transactional Processing**

- **Online Analytical Processing**

The only part that really matters is the difference between *Transactional* and *Analytical*.

Think of it like Waffle House[22].

A transactional system (OLTP) is the cook. Specifically, the cook at 3:00 AM on a Saturday. They are a chaos-tolerant deity who can juggle eggs, waffles, and twenty shouted orders from a crowd of drunk students ("scattered, smothered, covered!"). Their job is to perform lots of small tasks as fast as physically possible. They don't care about last month's potato usage; they care about *this specific order right now*.

An analytical system (OLAP) is the regional manager. They walk in with a clipboard, stop the music, and start counting inventory. They compare sales across multiple locations, forecast next month's syrup demand, and analyze why profitability drops on Tuesdays. Their job

---

[22] *For non-American readers:* **Waffle House** is a 24/7 diner chain across the Southern United States, famous for never closing. And when I say "never," I mean it literally—FEMA (the Federal Emergency Management Agency) uses the *"Waffle House Index"* as an informal metric to assess disaster severity. If the local Waffle House is serving a full menu, the area is fine. If they switched to a limited menu (usually meaning they are on generator power), there is significant damage. If Waffle House is closed, run—you are looking at catastrophic destruction. It's not an official government metric, but emergency responders genuinely check it because Waffle House has better disaster preparedness than most municipalities.

isn't to be fast — it's to be correct. They crunch massive amounts of data to find the "big picture."

The Golden Rule: You never want the regional manager standing in the cook's way during the lunch rush. If you ask the cook to stop flipping burgers and calculate the quarterly variance of cheese consumption, the kitchen stops, the customers riot, and the Waffle House burns down.

Databases follow the same logic. Some are built to handle thousands of tiny requests per second — they're the reason your online shop loads quickly and lets you instantly order that sequined Nicolas Cage pillow you absolutely don't need (no judgment). These are **OLTP** systems.

But behind that circus is a whole logistics network making sure that when you order your dream pillow, it actually exists in a warehouse. And that the price is high enough to cover shipping, yet low enough that fellow pillow connoisseurs will still buy it. These processes require crunching huge amounts of historical data, but only occasionally. That's **OLAP**.

Just like with 24/7 diners, small companies can survive with just the cook (OLTP). But once you scale, you need the manager (OLAP). They store and process data in very different ways because their jobs are contradictory.

All the cases in this chapter so far involved OLTP systems because, let's be clear: their failures are loud, public, and immediate.

OLAP failures? They're quiet. The reports just... lie. And nobody notices until the CFO makes a billion-dollar decision based on bad math.

Target Canada Master Data Disaster
When Your Database Thinks A Box Of Crayons
Is The Size Of A Fridge

Date: 2013–2015

Impact: 7B total losses; 133 stores closed; 17,000 jobs eliminated; customers found empty shelves while warehouses overflowed with unsellable inventory

Root Cause: Master data failure — incorrect product dimensions, weights, and units (imperial vs. metric)

When Target decided to expand into Canada, the plan sounded beautifully simple: copy the successful U.S. operation, paste it north of the border, and enjoy the profits. Instead, they created one of the largest retail IT disasters of the decade — powered not by outages, crashes, or cyberattacks, but by something far more mundane: bad metadata.

Target's U.S. systems weren't built for Canada, so the company rolled out a brand-new SAP environment coupled with a JDA supply-chain system, essentially buying a Lamborghini and then trying to drive it like a shopping cart.

This gleaming new system needed master data for roughly 75,000 products: dimensions, weights, case packs, pallet sizes — the invisible scaffolding that tells warehouses, trucks, and stores how much space things occupy and when to restock them. None of this was migrated automatically. Instead, it was — and I kid you not — entered by hand by rushed new hires and interns working under impossible deadlines. The results were exactly what you would expect when you combine a massive ERP[23] rollout, unrealistic schedules, and humans with keyboards.

In the U.S., product dimensions defaulted to inches. In Canada's system, employees had to choose units manually. Many didn't. Others mixed up centimeters and inches. Some entered numbers from U.S. spreadsheets but left the unit as metric. The database accepted every lie without complaint. And then the real world buckled.

A pack of crayons might be recorded as the size of a refrigerator, leading the system to conclude that a shelf could hold only two units when in reality it held fifty. Store systems happily reported "fully stocked" shelves that, to actual customers, looked deserted. The reverse happened too: a bulky product might be recorded as something tiny, prompting the system to order thousands of units. Warehouses clogged as trucks delivered goods that physically couldn't fit into aisles, onto pallets, or inside the outgoing trailers meant to carry them to stores. Employees found themselves navigating mountains of merchandise that the system confidently insisted should take up almost no space.

The expensive auto-replenishment system — designed to keep stores stocked with mathematical precision — worked flawlessly in theory. Unfortunately, it was doing math on nonsense. Leadership eventually shut it off entirely. For months, a multibillion-dollar corporation

---

[23] **ERP, aka Enterprise Requires Pain**

ERP stands for *Enterprise Resource Planning* — a giant system that claims it can manage everything: warehouses, logistics, invoices, purchasing, inventory, supply chains, the lunar cycle, and possibly your CFO's horoscope. In theory, it's the brain of the entire organization. In practice, it's usually an extremely expensive pain organ that starts working correctly approximately five minutes after the company goes bankrupt.

relied on employees walking through aisles with clipboards, visually checking what was actually on the shelves and trying to reconcile it with a system that lived in a parallel universe.

This was not an IT outage. The servers ran flawlessly. SAP didn't crash. The application layer didn't fail. Everything "worked." That was the terrifying part: the system executed perfectly according to specifications, but its understanding of the world no longer matched physical reality. And once that happens, no algorithm, no dashboard, and no KPI can save you.

LESSON LEARNED

- Metadata is not a formality — it is how your business understands the world.
- Wrong units lead to wrong decisions, no matter how perfect the software.
- Manual data entry at scale is a disaster wearing a name badge.
- A system that runs perfectly on bad data is more dangerous than one that crashes—at least crashes get fixed.

Master data doesn't sound dramatic until it costs you $7 billion and 17,000 jobs. Turns out 'is this in inches or centimeters' is an expensive question to answer wrong.

CHAPTER 14:
LOST IN MIGRATION

Data has many ways of dying. By now we've seen disks quietly forgetting their contents, databases corrupting themselves out of spite, backups vanishing into the void, and archives deleted in the name of cost savings. If information can rot, flip, drift, or immolate itself, it probably has. But there's one moment in a system's life where the odds of catastrophe spike dramatically: the moment you try to move anything.

If the previous chapters explored what happens when data stays still, this one looks at the danger that appears the second it starts walking. Migrations are the digital equivalent of a household move: everything is technically accounted for, nicely labeled, supposedly safe—and yet somehow you end up in the new place missing half a box, one chair leg, and your favorite mug.

In fact, my first job taught me this lesson the analog way. The company I worked for was moving offices—just three kilometers down the road. A trivial relocation. The moving crew managed to break one desk and *lose* another. To this day I have no idea how you misplace a desk. It's not a USB stick; it has a gravitational field. But there it was: gone, vanished, presumably living a better life somewhere.

Digital migrations aren't much different. Move data between systems, formats, APIs, or storage layers, and suddenly the universe reveals how many creative ways it has to sabotage you. Records vanish. Encodings mutate. Resumable transfers fail to resume. Partial writes masquerade as success. And the best part? By the time you notice something's missing, the old system has already been decommissioned.

So in this chapter we'll unpack the many layers of chaos hiding in that deceptively simple phrase: "just migrate it." Because nothing triggers failure quite like assuming the journey will be easier than the destination.

——————— TSB Bank Meltdown (UK) ———————

Date: April 2018

Impact: 2+ million customers locked out; fraud exposure; £330M in fines, compensation, and lost business; CEO resignation

Root Cause: Data and logic mismatch during cut-over; insufficient prod-like testing; rushed big-bang migration

When a bank tells customers a migration will be "seamless," what they usually mean is: please don't panic yet. In April 2018, TSB decided it was time to stop relying on the legacy core banking platform operated by its former owner, Lloyds Banking Group. The plan sounded simple enough: migrate five million customers — roughly 1.3 billion records — to Proteo4UK, the adapted UK version of Sabadell's core banking system. A clean break. Total independence. A triumph of engineering.

Instead, the bank spent six weeks starring in its own disaster documentary.

The moment TSB flipped the switch, reality fell out of the ceiling tiles. Customers logging into their accounts were greeted not by their own finances, but by other people's balances, loan information, or transaction histories. Some saw multiple strangers' accounts stitched together like a financial Frankenstein. Others saw negative balances that made no sense. Hundreds of thousands couldn't log in at all. Card payments failed. Fraud teams panicked. Branch staff were left explaining to furious customers that no, this was not a prank, and yes, the bank was technically still solvent.

The root cause wasn't a single catastrophic bug — it was a perfect storm of mismatches. The new system didn't fully replicate decades of legacy logic embedded in Sabadell's platform. Certain workflows were implemented differently, some assumptions were baked into the old codebase and never documented, and several data fields didn't map cleanly between systems. It was the migration equivalent of moving house and discovering the new apartment has doors in the wrong places.

Testing should have caught this. It didn't. TSB had done load tests, but only on partial datasets. They executed parallel runs, but not long enough to expose drift under real-world volume. Under the hood, IBM's later investigation concluded that "non-functional testing was insufficient," which is consulting-speak for: *we tested it in the lab and hoped for the best.*

Once the cut-over was done, there was no going back. Rollback wasn't an option — the old system had already been frozen. Engineers were stuck performing live surgery on a banking platform used by millions, while the press, regulators, and angry customers watched the patient thrash.

The financial fallout was brutal: £330 million in compensation and regulatory penalties. Customer trust evaporated overnight. Market share dipped. And eventually, the CEO stepped down — a reminder that in banking, nothing gets you fired faster than accidentally showing people other people's money.

LESSON LEARNED

- Big-bang migrations are just big explosions with better branding.
- "Test in production" isn't a strategy — it's a confession.
- Parallel runs only matter if they're long enough to mimic reality.
- Legacy logic is never "legacy" — it's infrastructure.
- If rollback is impossible, your plan isn't a plan; it's a wish.

TSB wanted independence from Sabadell. They forgot to write their own constitution and accidentally launched six weeks of full-scale financial anarchy.

The Great British Police Purge

Date: January 2021

Impact: ~209,550 criminal records deleted; 112,000 potentially dangerous individuals temporarily "cleared"; weeks of manual recovery; Home Secretary forced to apologize

Root Cause: Faulty housekeeping script; no peer review; confusion between "ready for deletion" and "under investigation"

Most government IT disasters are slow burns—projects that hemorrhage money for years before quietly dying of embarrassment. But in January 2021, the UK Home Office demonstrated a bold new approach: causing a national policing crisis instantly, with nothing but a script and misplaced confidence. The victim was the Police National Computer (PNC), a venerable mainframe that functions as the collective memory of British law enforcement. It knows who's been arrested, who's wanted, whose fingerprints match a crime scene, and who should absolutely not be walking free.

The job at hand was routine: delete old arrest records for individuals who were never charged—a privacy-driven spring cleaning, the kind of bureaucratic housekeeping no one expects to make headlines. Engineers wrote a script to automate it, intending a simple logical check: *If (record is old) AND (case is closed), delete it.* Unfortunately, what they deployed behaved more like: *If (record exists), delete enthusiastically.* The selection criteria were coded incorrectly, and the script plowed ahead with the serene confidence of a bulldozer in a greenhouse, ignoring case status entirely and focusing solely on the "delete" half of its job description.

When it finished, someone noticed that the digital equivalent of a massacre had occurred: over 413,000 database entries—comprising 209,550 offence records plus linked fingerprints, DNA profiles, and arrest histories —had evaporated. Suddenly, officers checking suspects discovered... nothing. Violent offenders appeared as first-time angels, and DNA swabs returned "No Match" because the reference samples had been lovingly scrubbed into oblivion. For days, the UK police operated in a state best described as "institutional amnesia," with detectives scrambling through paper notes, half-remembered histories, and pure panic.

Recovery was not a matter of hitting "Undo." The PNC is a living, constantly updated mainframe, and restoring the missing data without overwriting new legitimate arrests became a painstaking ordeal. It took months of forensic reconstruction—digital archaeology conducted under political pressure. Ironically, the engineers had set out to protect privacy. In a sense, they succeeded—they just protected the privacy of 112,000 criminals a little too thoroughly.

Recovery was not a matter of hitting "Undo." The PNC is a living, constantly updated mainframe; restoring the missing data without overwriting new legitimate arrests was a painstaking ordeal. It took months of forensic reconstruction—digital archaeology performed under political pressure.

Ironically, the engineers had been trying to protect privacy. In a sense, they succeeded—they just protected the privacy of **112,000 criminals** a little too thoroughly.

LESSON LEARNED

- A **DELETE** script is a weapon; write and review it accordingly.
- In critical systems you don't delete — you mark inactive. For a good reason...
- If you skip the dry run, you are not testing—you're gambling your career.
- Maintenance code causes the most spectacular explosions; review it like a feature.
- When 400,000 records vanish, monitoring should scream long before the job finishes.

Politicians had promised a 'clean slate' for the nation post-Brexit. The Home Office simply took them literally.

—————— **Canada's Phoenix Pay System** ——————

Date: February 2016 (Launch) – Ongoing

Impact: ~300,000 federal employees underpaid, overpaid, or not paid at all; estimated cost to fix >$2.2 billion; families forced into bankruptcy; a decade-long national embarrassment

Root Cause: Mass consolidation of 46 incompatible legacy systems into one rigid PeopleSoft instance; data accuracy issues ignored during transfer; governance by wishful thinking; "garbage in, garbage out" scaled to a G20 economy

The Canadian government decided it could save $70 million a year by firing hundreds of payroll specialists and replacing them with a central, elegant, modern super-system named Phoenix. What they built instead was a national poverty generator—an automated chaos engine that redistributed money according to planetary alignment.

This was not a small migration. It was a **mass consolidation of 46 departmental payroll systems**, many of them so old they predated the creation of the very ministries they served. Some stored data in bespoke formats. Some stored data in *other* bespoke formats. Some barely stored data at all. Every warning sign blinked red: pilot tests showed consistent miscalculations, the data-cleaning phase was absurdly behind schedule, and internal memos begged leadership to wait. Leadership instead chose the sacred path of "Go Live And Pray."

Phoenix did not pray back.

Within weeks, payroll melted. The logic engine couldn't handle Canada's Byzantine web of union rules—retroactive pay, acting pay, overtime, "higher duty" pay, seasonal pay, bilingual bonuses, Arctic isolation allowances, and the bureaucratic hydra known as *entitlements*. Phoenix looked at this glorious complexity and simply said: **no.**

What followed bordered on dystopian absurdism:

• Thousands of employees received **$0.00 paychecks** for months.

• Others were paid wildly too much—one employee woke up $600,000 richer and then was pursued by tax authorities for income they never earned.

• Maternity leave and disability cases were mangled so badly that families lost access to their legally guaranteed benefits.

• Some employees were simultaneously marked as overpaid *and* underpaid, a quantum-state salary paradox only a government system could invent.

Then came the real punchline: the old systems had already been shut down, and the clerks who knew how to fix payroll had been fired. There was no rollback. No undo button. No archive environment. Canada had successfully deleted its own payroll muscle memory.

To stabilize the situation, the government scrambled to hire thousands of emergency pay clerks, many of whom had to reverse-engineer individual pay histories with calculators, notebooks, and spreadsheets. Nearly a decade later, the backlog still exists. Tens of thousands of cases remain unresolved. Phoenix has become less a system and more a generational curse.

LESSON LEARNED

• Complex pay systems don't shrink when you migrate them — they explode when you pretend they will.

> - Removing human expertise before verifying the replacement system works is how you turn modernization into self-inflicted disaster.
> - Bad legacy data doesn't get cleaner in a new system — it just breaks louder.
> - Ignoring failed tests doesn't save time — it schedules the catastrophe.

Phoenix was supposed to rise from the ashes of outdated software. Instead, it set half the federal workforce on financial fire.

 **Explainer:**
What Encoding Actually Is (and Why It Breaks So Easily)

Before we get into Japan's My Number faceplant, we need a quick primer. A short one. The last version was basically a whole lecture — this one is the distilled, migration-relevant version.

Computers don't understand letters. They understand numbers — and those numbers only become text if you tell the machine which "alphabet" to use. That "alphabet" is called **encoding**.

Remember back in Chapter 1, when we talked about how computers interpret numbers depending on their encoding system? Text works the same way — except here the chaos multiplies. Computers behave the same way. A byte pattern like `01100001` might mean 97 or a — depending on whether the computer is expecting a number or text... and whether everyone involved is actually following the same agreed-upon standard.

For English letters, everyone *did* agree. For anything beyond that — ą, ö, ñ, 信 — things got messy. The encodings themselves existed long before the 1990s, but that decade (and the early 2000s) was when the chaos peaked. As the internet connected systems that had never "spoken" to each other before, all those regional encoding standards started colliding — and text turned into ?, □, or total garbage.

UTF-8 solved this problem by defining a universal system for *every* character in *every* alphabet — including emoji.

Fun fact: the Unicode Consortium — originally founded to unify the world's writing systems — now spends most of its time performing its sacred modern duty: voting on which emoji should be added next. Modern priorities.

The catch? UTF-8 only works if you actually use it. If one system exports data using an older encoding and the new system assumes UTF-8, you don't get an error — you get corrupted text. Or no text at all.

To be fair, most encoding bugs don't trigger disasters — at worst a few letters turn into gibberish, but you can still guess what the text was meant to say. That's true for languages using Latin-based alphabets... but Japan does not belong to that club. And it gifted us material for the next story.

—— **Japan's "Someone's Number" Meldown** ——

Date: May–August 2023

Impact: 7,300+ confirmed incidents of health data mismatched to wrong people; strangers receiving others' prescriptions; breakdown of trust in the national Digital ID; Prime Minister forced into a national apology

Root Cause: Legacy character-set limitations (Katakana vs. Kanji); fuzzy phonetic matching; assumption that Name + Birthdate = Unique Identifier

Japan is a technological paradox: a country capable of running trains so punctual they make Swiss watches look sloppy, yet in June 2024 triumphantly declared it had finally stopped using floppy disks in government workflows. This is the same nation that gave humanity Nintendo, but still treats fax machines like state-of-the-art cryptography and runs its banking sector on hardware that predates the Berlin Wall coming down.

Into this wonderland of contradictions came the "My Number" (MyNa) project — an ambitious, heroic, and ultimately unhinged attempt to merge every citizen's health, pension, and financial identifiers into a single digital ID. On paper, it was a sleek future. In execution, it was a paperwork landslide with Wi-Fi.

The core problem began with something deceptively simple: **names.** In Japanese. Which is to say: not simple at all.

A name like "Akira" can be written in dozens of Kanji variants, each with different meanings, strokes, and levels of existential despair for database architects. Meanwhile, private-sector bank systems — built during the floppy-disk famine of the 1980s — stored names only in their phonetic form, using *half-width Katakana*, a relic encoding invented solely to torment future engineers.

So the migration logic had to perform this magic trick:
- Gov Record (UTF-8/Kanji): 田中 (Tanaka)
- Bank Record (Legacy/Katakana): ﾀﾅｶ (Tanaka)

Unfortunately, there is no universal, deterministic, mathematically pure way to map Kanji to half-width Katakana. You can't even get close. So Japan did what every over-optimistic migration project does when faced with incompatible schemas: it guessed.

Specifically, it matched records based on **Phonetic Name + Birthdate** — essentially assuming that in a nation of 125 million people, this combination would uniquely identify a citizen.

It did not.

"Tanaka born on March 1st" is not an individual. It's a demographic cohort.

And so, automated batch jobs began linking government records to whatever "close enough" match they stumbled across, producing a nationwide data-identity lottery where the grand prize was someone else's medical records.

Citizens logged into the portal only to be greeted by long, intimate lists of medications prescribed to complete strangers.

Disability payments wandered into the wrong bank accounts.

Hospitals declared elderly patients "uninsured" because the system couldn't reconcile beautifully calligraphed Kanji with a budget-constrained 1980s Katakana encoding.

This wasn't a glitch. It was a structural failure wearing a nametag.

By mid-2023, over 7,300 confirmed mismatches had surfaced. Privacy regulators raided the Digital Agency. Public trust dipped below sea level. And the Prime Minister performed the dreaded political ritual of bowing in apology — the Japanese equivalent of a full-stack rollback.

Japan had attempted a sleek, modern digital revolution. Instead, it discovered that when your alphabets span 50,000 characters and your infrastructure spans four decades, the alphabet itself becomes legacy tech.

LESSON LEARNED

- Names are not primary keys — especially in a language with 50,000 characters and three writing systems.
- Phonetic matching is gambling; eventually the system will give someone else's heart medication to a man with the same birthday.
- Legacy encodings bite back: you cannot funnel 1980s half-width banking data into a modern UTF-8 system without manual verification.
- Even in a high-trust society, bad data migration is the fastest route to destroying public trust.

Japan's trains run with 18-second precision. Their national ID ran on 'sounds close enough.' Only one of these approaches scales.

MySpace Migration Meltdown
The Move That Bulldozed Home

Date: Migration (2016–2017); user reports (2018); official admission (March 2019)

Impact: 50+ million songs, plus untold photos, videos, and blogs (2003–2015) — permanently deleted.

Root Cause: Botched server migration; likely checksum validation failure during transfer...

Japan showed that a migration failure doesn't require broken IDs. MySpace showed you don't need a database at all.

MySpace wanted a comeback. Instead, it deleted a decade of internet culture — and waited two years to mention it. Twelve years of teenage oversharing, emo-band demos, and bathroom-mirror selfies went *poof* — not in a single moment of chaos, but in two years of slow decay, excuses, and quiet cover-ups.

Around **2016–2017**, MySpace started moving old data to new infrastructure. Think of it as spring cleaning by people who forgot to label the boxes. The process relied on automated **rsync** scripts — a kind of digital cloning tool that copies files from one place to another.

But there's a catch: if something interrupts the transfer — even a small network hiccup (remember those packets from Chapter 6?) — you might not get a perfect copy. That's where **checksums** come in: a digital receipt proving every byte made the journey intact. Without it, your clone can turn out more Frankenstein than Dolly the sheep — legs where the head should be, tails for arms, and a blinking neon "FREE BEER" sign in place of a tail.

MySpace, chasing speed, turned checksums off. Some files failed mid-transfer and were overwritten by garbage. Then, the cleanup scripts ran — deleting the old data. In short: the movers threw away the boxes before checking if the new house even had walls.

By 2018, users noticed their playlists didn't play, photos wouldn't load, and videos just spun forever. Support dismissed it as a "temporary issue." Behind the scenes, engineers already knew the data was toast. Support communications at the time only confirmed the outcome — *"files were corrupted and unable to be transferred... there's no way to recover."*

MySpace never published a technical post-mortem, so the details of how the migration failed remain unverified. The scenario described above follows the most widely accepted expert reconstruction of how such corruption typically occurs at scale — but while the mechanism is inferred, the scale of the destruction is absolutely confirmed.

In March 2019, MySpace finally confessed — via a tiny banner on its homepage. The message was corporate-speak poetry: "As a result of a server migration project, photos, videos, and audio files uploaded more than three years ago may no longer be available." Translation: "We fucked up, waited two years to tell you, and there's nothing left."

When users tried to log in, they found their profiles as empty as a dorm fridge the morning after a party. Entire garage bands lost their discographies, and even famous groups like the Arctic Monkeys lost early demos. MySpace had executed the largest accidental cultural purge of the 2000s — an extinction event for digital nostalgia.

Remember that database I dropped a few pages ago? I had a snapshot. MySpace didn't. Sure, their scale was massive and their budget was shrinking — but that's exactly when you *can't* afford to skip backups. Storage is cheap. Explaining to millions of users that their data's gone forever? That costs more.

Some users suspected this wasn't incompetence — it was cost-cutting disguised as a migration. Why pay for storage when you can just... not? Whether intentional or accidental, the result was the same: a digital extinction event that MySpace hoped nobody would notice.

LESSON LEARNED

- Never delete the source until the destination passes validation — especially when network transfers are involved.

- Backups are only as good as your last restore test, and you don't want that test to be the postmortem.

- "Performance optimizations" that disable data integrity checks are the corporate equivalent of driving without seatbelts because they slow you down.

- Despite what your CFO says, the cost of maintaining a proper backup is almost always smaller than the cost of explaining its absence.

In the end, MySpace didn't just lose its users — it lost proof they'd ever been there. Mission accomplished?

CHAPTER 15:
SCHRÖDINGER'S BACKUP – BOTH THERE AND NOT THERE UNTIL YOU NEED IT

There's an old IT saying: There are two kinds of people — the ones that make backups, and the ones that **will** make backups.

As you'll see in this chapter, there's also a secret third kind: the rare souls who actually test whether their backups work.

It's a funny line, but also painfully true — because few things in IT inspire more false confidence than the phrase "Don't worry, we have backups." It's the digital equivalent of carrying an umbrella that's always at home when it rains. Because, as countless admins have learned the hard way, having a backup isn't the same as having a *working* backup.

This chapter is a guided tour through humanity's most optimistic assumptions about data recovery. We'll meet companies that proudly discovered their backups contained nothing but empty directories, hospitals that realized their "disaster recovery" lived on the same power circuit as the disaster, and teams who learned that "restore test" is not a theoretical concept.

But it's not all doom and deletion. Sometimes, against all odds, backups actually do save the day — even when the day looks beyond saving. So while most of these stories begin with misplaced confidence and end with frantic swearing, a few remind us that hope, like redundancy, occasionally works as intended.

Before we tour the wreckage, let's establish what backups really are — and why the sheer number of related terms can make you feel like this is an entire scientific discipline of its own. (Spoiler: it kind of is.)

Explainer:
The Backup Bestiary—Choose Wisely, Regret Later

Imagine you're the proud collector of business cards — old-school, paper ones. They're your network, your livelihood, your analog LinkedIn. Every Sunday, you make photocopies of the entire binder, because you're a responsible adult (and you don't trust cloud sync). If your dog decides to eat the original — and dogs, as rumor has it, eat more than just homework — you can rebuild the binder using the copies. It'll take time, sure, but at least you'll still know who owes you coffee.

Two questions now define your fate:

- **RTO (Recovery Time Objective):** How fast can you rebuild your binder and get back to annoying your clients with follow-up calls? In IT, that's how long your systems can stay down before the business starts bleeding money.

- **RPO (Recovery Point Objective):** How much data can you afford to lose? If you make copies every Sunday and your dog strikes on Saturday, you just lost a week's worth of new contacts. That's your RPO.

From here, the backup world branches into multiple species:

- **Snapshots:** Freezing data at a specific moment — like making a quick photocopy. The data must remain in *exactly the same format*; it's that Sunday xerox of your binder. Fast and convenient, but they eat storage like there's no tomorrow.

- **Full Backups:** Copying *everything* (sometimes in a different format). Think transcribing all those cards into a spreadsheet. You can think of it as a snapshot, but one that allows you to change how data is stored during copying — easier to compress and archive, but slower to create.

- **Incremental Backups:** Recording only changes — every new or modified card gets logged. It's like making a copy of each new card as you add it... and if you remove a contact, that deletion has to be recorded too! Sounds smart, but you're building a chain — lose one link, and the whole restoration crumbles. Rebuilding means walking that chain link by link. Great for RPO, terrible for RTO.

- **Differential Backups:** A middle ground. Copy all new cards since the last full backup. Quicker than a full copy, heavier than incremental — like adding one more page of "new arrivals" each week.

Of course, both incremental and differential backups still depend on having a solid starting point — usually a full backup. Otherwise, notes like "I deleted Bob's card" are pretty useless without knowing who Bob was in the first place.

Now, choosing what to back up and how often is only half the battle. You also need to decide *where* to put it — and this is where things get interesting, expensive, or both.

- **Block Storage:** A bare, unformatted hard drive—pure chaos. Numbered containers of bytes with no labels, no folders, no meaning. The disk just says: "Here's block #4F2A. You figure out what's inside and how it connects to the next one." Lightning-fast, but completely useless on its own—you can't actually use it without a filesystem to organize the chaos.

- **File Storage:** Block Storage with an operating system. A filesystem (ext4, NTFS, FAT, whatever) sits on top of one or more raw disks and turns numbered blocks into `vacation_photos/2023/july.jpg`. One filesystem can span multiple disks, making them look like a single logical drive. Add network protocols (NFS, SMB) and you get a NAS (Network Attached Storage)—shared folders across the network. Convenient for humans, expensive and slow at massive scale. Perfect for teams sharing documents; awful for petabytes.

- **Object Storage:** Think AWS S3 or similar services. Cheap, redundant, and ideal for entire files or big blobs of data. But if you just want to edit a single sentence, tough luck — you'll need to replace the whole file. It's like rewriting a novel because you misspelled one word. Your English teacher would approve; your CFO, not so much.

- **The "Medium of Last Resort" (Tape):** While the above usually live on hard drives or SSDs, **Tape** is a physical medium that is still alive and kicking in 2025. It's the cheapest way to hoard data, but restoring from it requires a robot arm (or an intern) to physically fetch a cartridge. Think of it as "cold storage"—perfect for data you hope to never see again.

Oh, and since I mentioned *cold storage* — yes, that's an actual term. IT folks love talking about the "temperature" of backups. The easier it is to reach your data, the "hotter" (and pricier) the storage. A *hot backup* sits close at hand, spinning away on fast disks, ready for instant recovery. A *warm backup* might take a few minutes or hours to activate.

And a *cold backup*? That's the one you need to fetch from the basement, dust off, and hope it still speaks your current file format. In other words, the colder it gets, the cheaper it is — but don't expect any warmth when you're in a hurry.

But backups aren't just about the 'what' and 'where'— they're about the 'forever' and the 'oh shit' moments too. **Archives** are the attic box — indefinite retention, no guarantee you'll ever get it all back in one piece. It's the digital version of that box of cables you keep in the attic — all "just in case," yet every time you need one, it's faster to buy a new cable from Amazon than to dig through the mess. **Disaster Recovery (DR)**, on the other hand, is the fire drill: not the copies themselves, but the rehearsed plan to rebuild when the binder (and maybe the house) burns down.

If your head's spinning, good — that means you're getting it. The art of backup design is really the art of compromise. You trade time, space, and sanity to decide what's worth saving and how fast you'll regret not saving it. Because, let's be honest: not every piece of data is created equal.

You'll invest a lot more in preserving your wealthy uncle's will than in last week's to-do list. The same logic applies to your digital life: your wedding photos or the first steps of your child deserve far more protection than the snapshot of last Saturday's dinner. Unless you're a food influencer — in which case, I won't judge... but I also won't pretend to understand.

——— NASA Curiosity Rover Storage Leak ———

Date: 2013–2014

Impact: Flash storage exhaustion causing safe-mode loops, multi-day science downtime, and forced failover to the backup flight computer.

Root Cause: Orphaned temporary files left in non-volatile flash; file-handling subsystem failed to clean up working data; no automated housekeeping in the embedded OS.

Before we descend into earthly tales of vanished snapshots and ill-fated `rm -rf` moments, let's start somewhere a little more dramatic. Redundancy — the kind we'll spend a good chunk of the next part dissecting without mercy — is not a luxury in space. It's not a design choice, a budgeting argument, or an item in a quarterly roadmap. Out there, redundancy is survival. It's the only reason anything keeps working when no technician can quietly sneak in at 2 AM with a flashlight and a USB stick.

That's why Curiosity landed on Mars in 2012 with two nearly identical flight computers, Side A and Side B. Not because NASA likes symmetry, but because when your robot coworker lives 225 million kilometers away, "single point of failure" stops being a warning and becomes a death sentence. For the first year, everything behaved beautifully. The rover drilled rocks, shot lasers at things that couldn't file complaints, and sent home postcards like the world's most overachieving tourist.

Then something quietly unsettling started happening: Curiosity's flash storage began filling itself to death.

Not because of cosmic rays or aging hardware, but because the rover's file-handling subsystem did something embarrassingly human — it created temporary files and then forgot to delete them. Image buffers, telemetry fragments, instrument logs... all piling up in the rover's tiny, radiation-hardened flash storage. No garbage collector, no housekeeping routines, just orphaned files accumulating like digital dust bunnies under a Martian sofa.

Curiosity's flash memory isn't large. A couple of gigabytes — generous for a spacecraft, trivial for a phone. Every forgotten megabyte mattered. As storage filled, Side A began slipping into safe mode: the rover's equivalent of a panic attack. It shut down instruments, stopped science operations, and waited for Earth to explain why its internal closets were overflowing. Each safe-mode episode meant several days of lost research. And unlike your laptop, no one could walk over and hold the power button until the problem went away.

Telemetry confirmed the culprit, and simulations on the Earth-based testbed reproduced the behavior exactly: temporary files left behind by imaging and processing routines were choking the filesystem. Engineers prepared the only viable plan — fail over to the unused backup computer, Side B, reformat Side A, patch the cleanup routines, and try again.

In early April 2014, Side B took over flawlessly. Side A was scrubbed, fixed, and eventually restored to service. No science data was lost. The mission continued. Redundancy had done exactly what redundancy is supposed to do: catch the failure no one could afford to experience twice.

It's a perfectly simple story, and a perfectly embarrassing one: even a billion-dollar, radiation-hardened interplanetary laboratory can faceplant because it forgot to clean up its temporary files. And it belongs here — at the start of a chapter about backups, failovers, persistence, and the eternal struggle to keep data both available and alive — because it reminds us of the most universal truth in computing:

It doesn't matter if your system is running in a cloud, a basement rack, or on Mars.

If you don't take care of your storage, sooner or later it will take care of you.

LESSON LEARNED

- In space, every byte is forever—there's no cloud, no recycle bin.
- Test long-running file operations under real-world stress (radiation included).
- Redundancy matters—Side B was the real MVP.
- Even high-stakes, radiation-hardened robots can trip over leftover temp files.

Some failures feel tragic. This one feels like the universe reminding us that even on Mars, you still have to empty the trash.

GitLab Database Incident
`rm -rf` And Five Useless Backups

Date: January 31, 2017

Impact: 300 GB of live production data deleted; multiple backup systems failed; several hours of downtime.

Root Cause: Human error – accidental deletion of the primary PostgreSQL database using a destructive command.

GitLab — an alternative to GitHub for hosting Git repositories (see Chapter 16 for context) — has always been proud of its transparency. Which, as it turns out, made its most infamous disaster one of the best-documented in tech history.

It's late evening on January 31, 2017. Production feels sluggish, replication lag is building up, and an engineer decides to step in and "clean things up." He logs into what he *thinks* is a secondary database server and spots a stale directory that seems safe to delete.

So, he runs a familiar command: `rm -rf`

If you've ever seen hacker movies where someone types furiously and screens fill with scrolling code — yes, people really do use it, though it looks far less glamorous in real life. It's used to delete files or directories from the command line. Everything after the dash (–) are *flags*, which modify how the command behaves:

- r stands for *recursive* — it tells the system to delete not just the folder, but *everything inside it* (see Chapter 17 for more on recursion).

- f stands for *force* — basically, "I know what I'm doing, don't ask me to confirm."

Put together, `rm -rf` is the digital equivalent of striking a match. Normally, that's fine — maybe you just want to light a candle or, if you must, a cigarette. The problem comes when you do it while refueling your car. One typo in the path and the whole thing goes up in flames faster than you can say 'oops.' And honestly? I don't know a single engineer who hasn't done it at least once — though most will deny it if you ask.

This time, it wasn't a harmless mistake. The command was run on the wrong directory. On the wrong server. And not just *any* server — the **primary production PostgreSQL instance.**

In an instant, roughly **300 GB of live production data** was gone. Their RPO ballooned from hours to days; their RTO became a sleepless marathon.

But GitLab had five backup mechanisms. What could go wrong?

Turns out, everything:

- One was failing silently.

- Another hadn't run in six days.

- One was misconfigured.

- Another was corrupted.

- And the last one? Writing to the same disk that had just been erased.

No functioning backup. No easy rollback. It was probably one of those moments when someone discovered the third group of people mentioned in the chapter intro — the ones who actually test their backups.

The recovery effort was a mix of heroism, improvisation, and public therapy. Engineers worked through the night, piecing data together from a replica and whatever transaction logs survived. True to its values, GitLab live-streamed the process, allowing thousands of viewers to watch in solidarity (and mild horror). It was painful, chaotic, and — in its own way — beautiful.

> **LESSON LEARNED**
>
> - `rm -rf` has no "Are you sure?" in production. Before you ever press Enter on a command like this, ask a teammate to double-check your target path. Or use extra safety nets like `--dry-run` flags, `trash-cli`, or `rm` aliases with confirmation.
> - Backups that don't restore are just expensive placebo.
> - Redundancy means nothing if all your eggs live in identically broken baskets.
> - Always verify your safety nets before you need them — a five-minute restore test beats hours of frantic recovery and days spent writing the postmortem.

GitLab 2017: `rm -rf` 1, Five Backup Systems 0.

Toy Story 2
`rm -rf` Almost Deleted Pixar's Future

Date: 1998

Impact: 90% of Toy Story 2 production files deleted; project nearly lost; film release delayed by nine months and crew faced 100-hour workweeks.

Root Cause: Accidental execution of destructive delete command on the main production system.

At some point during the production of *Toy Story 2*, someone at Pixar ran a command that should never, ever be executed near valuable data: `rm -rf /`

You already know what `rm -rf` does — but that innocent-looking / at the end deserves its own moment of fame. In UNIX-like systems (which covers basically everything except Windows), / means "everything this computer can see." Not just one folder or one drive — *every single thing*, across all connected storage. Running `rm -rf /` isn't just lighting a match near the gas pump; it's more like setting off a barrel of dynamite in the middle of a refinery.

Within seconds, **90% of the movie's production files vanished** — models, animations, textures, renders, everything. One mistyped command, no directory scope, and Pixar's biggest sequel-in-progress was gone.

Had those files been truly lost, Pixar's future could have been in serious trouble. The company wasn't on the brink of bankruptcy, but the additional costs, production delays, and reputational hit could have led to mergers, acquisitions, or worse — though that's speculative. What's certain is that the studio came terrifyingly close to a catastrophe that might have reshaped its history.

But surely there were backups, right?

Well... sort of. Pixar's automated backups had quietly stopped working months earlier because the central backup server had been unplugged for 'maintenance' — and then forgotten. Nobody noticed. The realization triggered instant panic, shouting, and the kind of existential dread usually reserved for philosophy majors. This wasn't just lost work — it was years of creative effort evaporating before their eyes.

Enter Galyn Susman, the film's technical director. She happened to be working from home to care for her newborn child — and, crucially, she had a personal copy of the film's working files on her home computer. Technically, that local copy went against company policy for production data, but an exception had been made due to her maternity leave. Luckily for Pixar, that small breach of protocol became their salvation.

Her home system was physically carried into Pixar's offices in her private Volvo — instantly making it the most valuable Swedish car in history, worth nearly $100 million in recovered assets. The team then spent days rebuilding from that accidental, life-saving backup. The recovery pushed the film's release back by nine months and led to countless 100-hour workweeks for the exhausted crew.

LESSON LEARNED

- `rm -rf /` is the most expensive typo in Unix history. There's a reason this command appears twice in one chapter. That should tell you something.
- Backups that no one checks might as well not exist.
- The best disaster recovery plan is sometimes the one that wasn't officially approved.

Toy Story 2: saved by maternity leave, a Volvo station wagon, and corporate policy exceptions.

HP/HPE vs Academia
Drama In Two Acts

In November 2015, Hewlett-Packard split into two companies: HP Inc. (handling PCs and printers) and Hewlett Packard Enterprise (HPE), responsible for servers and enterprise infrastructure. At King's College London, the system was still branded HP; by the time Kyoto's supercomputer met its fate, HPE had fully inherited the throne — and the responsibility.

Note: You already know what availability and durability mean. What remains is the magical incantation known as "five nines of availability." We'll explain it properly in the next part, alongside SLAs and disaster recovery. For now, just know it describes a level of perfection that reliably triggers *nerdgasms* among system administrators.

Act I – King's College London:
The Patch That Never Was

Date: October 17, 2016

Impact: Terabytes of research and administrative data lost; weeks of downtime; partial recovery with permanent data gaps.

Root Cause: Unpatched HP 3PAR controller firmware failed after hardware replacement, crashing the entire storage array.

The HP 3PAR StoreServ system came with glossy brochures full of promises — near-perfect availability (five nines!), bulletproof durability, and enterprise-grade reliability. King's College London believed those claims — it turns out, "enterprise-grade reliability" mostly meant "reliable until you touch it."

It started as a perfectly ordinary Monday at the Strand Data Centre. A failed storage controller needed replacement — standard maintenance procedure. But the replacement controller wasn't running the same firmware as the rest of the array, and a patch to fix that mismatch had been available for weeks. It just hadn't been applied. Once the new controller came online, the unpatched logic promptly lost its mind. The array collapsed, drives went dark, and twenty years of irreplaceable research fell into digital purgatory.

The IT team soon realized the disaster was much larger than a bad patch day. HP 3PAR's own marketing promised both high availability and near-perfect durability —

features meant to ensure this *couldn't* happen. Yet one missed patch and a single failed controller managed to sink the entire setup. As if that weren't enough, the backups joined the mutiny. NetBackup tapes were outdated, Veeam snapshots hadn't been verified in months, and some researchers had been keeping their only copies of data on shared drives that weren't backed up at all — cold tapes, warm snapshots, both failed when it mattered. The result was chaos: days of finger-pointing, weeks of reconstruction, and multiple research groups realizing they'd lost years of work forever.

One internal review dryly described the event as "a cascading failure of confidence, competence, and communication." In other words: everything that could go wrong, did — and then a few things that shouldn't have.

LESSON

Patching feels like paperwork until your "high-availability" system becomes a highly-unavailable one. And never assume a glossy SLA means you can skip the boring parts.

Act II – Kyoto University:
When The Patch Became The Problem

Date: December 14–16, 2021

Impact: 77 TB of data deleted (28 TB unrecoverable) from 14 research groups; supercomputer operations halted.

Root Cause: Faulty HPE backup script update caused mass file deletion during log cleanup.

Five years later and half a world away, Kyoto University provided a grim counterpoint to King's story: what happens when you *do* apply the patch — without testing.

During a routine maintenance update, HPE pushed a modified backup script to Kyoto's Cray XC40/CS400 supercomputer cluster. The intention? Simple housekeeping — delete a few old log files. The outcome? A system meltdown so spectacular it could have been directed by Michael Bay.

Inside the script lurked a small but catastrophic bug. It overwrote a running process, left key variables undefined, and in a perfect storm of Bash logic, it transformed `rm -rf $LOGDIR/*` into the infamous `rm -rf /` due to an empty variable, proceeding to delete *live* user files instead of logs. Thirty-four million files disappeared in hours. Seventy-seven terabytes of research data evaporated; twenty-eight of them gone forever. Entire research projects — from quantum chemistry to immunotherapy simulations — were wiped out because of one line in a shell script.

Unlike KCL, the culprit here wasn't neglect but misplaced trust — apparently "tested in production" was part of the premium package. The update came straight from HPE, a major vendor, and went live without staging or verification. Within days, operations froze, researchers scrambled for fragments of their lost data, and HPE issued a rare public apology, taking full responsibility. Kyoto's high-performance computing division rebuilt systems piece by piece, but the lost data never returned.

LESSON

Not every patch makes things better. Sometimes the cure wipes out the patient. Always test your fixes before trusting them.

HP/HPE: Damned if you skip the patch (KCL), damned if you apply it blindly (Kyoto).

LESSON LEARNED

- Firmware patches are not optional — they are seatbelts for your data.
- Vendor updates deserve the same suspicion you reserve for forwarded emails promising free iPhones.
- Backups are only as good as your last restore test.
- Even "five nines" of reliability won't save you from one well-placed human error.
- Whether you skip the patch or deploy it sight unseen — either extreme will get you burned.

Disclaimer: This story isn't meant to mock a specific company. It's a reminder that failure thrives on both extremes: negligence and overconfidence. Ignoring updates invites chaos, but rolling them out without testing isn't resilience — it's roulette with enterprise data.

————————— **From My Own Burn File** —————————
The Snapshot That Saved My Ass (~2018)

Sometimes it's good to take a breather from other people's disasters and confess to one of your own. Consider this a palate cleanser — with a faint smell of smoke.

It was sometime in the fall of 2018, if memory serves. My team was handling a particularly gnarly upgrade for a client we had just inherited. As usual with handovers, the documentation was thin, the processes creative, and the infrastructure a museum of bad decisions — or at least that's how it usually looks from a successor's perspective. In reality, there's usually a reason behind every choice: a deadline, a crisis, or the allure of some shiny new technology that promises to solve all problems, cure world hunger, and maybe even discover the secret to immortality... until its creator gets bored and moves on.

In any case though, we had to work with what we had so releasing a new version required a sequence of manual steps so delicate it felt like walking a tightrope... in high heels.

The deployment day began early. Following the plan, we shut down the client's website, replaced it with everyone's favorite *"scheduled maintenance"* page, and got to work.

When we were about to upgrade the main database, I decided to take a quick snapshot — just in case. It took about an hour and a half, during which my CTO began questioning whether we were wasting time. I insisted it was worth it.

A few hours later, deep into the upgrade, I noticed that one of the update procedures didn't work properly on the test environment. I figured I'd drop the test database and re-run it cleanly. Simple enough.

CTO: "Wait, are you sure you're dropping the right database?"

Me: "Of course I am, sss... SHIT!"

Let's just say my confidence turned out to be about as trustworthy as a politician's campaign promise. I had just nuked the production database — the client's actual data — with surgical precision.

Me: "See? I told you we needed that backup!"

We restored the snapshot, completed the upgrade, and lost about four hours in total — but zero client data. My screw-up cost us an afternoon instead of a catastrophe.

I'm not telling this story to brag. The point is simple: mistakes happen. Experienced engineers don't mess up less often — they just plan for it better. They know that one day, something *will* go wrong... and they make sure it's survivable.

LESSON LEARNED

- Ninety minutes is a small price to pay for insurance.
- Before touching any production system, always assume something will go wrong — because one day, it will.
- Test your restores – a dry-run beats a live panic.

T-Mobile Sidekick Outage
When the Cloud Forgot Backups

Date: October 2–12, 2009

Impact: Around 800,000 U.S. users lost contacts, calendars, photos, and messages

Root Cause: Botched SAN (Storage Area Network) upgrade by Hitachi for Microsoft's Danger subsidiary; both primary and backup data stores corrupted.

The cloud didn't appear overnight. Amazon, the first real cloud pioneer, began slowly: in July 2004 it launched SQS (will cover queues in chapter 17), followed by S3 in March 2006 (also a key player in that same chapter). By 2009, Amazon offered around 15 cloud services; for comparison, by 2025 that number has exploded to roughly 350. Not bad for a company that originally monetized unused computing capacity from its e-commerce business.

The years 2008–2009 marked a strange adolescence for this technology. People had finally realized the cloud was more than a passing fad — though not yet the unstoppable force it is today.

Enter the **T-Mobile Sidekick**, a line of "business phones" from the pre-iPhone era. Imagine a chunky, slide-out keyboard device that lets you send emails, browse the web, and chat on AOL, MSN, or Yahoo Messenger — the ancestors of WhatsApp, Telegram, and Discord. In short: everything a modern smartphone does, minus Netflix, TikTok, and the countless apps whose main feature is showing you ads. Back then, the Sidekick felt like a Tesla parked next to a 1998 Toyota Corolla.

Its defining feature was something truly futuristic: **online synchronization**. Every message, contact, and calendar entry was mirrored on Microsoft's servers through its Danger subsidiary — a company that built a dedicated mobile OS so obscure that today only IT archaeologists (myself included) remember it existed. Users didn't call it "the cloud" yet — but that's exactly what it was. Your phone could be lost, dropped in a puddle, or run over by a bus, and your data would still be safe "up there." At least, that was the theory.

Then October 2, 2009 happened.

During what was supposed to be a simple infrastructure upgrade, a contractor at Hitachi performed maintenance on Danger's **Storage Area Network (SAN)** — a system based on block storage that synchronizes hundreds of disks. If that sounds complex, it is. Think of the earlier unicycle metaphor: juggling knives while riding one. Now imagine that instead of a single juggler, it's an entire small town tossing those knives between them. When it's done right, it's beautiful. When it goes wrong... well, you get the Sidekick outage.

The upgrade corrupted the main database. Worse: in an act of perfect symmetry, it corrupted the backups too. Primary and secondary, both toast — a synchronized catastrophe worthy of an Olympic diving team. Same location, same logic, same fate.

When users woke up the next morning, their Sidekicks were eerily empty. No contacts, no notes, no messages. Because the devices themselves had almost no local storage, all their personal data was gone. Microsoft and T-Mobile initially assured users that service would return shortly — but as engineers sifted through corrupted logs and mangled files, it appeared there was nothing to restore. Roughly 28 terabytes worth of user data had evaporated.

T-Mobile suspended Sidekick sales and offered $100 credits and a month of free data as a peace offering — the digital equivalent of bringing chocolates to apologize for burning down someone's house. Microsoft's CEO Steve Ballmer — a man famous for yelling *"DEVELOPERS! DEVELOPERS! DEVELOPERS!"* at conferences — downplayed the catastrophe as an "outage," but for 800,000 customers who lost years of memories, it was more like a digital lobotomy.

Before we get to the aftermath, one clarification matters. In the early days of the crisis, both T-Mobile and Microsoft publicly stated that the data was likely gone forever. That messaging wasn't spin — engineers genuinely believed the SAN corruption had annihilated every recoverable copy. But after nearly a week of forensic work, Microsoft managed to recover most, if not all customer data. It didn't matter. The trust damage was done. Users behaved as if everything had vanished, switched devices, abandoned the platform, and the Sidekick brand never recovered from those first catastrophic days.

The event became one of the first high-profile demonstrations that "cloud" did not mean "invincible." Lawsuits followed, user trust evaporated, and the Sidekick line quietly died. Ironically, the device designed to showcase the power of online syncing ended up as a cautionary tale for why cloud reliability and durability are not the same thing.

LESSON LEARNED

- Cloud synchronization is convenient, but it's not the same as having an independent backup.
- Redundancy means nothing if all your copies share the same fate.
- A disaster recovery plan isn't truly a plan until it's been tested.

When the T-Mobile Sidekick launched, no one expected that its software maker's name — "Danger" — would turn out to be the most accurate description of their data strategy.

PART III: SUMMARY
WHEN DATA FIGHTS BACK

Digital systems like to pretend they're permanent. Marketing decks tell us that data is "forever," that the cloud is "reliable," and that once something becomes a row in a database it has achieved immortality. This part of the book should have thoroughly cured you of that illusion.

Across these chapters, we've watched data die in every way imaginable — quietly, suddenly, stupidly, predictably — and all for variations of the same underlying theme: its fragility is a human invention. Sometimes it decayed in place, sitting on disks that forgot their contents or in databases that corrupted themselves out of boredom. Sometimes it vanished because backups were missing, mislabeled, or sacrificed on the altar of cost-cutting. But the deeper truth revealed across this entire part is simpler and more painful:

Data is fragile not because of technology, but because of humans.

Humans who assume instead of checking, optimise costs over preservation, rush deadlines, skip validation, delete the backup folder because it's "too big," or believe a system built on tangled interdependencies will obediently survive being unplugged and dropped into a new environment.

We saw systems lose track of their own identities — IDs drifting apart, relationships collapsing, references dissolving. We watched encodings betray entire alphabets. We saw migrations fail not because petabytes were too heavy to lift but because someone forgot that text has rules, schemas have meaning, and files don't magically realign themselves when dropped into a new home.

And then there were the non-technical failures: the places where corporate strategy did more damage than any corrupted sector. Systems "optimised" into oblivion. Archives trimmed. Services shut down. Cultural memory treated as a rounding error on a balance sheet. The kind of digital amnesia that doesn't happen by accident — but conveniently looks like it did.

If the early chapters showed how data can rot in storage, and the later ones showed how it can evaporate during movement, the theme that unifies this entire part is the same one that unifies most of engineering:

Everything works... until someone touches it.

Data doesn't want to move or change shape. Every transformation — whether migrating, re-encoding, merging, splitting, translating, or reconciling — is an invitation for entropy to sit at the table and ask, "What happens if I flip *this* bit?" Unless we check, validate, rehearse, test, simulate, and monitor, the answer is usually some flavor of failure: sometimes small, sometimes catastrophic, occasionally irreversible.

The systems we build are only as reliable as the people who design, maintain, and migrate them — and people, as the evidence shows, are not a reliable storage medium.

So as we leave this part behind and turn toward the next, keep one thought close:

Data is only as durable as the discipline around it. And discipline, unlike disks or databases, cannot be provisioned on demand.

We've now wrapped up the fundamentals: how computers **think** (compute), how they **talk** to each other (networking), and how they **remember** (storage — or fail to). In the next part, we'll turn to a topic that humanity consistently overestimates: **security**, and our touching, almost childlike faith that the things we build are safe simply because we'd prefer them to be.

IV. THE ILLUSION OF SAFETY

PART IV:
THE ILLUSION OF SAFETY
— WHEN CLOUDS BITE BACK

Up to this point, we've explored how the digital world stands on fragile foundations — code, protocols, and timing mechanisms that can bring half the Internet to its knees when they misfire. But there's another kind of fragility: the one we build ourselves. The next chapters move from the giants' mistakes to our own — the flawed ways we use, extend, and overtrust the systems they've given us. This is the realm of misplaced confidence, where convenience breeds carelessness and automation lulls us into a false sense of control.

Across this part, we'll explore three main flavors of self-inflicted chaos. First, **data safety in the cloud**, where engineers misread shared responsibility and accidentally gift-wrap their data for the public. Then, **cost illusions**, where the same scalability that makes the cloud powerful also multiplies bills faster than common sense. Finally, **security tools** — the guardians that occasionally turn on their masters, when hubris and overlooked toggles transform protection into a weapon.

Together, these chapters form a field guide to modern overconfidence. They remind us that while the cloud may float above us, its mistakes still land squarely on our heads.

In short: if Part II showed how the Internet's plumbing can burst, Part III is about the leaks we drill into the pipes ourselves — sometimes with the best of intentions.

A NOTE ON PERSPECTIVE

Before we get to the first explainer, a quick note on perspective. In this part of the book, I'll occasionally use the form "we can." It's deliberate. We're entering territory that's open to nearly everyone — the world of cloud tools you can spin up with nothing more than a credit card, just like subscribing to Netflix or ordering coffee beans online. Sure, it takes a bit more technical knowledge, and as you'll see, the consequences can be far nastier than running out of shelf space for unwanted beans or paying for a forgotten subscription. Still, they're just as easy to reach. So when I say we can, it's because we really can — and sometimes, that's the problem.

For the same reason, some of the stories in this part may seem smaller in scale. These aren't world- stopping outages — but for those involved, they hit just as hard.

In a few of the smaller cases, I'll also skip the exact company or organization name. Don't worry — the online bibliography will include all the relevant references for those curious enough to dig deeper.

Explainer:
The Shared Responsibility Model

Before diving into the case studies, we need to pause for a short reality check. Every story in this part—whether about leaking data, runaway bills, or overzealous security software—stems from the same misunderstanding: who's actually responsible for what. The term *Shared Responsibility Model* may sound like compliance jargon, but it's the backbone of how modern cloud computing distributes risk. It defines where the provider's duties stop and where yours begin—across safety, cost, and security tools alike. Get that line wrong, and everything built on top starts to wobble.

Imagine the cloud as a car. The manufacturer promises that the brakes stop you, the airbags deploy when they should instead of when they feel like it, and the steering wheel connects to the wheels, not the radio. That's **safety of the car** — the vendor's responsibility.

But if you drive that same car full speed into a wall and call it a stress test, that's **safety in the car** — your problem entirely.

In general, we can trust that car manufacturers do their job properly — at least well enough that most of us don't feel the need to recheck the bolts before every trip. Still, as we'll learn much later in Volume 4 on corporate hubris, that faith isn't always rewarded.

The same principle applies to digital infrastructure. Cloud platforms follow the same logic: providers handle the **security of the cloud** — the physical infrastructure, the hardware, and the core services. Everything above that layer — access permissions, data handling, encryption, configurations — falls under **security in the cloud**.

It's a deceptively simple idea that fails in predictably creative ways. Users overestimate what's "covered," misread the fine print, or assume that a checkbox labeled "secure by default" actually means what it says. The result: public data, overprivileged roles, and data that was never supposed to see daylight.

CHAPTER 16:
WHEN STORAGE BECOMES BILLBOARDS

We love the cloud because it promises simplicity, scale, and safety — a digital autopilot that never sleeps. Yet that promise hides a trap. When everything feels taken care of, it's easy to forget where the line of responsibility actually lies. Most breaches in the cloud don't come from hackers breaking in; they come from engineers accidentally leaving the door open and wondering later why the neighbors moved in.

In the next pages, we'll see how a single checkbox can turn a fortress into a free-for-all. When safes meant for confidential data morph into public book-exchange clubs, the illusion of safety becomes worse than no security at all — at least then you'd know the door was open.

Case Set: When Data Is Left in Public

In 2017, a cybersecurity consultant was Googling for exposed AWS buckets as part of a security audit. Within minutes, he found Accenture's internal credentials sitting in public storage. Accenture is a $50 billion company that literally sells cybersecurity services to governments. Their most sensitive internal data was accessible to anyone with a search query and fifteen seconds of patience.

But let's take a step back.

One of the most basic services offered by every major cloud provider is file storage. As we'll already saw back in Chapter 15, these services proudly advertise their *infinite capacity*. Of course, that claim is an oversimplification—but a useful one. The reality is that these companies have enough storage to make sure their customers never hit a hard limit. And if anyone ever tries to challenge that promise, the sheer scale (and budget) of these providers guarantees that the challenger will go bankrupt long before the clouds run out of disks.

At their core, these object storage systems are simple: you upload a file, and the cloud keeps it for you. Files are stored inside so-called *buckets*, and each file becomes an *object*. You can think of buckets as individual drives, and objects as the files sitting on them. Yes, engineers could've just called them that—but apparently there's a professional fetish for inventing new names every five minutes. And while there are subtle architectural differences between these concepts, none of them matter here: the problem isn't terminology—it's the open doors.

These services also offer a variety of advanced features — from controlling who can see what, to keeping old versions of files, even hosting full websites directly from storage. Useful? Absolutely. Instantly intuitive? Not really.

For now, let's focus on the simplest expectation: that the data you store remains private.

That, unfortunately, is where things start to fall apart. Because again and again, companies forget to properly secure their buckets. The result? Publicly exposed customer data, internal credentials, and proprietary documents—left wide open for anyone with a browser or a bit of curiosity.

Rather than dissecting each incident separately, let's look at several of the most famous examples together.

Verizon

Date: 2017

Cloud Provider: AWS (Amazon Web Services)

Impact: Personal data of millions of customers exposed, including names, phone numbers, and account PINs (Verizon claimed 6 million; researchers estimated up to 14 million).

Background: A third-party vendor managing customer support left a massive S3 backup publicly accessible. The configuration allowed anyone with the URL to download entire datasets—no authentication required.

Accenture

Date: 2017

Cloud Provider: AWS (Amazon Web Services)

Impact: Internal credentials, private keys, and system logs exposed across four unsecured AWS S3 buckets.

Background: The consulting giant stored sensitive infrastructure data in S3 without proper access controls. Anyone with the link could access credentials capable of reconstructing parts of Accenture's internal network. In other words: a global cybersecurity contractor left the keys to its own kingdom under the doormat.

———— BlueBleed (Microsoft) ————

Date: 2022

Cloud Provider: Microsoft Azure

Impact: 2.4 TB of customer information exposed, affecting more than 65,000 companies worldwide.

Background: A Microsoft endpoint associated with internal support systems was left publicly accessible via Azure Blob Storage. Ironically, the company leaked its own clients' data while using its own cloud service—proving once and for all that dogfooding can occasionally turn into self-cannibalism.

———— Alice's Table ————

Date: 2024

Cloud Provider: Google Cloud Platform (GCP)

Impact: 37,349 files containing the personal data of roughly 83,000 customers exposed.

Background: The Boston-based event-florist startup, known from *Shark Tank*, left a Google Cloud Storage bucket publicly open. The exposed files included invoices, event details, and customer communications. It turns out that "blooming business" wasn't meant to describe their data exposure. This case also proves the problem isn't limited to tech giants—small startups stumble on the same misconfiguration traps.

What these cases show is that the problem isn't the provider—it's how the service is used. AWS, Azure, GCP—all of them provide mechanisms to keep your data private. The leaks happen because someone, somewhere, forgets to flip the switch from "public" to "private," or assumes that obscurity is a form of security. It isn't.

It's worth noting that AWS named its storage service **S3**, short for *Simple Storage Service*. A cute name, implying ease and elegance. But given how many headlines it's responsible for, perhaps they should rename it **S4: Sometimes Secure, Sometimes Screwed**. Because clearly, "simple" is not how this story plays out.

Think of this as the digital equivalent of leaving your office lights on overnight with the door wide open. Most of the time, no one walks in. But when they do, the results tend to make headlines—and occasionally careers in cybersecurity.

The issue became so common that an entire ecosystem grew around it. Security researchers (and less ethical actors) started using *Google Dorks*—special search queries that dig through indexed results to find exposed storage, log files, and credentials. Entire websites now catalog these queries, turning the Internet itself into a scavenger hunt for forgotten data.

LESSON LEARNED

- Object storage is simple, but access control isn't.
- Trusting obscurity is not security.
- The provider isn't the problem—human configuration is.
- If your data can be found through a Google search, it's not a vulnerability scan—it's an open invitation.
- "Simple" services rarely are. Especially when humans are involved.

If you think this risk spares even the most secure or classified sectors—well, I have bad news for you.

—— Bonus Case: U.S Defense Contractor ——

Date of Discovery: September 6, 2017

Cloud Provider: AWS (Amazon Web Services)

Impact: Roughly 1.8 billion social media posts scraped from 2009–2017, collected from platforms, forums, and comment sections across multiple languages and regions, including Arabic, Farsi, and Central/South Asian dialects.

Background: An unnamed U.S. defense contractor (referred to as 'VendorX' in the exposed data) was quietly building a portrait of the Internet. They had scraped nearly two billion public posts—names, locations, political views, relationship networks—and indexed them into a searchable intelligence database. The kind of tool used to track extremists, identify influencers, or map the social fabric of entire regions.

Then they put it in an Amazon S3 bucket. And forgot to lock the door.

No authentication. No password. Just a URL. Anyone who found it could download the whole thing—400 gigabytes of surveillance-grade intelligence, compiled from public data but suddenly very, very public itself.

The irony was exquisite: a tool designed to monitor the world accidentally broadcast itself *to* the world. It wasn't classified information, the contractor later argued.

Sure. Not *classified*, merely *CIA-ready* surveillance data now free for anyone with decent Wi-Fi. *Oopsies*.

Capital One
The Bank That Outsourced Its Locks

Date: July 2019

Impact: ~100 million customer records exposed — names, addresses, SSNs, credit card numbers, and loan applications.

Root Cause: A Server-Side Request Forgery (SSRF) exploited through a misconfigured web firewall, leaking credentials with full access to customer data.

In 2019, Paige Thompson, a former engineer at Amazon, showed the world just how fragile cloud security can be when people trust the wrong part of the system. She found a hole in Capital One's online defenses — specifically in its Web Application Firewall, or WAF. If you remember from the Cloudflare case in Part II, a WAF acts like airport security for websites: not only checking luggage tags but also opening each suitcase to look for suspicious items. Capital One's version of this guard was a little too trusting — more like a bouncer who lets anyone in as long as they wave a note saying "VIP." It let Thompson send a crafted request that made the system ask internal services for secrets on her behalf.

Explainer:
SSRF, Or How To Trick A Librarian Into Betraying Their Own Library

Let's bring back our favorite trio: Alice, Bob, and Eve.

Eve, our ever-curious eavesdropper, wants access to Bob's secret room full of priceless manuscripts. Bob is a well-meaning librarian who carefully guards that room and only opens it when a trusted assistant brings him the right key. The assistant, loyal and efficient, never questions Bob's requests.

Now Eve sends Bob a cleverly forged letter that looks like a normal note from Alice — a visiting scholar — but secretly says: *"Hey Bob, please ask your assistant for that key and send it to me."* Bob, polite and a bit naive, complies. The assistant sees Bob's familiar handwriting, hands over the key, and Eve walks straight into the vault.

That's SSRF in a nutshell: tricking a trusted system into doing the dirty work for you.

Back to the cloud, Thompson's forged "letter" was a crafted web request that convinced Capital One's firewall to fetch and forward sensitive credentials. These were cloud access keys for an internal role — the digital equivalent of Bob's master key. And just like our librarian, the system handed them over without asking questions.

Identity and Access Management (IAM) — the cloud's central service that defines who can do what — was meant to limit those keys to what each role needed. But Capital One's configuration was far too generous.

In cloud security, this is the equivalent of giving your gardener a master key to the entire mansion because he occasionally needs the toolshed. It's convenient — until you find him in the wine cellar, drunk, while the dog's gone missing and someone's playing with the lawnmower in the hallway. To prevent that kind of chaos, you'd give each employee their own dedicated keys — only to the rooms they actually need to enter.

This approach is known as the *Principle of Least Privilege* — the simple idea that every account or system component should only have access to what it truly needs, and nothing more. Engineers have a well-known fetish for inventing names for plain common sense, but let's be honest — creativity has never been their strongest side.

With those credentials, Thompson could browse Capital One's storage like a well-stocked supermarket with no cashier in sight. She quietly copied data, stored it on her own server, and — in a twist that could only happen in the age of the internet — bragged about it on GitHub. Capital One didn't detect the breach through any internal monitoring; they found out because someone scrolling through GitHub noticed the post and reported it.

The aftermath was predictable: over 100 million records leaked, lawsuits, an $80 million fine from regulators, and a few billion memes about "cloud trust." AWS insisted the tools were safe; Capital One admitted the configuration wasn't. Everyone technically told the truth.

The irony? This was exactly the kind of incident cloud evangelists claimed could never happen. The shared responsibility model — the idea that the provider secures the infrastructure and the customer secures their use of it — became the punchline of every security talk for months. Shared responsibility, it turned out, often means shared regret.

The moral of the story? You don't give your gardener the master key to the mansion just because it's convenient. Least privilege isn't just a security mantra — it's common sense with better marketing.

And as for Paige? She didn't just exfiltrate the data — she posted about it on GitHub and Slack, where security researchers and Capital One's competitors could see it. Unlike the ethical disclosure process used by researchers in the previous cases, Thompson's approach was public, uncoordinated, and—prosecutors would later argue— boastful.

Thompson's defense? She claimed she was just doing security research and wanted public credit. The jury wasn't impressed.

Prosecutors demanded seven years; the court initially handed down time served plus five years' probation, but in March 2025, a federal appeals court tossed that as too lenient, sending it back for resentencing. As of October 2025, the new hearing looms, and Paige might finally get her day in a cell – or at least a stricter leash.

Capital One, meanwhile, had no idea the breach happened until an outsider pointed it out — proof that sometimes the internet knows about your security problems before you do.

LESSON LEARNED

- Least privilege is not optional — it's a must-have. If someone only needs the toolshed, don't hand them the wine cellar too.

- Never assume your WAF is infallible; sometimes the guard opens the door for the thief — as long as they flash a fake VIP note.

- IAM roles should be treated like spare keys — keep them few, specific, and never universal.

- Detection matters as much as prevention. Capital One had no internal alerting that someone was accessing millions of records. If you can't detect a breach, you can't respond—and the internet will respond for you.

- The cloud doesn't absolve you of mistakes; it just helps you make bigger ones faster.

Capital One gave its gardener the keys to the mansion — and then blamed the locksmith when the wine went missing

Explainer:
What The Hell Is GitHub?

I've mentioned GitHub and repositories a few times already, but never actually stopped to explain what the hell they are. Let's fix that before diving into the Uber mess.

Git is what's known as a *version control system.* There are others out there, but this one became the de facto standard of the software industry. Think of Git as a meticulous archivist who tracks every project along with its full history of changes — who edited what, when, and why. It's the core tool that lets programmers undo their late-night "brilliant" ideas or decipher what on earth they meant when they wrote a line of code a month earlier. In truth, Git can store almost any text-based content — including, say, early drafts of books. (Not that I'd know anything about that.)

And a *repository*? For once, engineers didn't invent a new name. They just borrowed an existing word — *repositoire* in French, *repositorium* in Latin — meaning a vessel, a storage place. In practice, a repository is a collection of files that belong together, like chapters of a book in separate documents or, in our case, chunks of code that make up a program.

GitHub, meanwhile, is the world's largest hosting platform for those repositories. It's estimated to hold over 420 million of them, with at least 28 million publicly accessible — the rest marked 'private,' visible only to authorized users. Which, as Uber would soon discover, is not the same as 'secure.'

Giants like Microsoft, Google, Facebook, Red Hat, and Amazon use it every day — as does the not-so-humble author of these words (on a slightly smaller scale).

Attentive readers might have noticed a small red flag in the phrase *"full history of changes."* Since Git keeps track of practically every modification ever made, anything you commit there tends to stick around. Sure, you can technically rewrite history or delete entire repositories, but it's neither simple nor foolproof. Which means GitHub is *not* a great place to store things that should remain confidential — like passwords, credit card numbers, or a diary full of unfiltered thoughts about your boss.

Uber

GitHub As A Bag Of Keys And A "Bug Bounty" For Silence

Date: October 2016

Impact: Data of 57 million users and drivers exposed — names, emails, phone numbers, and driver's license details.

Root Cause: AWS access key with full S3 permissions — over-privileged, no rotation, no expiration, no MFA — accidentally committed to a private GitHub repository.

In 2016, Uber learned the hard way that "private repository" doesn't mean "invisible." Hackers discovered an AWS access key inside a GitHub repo used by Uber's developers — a small oversight that turned into a massive breach. With that single key, the attackers gained full access to Uber's S3 Datastore and quietly downloaded the personal information of 57 million people. It was like leaving the company vault open with a sticky note saying "back in five."

How did the hackers find a key in a private repository? Uber had granted access to dozens of engineers and contractors. One of them — either malicious or careless —

appears to have been the leak vector. Or perhaps the repo was briefly public during development. The exact pathway remains murky, but the lesson is clear: "private" on GitHub means "private to everyone you've invited" — and invitation lists grow fast.

A quick sidebar here: *MFA*, or **Multi-Factor Authentication**, is the simple idea that logging into something should require more than just one thing you *know* (like a password). It should also involve something you *have* (like a phone or hardware token) or something you *are* (like a fingerprint). In Uber's case, none of that was in place — one static key unlocked everything. You didn't even need to pretend to be an engineer; just copy and paste the credentials and voilà, instant admin access.

The breach was a perfect example of *cross-dependency chaos*: GitHub, a platform for storing code, became the attack vector that led straight into Uber's cloud infrastructure. By hardcoding credentials in code, the team had what you might call an industry-grade safe — complete with a key dangling from a string tied to the wheel that opened it. Then they left the safe out on the front lawn for anyone to try. It was a comedy of errors that stopped being funny the moment regulators got involved.

Before we get to Uber's internal response, a quick digression on what a **bug bounty** actually is. In the IT world, it's a kind of open challenge — companies publicly declare, "Go ahead, try to hack us, we dare you," and promise a reward to anyone who finds a flaw responsibly. It's like a friendly wager with the entire internet: if you can break something, we'll pay you, but you must tell us how so we can fix it. The crucial part is that the bounty must be public, and the instructions or proof of concept must go *to the company*, not to Reddit.

Uber, of course, managed to misunderstand the assignment spectacularly. When hackers contacted them, the company decided to pay $100,000 under the guise of a *bug bounty reward* — with one small condition: keep quiet. This happened in late 2016. Uber kept the breach hidden for over a year, until November 2017, when *Bloomberg* broke the story and the cover-up collapsed. Essentially, Uber paid hush money for a hack and called it a feature. Somewhere, a PR person probably thought this counted as "community engagement."

When the truth surfaced a year later, it detonated with predictable force. Uber settled for $148 million with attorneys general from all 50 U.S. states and the District of Columbia for concealing the breach, alongside smaller fines from European regulators totaling around $1.7 million. The company's then-CEO, Travis Kalanick, stepped down, and the new leadership was left to mop up both the legal and reputational mess.

The irony? Uber's entire business model revolves around tracking people and their locations in real time. Yet it couldn't track where its own access keys were. The engineers who stored them on GitHub didn't just open the door for hackers — they built them a red carpet. It's as if the company famous for knowing exactly where every driver is had somehow lost track of its own digital car keys.

By 2025, GitHub's secret scanning (since 2018) blocks over 10 million leaks yearly, yet human errors persist — proof the lesson lingers.

Security isn't about how private your repo is; it's about what's inside it. If it contains secrets, it's not a code repository — it's a time bomb.

LESSON LEARNED

- Access sprawl kills security — if dozens of people have repo access, your private key is only as secure as the least careful person on that list. Never hardcode credentials, and use secret managers instead of wishful thinking. Audit access regularly.
- Rotate and expire IAM keys regularly; if it can live forever, it will die badly.
- Always assume your credentials will leak sooner or later — that's why MFA isn't optional. A second factor can't stop stupidity, but it can at least slow it down.
- Use secret-scanning tools on every commit (GitGuardian, TruffleHog, Gitleaks).
- Private repos are not safe vaults: assume anything online can leak.
- Transparency after a breach costs less than silence. Cover-ups compound damage.

Uber left its keys on GitHub, paid the thieves to stay quiet, and called it "responsible disclosure."

Dow Jones
& The Accidental Billboard of Risk

Date: February 5, 2019

Impact: 2.4 million sensitive records within a 4.4 GB Elasticsearch dataset exposed.

Root cause: Misconfigured Elasticsearch instance managed by a third-party vendor.

Dow Jones built its reputation on tracking risk. Its Risk & Compliance Watchlist was a premium product used by global banks to flag politically exposed persons (PEPs), sanctioned entities, and individuals linked to corruption, terrorism, or major crimes. In theory, it was meant to help prevent bad actors from hiding in plain sight. In practice, for nearly two weeks in 2019, it *was* hiding in plain sight—on the open internet.

An unsecured Elasticsearch cluster sitting on AWS exposed the entire 4.4 GB dataset to anyone with a browser and a bit of curiosity. The exposure was discovered by security researchers scanning for misconfigured databases —the same tools that anyone with malicious intent could use. No password, no firewall, no authentication—just 2.4 million entries of global financial red flags indexed neatly for the world to browse. It was like finding a neon-lit billboard saying: *"Confidential Compliance Data Here!"*

The database was operated by an authorized third-party vendor, who misconfigured the instance while managing it for Dow Jones. Elasticsearch, the technology behind the leak, is a database specifically designed for storing and searching through text and documents. (There are, of course, many other kinds of databases optimized for different use cases—but that's a story for another day.) It's fast, powerful, and, as this case proved, dangerously easy to misconfigure.

In this instance, the vendor left the cluster accessible from the public internet with no authentication. Elasticsearch instances should be deployed behind firewalls, with authentication enabled and IP whitelisting configured—basic protections that take minutes to set up but are often skipped in the rush to production. Tools like Shodan and BinaryEdge—search engines for exposed devices—quickly indexed it. Within hours, it became visible to anyone who knew where to look.

The data itself wasn't exactly top secret, as it was aggregated from public and government sources, but its value came from Dow Jones' curation: relationships, context, and annotations drawn from law enforcement and financial agencies. For example, while a person's name and nationality might be public, Dow Jones' notes connecting them to shell companies in three countries and flagging offshore accounts—that's the intelligence banks pay for. In the wrong hands, that's a goldmine for phishing (fraudulent attempts to trick people into revealing personal information), doxxing (publishing private or identifying data about someone online), or social engineering (manipulating people into compromising systems or data).

Once notified, Dow Jones took the database offline immediately. The company emphasized that the data originated from public sources and therefore didn't trigger a GDPR breach. For context, GDPR is the nightmare of anyone who has ever stored data in Europe—a set of painfully detailed legal regulations defining exactly who can collect, process, and store personal information. From the average user's perspective, it's the reason every website now greets you with a wall of cookie banners, making you feel like you're selling a kidney just to read the news. (Don't worry, other regions have their own equivalents.)

Still, the irony was too rich to ignore: a company that sold risk intelligence had just created its own. And while Dow Jones stressed that the data came from public sources, it also made sure to highlight that the database was managed by an "authorized third-party vendor." Conveniently, the vendor's name was never disclosed— leaving us to wonder how "third-party" it really was. We'll revisit this theme in Part VI, Volume 2, where we'll look at how complex chains of dependencies turn accountability into fog.

This wasn't a hack. No zero-day exploit, no sophisticated adversary—just another case of *security by assumption*. Vendor oversight, missing access controls, and the classic "it's only temporary" mindset combined to expose one of the most sensitive commercial datasets in the financial world.

The deeper problem lies in how common such lapses are. Elasticsearch has a long history of being the database equivalent of leaving your diary on a park bench. In 2019 alone, similar misconfigurations exposed billions of records across industries—from marketing CRMs to voter databases. When convenience and speed trump governance, you get what we might call *accidental transparency*.

LESSON LEARNED

- Visibility without control is exposure: Search-optimized tools are great, but make sure only the right people can search them.
- Outsourcing doesn't outsource responsibility: Third-party vendors are extensions of your security perimeter.
- Elasticsearch is not plug-and-play: Know what you're deploying, how it authenticates, and what happens when it doesn't.
- "Public data" aggregation creates new attack surfaces: Just because individual pieces are public doesn't mean their combination should be freely accessible. Context is power—and a vulnerability.

> • If your product is about spotting risk, maybe start with your own servers.

By 2025, Elasticsearch misconfigs still leak millions of records yearly, per security scans—a reminder that speed still trumps governance.

CHAPTER 17:
WHEN "SCALE" SCALES YOUR BILLS

DISCLAIMER

Let's be honest: companies don't like to brag about accidentally setting their own money on fire. When it comes to data leaks, they have to disclose them. But when it's a pure case of financial self-immolation, the only ones notified are accounting and therapy. That's why most incidents in this chapter are thinly documented — not because they didn't happen, but because nobody enjoys tweeting "we accidentally spent a car's worth of money heating AWS, Azure, and GCP data centers."

That doesn't mean the affected companies didn't perform their own post-mortem (see Chapter 0) and soul-searching. You can bet they did. In business, a furious finance controller is as strong a motivator as a school janitor guarding freshly waxed floors. You don't step on either twice.

For that reason, in the bibliography you'll often find links to Reddit threads, X (Twitter) posts, and similar confessions. While corporations stay silent, their engineers — safely anonymized — are surprisingly eager to share "what not to do." I've filtered every example here through a healthy dose of skepticism and engineering common sense. If it made it past that filter, it's because it sounded both stupid and entirely plausible

The cloud was supposed to save us money. And it did— right up until we realized that eliminating friction for hardware expansion also meant eliminating friction for spending.

Back then, adding a new server meant paperwork, waiting lists, and a few rounds of swearing in the data center. Now it's one click or script away. We welcomed agility, and with it, the ease of financial self-harm.

Today, small mistakes don't just cause inconvenience— they send invoices. Because in the cloud, every extra process, request, or byte transferred comes with a price tag. And while "scale" sounds glorious in press releases, in billing dashboards it means only one thing: multiplication.

The cruel beauty of the cloud is that it scales everything —speed, ambition, and costs alike. The same elasticity that lets a startup handle a sudden flood of users also lets a careless configuration or overlooked setting push monthly bills into the stratosphere. Scalability of compute power comes with scalability of invoices. A detail easy to forget until your CFO reminds you.

One more note. Compared to billion-dollar breaches or half-the-internet outages, the examples here may seem small. But remember—most of them happened to small teams or individuals. For a Fortune 500 company, a $20,000 bill is pocket change; for a bootstrapped startup, they can mean the difference between ramen and bankruptcy. Imagine one landing in your own inbox — the perspective changes fast.

From my own experience, I can confirm how real this is. I've personally experienced (and yes, at times triggered) cost spikes that multiplied project bills by an order of magnitude. Thanks to good monitoring and quick reactions, the damage never exceeded about $1,500 in a single day—but trust me, it was stressful given that in some cases the entire project's monthly budget was under $500. I've seen (almost) every flavor of these mistakes firsthand.

This chapter looks at how convenience quietly became a cost amplifier: how a missing cap, an innocent test, or a too-generous autoscaling policy can turn curiosity into a five-figure invoice.

Because in the cloud, there are two kinds of limits—technical and financial—and you usually find the second one first.

Compromised API Key
When Translation Becomes A Tax

In the previous chapter, we saw how bad security decisions can spill confidential data into the open. But sometimes, the fallout isn't about reputation or privacy — it's about the invoice. When credentials fall into the wrong hands, the consequences can be brutally, painfully direct.

The $450,000 Bill In 45 Days
Anonymous Startup (2025)

Picture this: a small startup happily coasting along, paying about $1,500 a month to Google Cloud. Then one morning, someone checks the billing console and sees a number that looks like a phone number. The total? $450,000. The cause? A single compromised API key.

Once leaked, that key became a public invitation to freeload. Whoever found it apparently decided to run 19 **billion** characters through Google's Translation API —

because why not translate *everything* when it's not your credit card on file?

The engineers described the moment of discovery as "a slow-motion heart attack." For weeks, logs had shown a gentle but relentless climb — a quiet financial avalanche nobody thought to question. By the time they caught on, the billing chart was pointing straight at orbit.

To Google's credit, support responded fast but with the empathy of a parking inspector: usage was legitimate, credentials were valid, and while no full refund was possible, the company eventually received about $50,000 in credits after weeks of back-and-forth — leaving roughly $400,000 still owed. The summary fit neatly into one line: *"Protect your keys."* Translation: this one's on you.

Among cloud veterans, the story became instant folklore — a perfect storm of automation, misplaced trust, and indifference from billing algorithms. No systems were breached, no data stolen, no users harmed. Just a half-million-dollar bonfire ignited by a string that should've stayed secret. The founders soon migrated away from GCP, still debating legal options and crowd-sharing the lesson that "cheap cloud" becomes very expensive the moment you stop watching it.

And, true to the internet's eternal wisdom, Reddit filled up with post-mortems by armchair experts and genuine engineers alike: confident after-the-fact analyses — mostly lists of "where things could've been better": quotas, alerts, anomaly detection. In other words, all the right advice, delivered exactly one billing cycle too late.

LESSON LEARNED

- Treat and rotate API keys like passwords — because they are.

- Implement request caps and monitoring alerts; silence is expensive.
- Never assume "read-only" or "demo" keys can't incur costs — hackers don't care what your documentation says.
- Financial firewalls matter as much as security ones.

Sometimes, the scariest hack isn't about stealing data — it's about realizing someone just bought themselves a linguistics PhD on your dime.

 **Explainer:**
Recursion — Not Just a Random Bunch of Letters

In academic terms, **recursion** is when a function calls itself. It's the programming equivalent of saying "I'll explain that later" and then referring back to the same explanation. In theory, it's elegant. In practice, it's a wonderful way to make both computers and humans spiral into confusion.

If that sounds abstract, imagine a dog chasing its own tail. The action makes perfect sense from the dog's perspective — something's moving, must catch it — but to an observer, it's an endless loop of enthusiasm and poor life choices.

Or, for a more reflective example: stand between two mirrors. In the first, you see yourself. In the second, you see your reflection's reflection. In the first again, you see the reflection of the reflection of the reflection... and so on, until you either get bored or question the nature of existence. That's recursion in visual form.

Still too abstract? Fine. Picture typing *"what is recursion?"* into Google. The search engine replies: *"Did you mean:*

recursion?" You click it. Same result. You click again. Same result. You click again… and if no one stops you, congratulations — you've just discovered infinite browsing mode.

In software, that kind soul who stops you before disappearing into the void is called a *stop condition* — the built-in rule that says, "Alright, enough of this." When recursion includes a proper stop condition, it becomes an elegant trick for expressing complex ideas in compact, reusable ways. When it doesn't, it becomes a horror story about CPUs, memory, and your sanity.

Now imagine that looping chaos in a cloud environment, where every click triggers a cascade of services. With hundreds of interconnected systems and automations, that simple "stop condition" often goes missing. One careless setup triggers another, which triggers another, which wakes the first one up again. Logs call APIs, APIs spawn processes, processes write more logs, and suddenly you've built an accidental perpetual-motion machine that bills by the millisecond.

Let's just say: the number of ways recursion can appear in modern cloud systems makes the variety of Kit Kat flavors in Japan look minimal by comparison.

DISCLAIMER

Since mid-2024, major cloud vendors have introduced Recursive Loop Detection — a diplomatic label for "we finally started killing the infinite loops you people keep unleashing on our infrastructure."

Yes, you can disable it. But doing so now requires explicitly confirming that financial self-destruction is part of your long-term career plan.

As a result, the cases described on the following pages are harder to reproduce today — not impossible (a sufficiently convoluted chain of triggers can still outsmart anything), just blessedly less likely.

$4,500 in Two Days
The Thumbnail That Wouldn't Stop

In a modern product image pipeline, automation is supposed to make life easier — not bankrupt you. This story centers on a **Lambda**, a small cloud program that runs automatically when something happens — in this case, when a user uploads a photo. It's part of what cloud providers call **serverless** computing: the servers still exist, of course, but they're someone else's problem. You just write the code, tell the cloud when to execute it, and trust that the universe (or AWS) will take care of the rest.

The plan was simple: each time a new image was uploaded, the Lambda would generate a smaller version — a thumbnail — and save it in the same storage space, just in a different folder. Elegant, efficient, and easy to maintain.

Except someone forgot one tiny rule: don't make thumbnails of thumbnails.

The missing condition — the digital equivalent of "stop chasing your tail" — meant that every time a new thumbnail appeared, the same Lambda would wake up again and proudly generate another one. And another. And another. Each copy landed in the same place, retriggering the process in a beautifully stupid feedback loop.

Within hours, a thousand instances were running simultaneously, nonstop. The result: a $4,500 bill in just two days, with a monthly projection of around $63,000 — all for resizing the same handful of images over and over.

It took 36 hours, several cups of coffee, and one very tired engineer to figure out what was happening. The fix? Add a simple input check in the code — "only generate thumbnails for images from the original folder" — and separate the folders (which, in keeping with IT's sacred naming tradition, are called *prefixes* in S3) so the system could finally tell originals from copies.

LESSON LEARNED

- Never let your code admire its own work.
- Add input filters before you add caffeine.
- Always set concurrency limits — they won't stop infinite loops, but they'll at least slow down your financial collapse.
- Automation without boundaries is just recursion with billing enabled.

In the cloud, even something as innocent as a picture resize can turn into a thousand-dollar self-portrait.

$10,000 Bill From CloudTrail-S3 Loop
Recursion In Sour Flavor

In many places, logs are a form of accountability — a trail of who did what, when. Government buildings track entries and exits, vehicle inspectors record every check, and IT systems... well, they log *everything*. Those records are called **logs** — a boring but essential breadcrumb trail that helps future engineers figure out what went wrong (or at least try to).

In the world of **serverless** computing, those logs are handled by services like **CloudTrail**, which dutifully records every action taken by your code. Each log entry is then saved to a dedicated storage bucket — yes, the same S3 buckets we've already met, those multipurpose containers of joy and pain.

Now, let's try a quick thought experiment. Imagine that every time a new log file appears in that bucket, another small cloud program — a **Lambda** — wakes up, reads the log, and writes a confirmation entry: "Hey, I just read this log!" Sounds innocent enough, right? Until you realize that the confirmation entry *itself* gets logged by CloudTrail... and saved to the same bucket... triggering the same Lambda again.

That's exactly what happened here. A startup accidentally created a beautiful, self-sustaining ouroboros of logging — a Lambda triggered by new logs, which produced new logs, which retriggered the same Lambda, and so on. Within a few hours, the system had gone from "quietly monitoring events" to "making events just to have something to monitor."

By the end of the week, daily costs had exploded from under $5 to roughly $1,400 — totaling about $10,000 before AWS alerted the team mid-incident, capping the damage. The engineers temporarily set all concurrency limits to zero to stop the bleeding and buy time. They first disabled the triggers, then reworked the setup so CloudTrail logs landed in a different location — one that didn't trigger the same Lambda ever again.

LESSON LEARNED

- Monitoring systems can watch themselves — but their logs shouldn't trigger new logs in response.
- Logs are supposed to record events, not create them.
- When shit hits the fan, stop the fan first. Then look for the guy with the hose.
- Before wiring automation, draw the arrows first. If they form a circle, stop.
- When AWS emails you mid-incident, it's rarely to say "nice job."

If hell had a cloud plan, it would probably bill by the log entry.

$72,000 Overnight
Recursion, Burning Hot Edition

Different cloud providers may call things by different names, but the magic trick is the same. Just like storage "buckets" come under a dozen different brand labels, the idea of **serverless** computing also wears many hats. On AWS, it's called *Lambda*. On Google Cloud, it goes by *Cloud Run*. But for the sake of sanity — and consistency — I'll keep calling it Lambda. Everyone does eventually.

Now, onto the fun part: *web scraping*. Think of it as digital dumpster diving, except you're looking for data instead of pizza crusts. It's when a program automatically visits web pages, reads their content, and extracts useful bits — prices, product names, or whatever the user wants. Done responsibly, it's a handy automation trick — and in fact, one of the world's best dumpster divers is Google itself.

Thanks to that habit, you can type something like *"topological implications of potato salad"* into the search bar and still get dozens of links, a few of which might even be relevant.

In 2020, the founder of a small startup called *Milkie Way* decided to test a scraper using Google Cloud Run. The budget? Seven dollars. The database? This time a free-tier Firebase instance (different from the ElasticSearch mentioned earlier). What could possibly go wrong?

Plenty, as it turns out.

A bug in the code caused repeated timeouts — each one prompting Cloud Run to restart the same function over and over again in a heroic but utterly pointless attempt to make it work. In a dynamic, ever-changing internet, this kind of retry loop often succeeds after a few tries. But this time, the failure wasn't due to a temporary glitch — it was baked right into the application. And this kind of small glitches likes to snowball straight into chaos.

The result? Thousands of restarts, each performing massive I/O operations — reading and writing data to Firebase at industrial scale. At first glance, the cost per operation seems laughably small: just $0.06 for every 100,000 reads or writes beyond the free tier. Unfortunately, over the course of one night, the system generated 116 billion operations, which translated to roughly $69,600 in database charges alone. Add the 16,000 hours' compute toll, pushing it to $72,000, and you get a $72,000 lesson in compounding stupidity.

For the curious: compute time in cloud systems is billed per instance. If ten copies of your function run for one minute each, that's ten minutes of billable time — kind of like hiring ten cleaners and paying all of them for the same hour. Efficient? Might be. Expensive? You bet.

After a frantic call and some explaining, Google waived the fee, noting that the runaway costs were exacerbated by delayed billing synchronization — in other words, the system didn't reflect real-time usage, sometimes lagging by up to 24 hours. Which meant that by the time you saw the problem, it had already run wild.

LESSON LEARNED

- Retry loops are great — until they're not.
- Always test with spending limits, even on "free" tiers.
- Monitor API calls and I/O usage before they monitor you.
- Prices in cloud pricing sheets may look tiny — until billions of operations hit.
- In cloud computing, "it'll fix itself" is famous last words.

Sometimes, the bug isn't what crashes your system — it's what crashes your wallet.

$75,000 in 48 Hours
Victim Of Its Own Success

Alright, enough recursion for one chapter.

This one happened in mid-2025 — so naturally, it had to involve AI. Don't worry, we won't dive into that particular rabbit hole here. There are whole two Parts in Volume 2 for AI and algorithm chaos where we can really let loose.

In this case, the disaster didn't come from a forgotten stop condition or a self-triggering loop — at least, not directly. Instead, it was the perfect storm of success, bad timing, and worse error handling.

A company had built a Lambda-powered API for real-time AI image processing — a clever setup that scaled automatically with demand. During a viral marketing campaign, that demand arrived all at once. In less than twelve hours, traffic skyrocketed from roughly 10,000 daily invocations to more than 10 million.

So far, so good — that's what serverless is supposed to handle, right? Except the system's error-handling logic had a dark side. Every failed invocation triggered chained retries across multiple connected services, each spawning more functions and generating even more logs. Instead of scaling gracefully, the system started echoing its own failures at industrial scale.

By the end of the weekend, the damage was done: $75,000 in charges for two days of "success."

The team fixed it by introducing *message queues* (SQS) between services, setting retry limits to five, and capping concurrency across all functions. A message queue is basically the cloud's way of saying "calm down, everyone will get their turn." Imagine halftime at a Yankees-Red Sox game — the whole stadium rushes for hot dogs. In the old setup, the vendor tried to serve everyone simultaneously by hiring a small army of students. The new setup? A single orderly line, serving each fan at a manageable pace.

They also tuned alarms to detect abnormal spikes earlier.

LESSON LEARNED

- Success can be more expensive than failure if you're not watching your scaling behavior.
- Always put a queue or buffer between chatty services.

> - Limit retries, cap concurrency, and test alarms under load.
> - Going viral is every marketer's dream — but make sure your monetization plan is awake for it.
> - Viral traffic tests your marketing and your architecture.

Sometimes, it's not the hackers, bugs, or outages that kill you — it's popularity.

And the same thing could just as easily happen with a sudden spike in requests to Google Maps, translation APIs (been there, seen that), , email delivery systems (that was a *fun* day), or any of a myriad other scenarios.

Cryptojacking
Mining Coins, Burning Cash

If there's a recurring theme in this part, it's that cloud resources don't discriminate between legitimate workloads and very creative theft. Enter cryptojacking — the art of hijacking someone else's compute power to mine cryptocurrency. In theory, it's a victimless crime. In practice, it's like stealing electricity — except the power bill comes in six figures and your CFO suddenly starts Googling "can you sue the blockchain?"

Let's start with a celebrity case: Tesla, 2018. Hackers gained access to one of Tesla's cloud management consoles, which wasn't properly secured. From there, they obtained AWS credentials, accessed S3 buckets containing telemetry data, and installed mining software. For several weeks, Tesla's infrastructure quietly mined cryptocurrency for someone else's benefit.

Reports estimate the attackers mined about 0.9 Bitcoin, worth roughly $6,000 at the time. Tesla never disclosed its cloud bill, but given similar incidents, we can make an educated guess. According to Sysdig's Threat Research Team, the cryptojacking group TeamTNT earned about $8,100 in crypto — while inflicting $430,000 in cloud costs on their victims. If we assume similar mining efficiency, Tesla's silent detour into the crypto business likely cost around $320,000 in wasted compute — not counting the priceless embarrassment of realizing your electric cars weren't the only things burning energy.

And Tesla wasn't alone.

Another case, documented by Palo Alto Networks' Unit 42 in 2022, involved an anonymous organization using Google Cloud App Engine. Attackers stole a service account key with excessive permissions, escalated privileges, and reconfigured the project's firewall. They spun up more than 1,600 virtual machines, often equipped with four GPUs, across multiple regions.

To maintain persistence, they created new service account keys and connected through Tor nodes to conceal their origin. Within hours, the compromised environment became a distributed mining farm — burning money faster than it mined coins. Teams scrambled to kill the miners (don't worry, we're talking about applications, not hackers)

How fast? Well, let's take popular types from GCP's offering: n1-standard-2. The naming may sound a bit odd at first, but over time you get used to it — the pattern is actually quite practical, and at least Google avoids potential licensing issues if they ever decide to name their servers after Pokémon.

Each n1-standard-2 VM with four GPUs costs between $1,100 (Nvidia T4) and $7,300 (V100) per month, depending on the region. Multiply that by 1,600 instances and you get a bill somewhere between $1.7 and $11 million per month — before storage, bandwidth, or network fees. In reality, large enterprises often enjoy discounts of up to 60%, but even then, the cost would still be astronomical — and here, we can only guess.

Even if the intrusion was detected quickly, the damage would still land in the hundreds of thousands range. That's a lot of money for coins you don't even own — or, as one engineer probably muttered, "at least we didn't mine Dogecoin."

—————— From My Own Burn File ——————

A few years back, a company I worked for narrowly avoided a similar financial hit — but only by shutting down the entire service and rebuilding it from scratch in emergency mode. During the investigation, we found mining software quietly generating **Monero** in the background. The catch? The client's online store stayed offline for two days... right in the middle of the holiday season. I never found out how the client felt about the *savings*.

LESSON LEARNED

- Your cloud account is a gold mine — sometimes literally — for attackers.
- Credentials without limits are an open invitation to free enterprise.
- Monitoring GPU and compute usage isn't optional.

> • When someone mines crypto in your cloud, you're the one paying the electric bill.

In short: when the cloud starts making money for someone else, they won't care for efficiency — or your quarterly budget.

NASA's $30 Million Oversight
The Egress Surprise

NASA's $30 Million Oversight — The Egress Surprise
The problem with clouds is that while they make data float effortlessly, gravity always shows up in the invoice. Even giants like NASA overlook this — imagine the hit on a startup. Case in point: NASA's Earthdata Cloud project, a massive 2020 migration that nearly turned into a budgeting black hole.

NASA planned to move 247 petabytes of Earth science data — satellite imagery, climate records, environmental readings — into Amazon Web Services (AWS) under the Earthdata Cloud initiative. The goal was noble: give scientists around the world faster, easier access to decades of open data.

For scale: 247 PB is enough to fit the *entire extended Lord of the Rings trilogy* in 4K roughly 450,000 times — which, coincidentally, is about how many times someone in the cloud industry says across their career *"we'll optimize costs later."*

The catch? Someone forgot to ask a crucial question: What happens when those scientists start downloading it?

In cloud lingo, there's ingress (uploading data into the cloud) and egress (downloading it out). AWS charges for egress whenever data leaves its cloud — and NASA, in its budget plan, accounted only for ingress, the one-way trip up. Every time a researcher downloaded a terabyte of satellite data, NASA would quietly pick up the tab. The Office of Inspector General (OIG) audit later found that these unplanned costs could hit tens of millions of dollars per year — projected to hit up to $30 million annually, depending on usage.

NASA has always been obsessed with space. Without the OIG audit, their data egress bills might have joined the mission: escaping Earth's gravity and heading straight into orbit.

The audit triggered a course correction. NASA began implementing data caching (think of it like the content delivery tricks we discussed in the Fastly case back in Part II, Chapter 10) and other optimization techniques that don't need unpacking here. Thankfully, the oversight was caught early — before it could consume enough budget to fund a small satellite mission.

This wasn't a technical failure. It was a budgeting one — a reminder that even the smartest engineers sometimes forget that the laws of finance, much like gravity, apply everywhere.

LESSON LEARNED

- In the cloud, what goes up will come down — and you'll pay for the return trip.
- Always account for egress costs; they're the fine print of scalability.
- Free public access doesn't mean free infrastructure.
- "Unlimited data for everyone" sounds great until the invoice arrives.

> - Before you move anything to the cloud, make sure you actually understand how you'll be billed — there are plenty of surprises hiding in the pricing model.

Or, to put it another way: space may be infinite, but your budget isn't.

To close this chapter, let's admit — there's a small silver lining. Cloud providers often show surprising generosity when faced with honest mistakes. Their business depends on customer growth, not financial exorcisms, so they rarely want to crush small companies before they start paying real money. For the giants, those refunds are smaller than their office coffee budget. Still, it's entirely discretionary — and as we saw in the first case, that $450,000 bill wasn't forgiven.

CHAPTER 18:
WHEN SECURITY TOOLS BECOME THE THREAT

We've seen what happens when cloud safety turns into self-exposure and when "scalable" turns into "financially suicidal." But there's one more illusion left to break: the belief that our security systems are somehow above all that.

The irony of modern defense is that the same tools meant to protect us can just as easily cause harm. Antivirus updates crash kernels, endpoint agents choke servers, and automated "protections" quietly lock out their own teams. It's like hiring a bouncer to keep the club safe only to watch him hand every guest a knife at the door — and then lock the doors so no one can get out.

When automation stumbles, even protection itself can become the problem. Endpoint Detection and Response (EDR) platforms designed to guard against unseen threats can unintentionally take down entire fleets. VPNs meant to connect remote workers throttle entire companies instead. Even Single Sign-On — humanity's collective wish to remember one password — can pull the plug on an enterprise with a single expired token.

In this chapter, we'll explore what happens when caution overreaches — when patches misfire, monitoring tools melt production, and "secure by default" quietly turns into "broken by design." Because sometimes, even the best shields have sharp edges — and learning where they cut is the only way to stay safe.

 **Explainer:**
When the Watchdogs Go Rogue — Kernel, Antivirus, and EDR

Imagine your computer as a city.

Not a flashy cyberpunk metropolis with flying cars, but a regular, busy place — streets, houses, utilities, grumpy residents, and a few shady bars where strange processes hang out at night.

At the center of it all is **the Kernel** — the city hall, the government, the one place that decides who gets access to what. The kernel doesn't build houses or deliver mail itself; instead, it coordinates the city's essential services. It keeps the water running (*I/O*), ensures power and heating (*CPU and resources*) reach everyone, and stops your neighbor from building a swimming pool on your plot (*process isolation*).

Think of *memory* as city land — the plots, courtyards, and backyards where residents build their houses and store their stuff. The kernel allocates these parcels, making sure nobody starts expanding over someone else's fence. And if a resident overstays? The kernel evicts them—sometimes mid-party, leaving digital debris everywhere (*process termination*). It's valuable real estate, and the kernel acts as zoning authority and land registry in one.

In short: it governs who can do what, and where.

Every application — your browser, text editor, or music player — lives in the city as an ordinary resident. They operate in the **user space**, a polite suburb where everyone minds their own business (mostly). Each resident can use public infrastructure — read files, connect to the internet, play sounds — but only by asking permission from the city hall. The kernel decides what's allowed and what's not.

When the City Needs a Watchdog

Now, even in the best-run cities, not every resident behaves. Some throw wild parties (malware), some build secret tunnels (rootkits), and others start fires just for fun (ransomware). That's where security services come in.

In the early days, this job belonged to the **antivirus** — think of it as the city's first security guard, part police officer, part firefighter. Its job was simple: walk around with a list of known troublemakers (virus signatures) and arrest anyone matching the description. "Aha! You're the 'ILoveYou' worm! You're coming with me."

It worked — until it didn't. The criminals got creative. They changed disguises, altered behavior, and started committing crimes the guard had never seen before.

So, the antivirus had to evolve. Instead of just matching names on a list, it had to learn to recognize *behavior* based on general instructions. In the old days, it was enough to follow a rule like "don't light a fire in the living room." Today, the guard has to infer that lighting fires in the bedroom is probably also bad — and react to the mere sight of smoke before the flames even start. This shift is what we call *heuristic or behavioral detection* — a kind of intuition trained to see trouble coming.

Still, that only covered so much. The next generation arrived: **EDR**, or **Endpoint Detection and Response**. If the antivirus is your neighborhood cop, the EDR is a mix of detective, counterintelligence agency, and public health department.

An antivirus deals with individuals — it catches one infected resident and calls it a day. The EDR looks at the *patterns.* It investigates: Who's talking to whom? Why is that office worker sending encrypted messages to strangers in another city at 3 a.m.? Are several employees simultaneously buying identical shovels and rope? Something's up.

EDR tools don't just patrol one block; they wire up CCTV across the city (*telemetry collection*) to spot gang activity before it escalates, tracking digital epidemics like a CDC for code, quarantining whole neighborhoods if a virus starts coughing. In other words, EDR tools don't just stop attacks; they collect data for later investigation — detailed logs, timelines, and traces that let forensic teams retrace every suspicious move. If malware is a local crime, EDR handles organized conspiracies *and* builds the case file afterward.

And it doesn't stop at one city. Zoom out: your computer is one city in a federation of devices. The EDR's jurisdiction spans the whole nation — in this metaphor, that's your *corporate network*. Each city (*an endpoint* — laptop, phone, or server) has its own local police, but the EDR connects them into a federal security service watching for coordinated threats across borders.

Why the Watchdogs Need Special Privileges

But every utopia has its underbelly: to spot misbehavior, these guardians need to see things others can't. They must peek into everyone's homes, check the wiring, and occasionally search through the trash. In the digital city, **that means operating not in user space, but in kernel space** — the secure district where the city's core decisions are made.

It's a bit like giving your security team the keys to every building in town. Necessary, yes — but risky. One bad command, and the whole city grid can go dark. These watchdogs operate with the authority of city hall itself — which means that if they screw up, it's not just a local problem. The entire hierarchy is compromised.

It's like the **Watergate scandal of 1972**: a few guys break into an office building to plant recording devices, but when the story comes out, it doesn't just end with their arrest — the whole administration collapses. The trust chain breaks, and suddenly, chaos reigns.

The same thing happens inside a computer. Processes running in kernel space aren't just privileged citizens — they *are* the system's law enforcement. When they malfunction, there's no higher authority — if the watchdog bites the mayor, there's no one left to call animal control to correct them. One faulty driver or botched security update, and the city goes into full anarchy: lights out, sirens blaring, total collapse. The digital equivalent? A cheerful Blue Screen of Death on Windows, or a kernel panic's cryptic poetry on other systems.

As you'll see in the case studies below, that's exactly what happened: the very watchdogs meant to protect the city started clubbing random bystanders and pulling the plug on the power plant — as you'll soon see in action.

In security, power and fragility go hand in hand. The kernel is the mayor, antivirus the patrol officer, and EDR the national security agency — but when any of them lose control, the result isn't peace.

It's chaos, with a blue screen.

CrowdStrike Kernel Panic

Date: July 19, 2024

Impact: Faulty Falcon update triggered BSODs on 8.5 million devices globally, disrupting enterprises, hospitals, and airlines; cost exceeded $5.4 billion.

Root Cause: A kernel driver logic error — the Falcon sensor attempted to load 21 modules into a memory space reserved for 20, causing the OS to terminate the process and crash itself.

The July 2024 CrowdStrike incident is remembered as the day a security update triggered a digital apocalypse. The company's Falcon sensor — a kernel-level driver used for real-time threat detection — received an automated update that, quite literally, broke the operating system it was meant to protect.

As explained earlier, the kernel is the OS's guardian and referee. But in this case, the guard tripped over its own rulebook. The update introduced a logic error in Falcon's driver that asked the kernel to allocate memory for 21 `sensors`, while the predefined buffer allowed only 20. When the kernel noticed that the program wanted to write beyond its assigned space, it did what it was designed to do — it terminated the offender immediately to protect the system's integrity.

That's a sensible decision when the offender is a misbehaving app or service. The user might lose a window, maybe a bit of work, but the system survives. Unfortunately, this time the misbehaving code was *inside the kernel itself* — so when the OS decided to shut down the offending program, it shut down *itself*.

What made matters worse was automation. The update was pushed globally through CrowdStrike's cloud distribution network within minutes — no staged rollout, no early warning, no graceful rollback. In modern infrastructure, that kind of speed is both a blessing and a curse: when things go right, everyone applauds the efficiency; when they don't, you get the largest IT outage in history.

Within hours, airports were grounding flights, hospitals were reverting to pen and paper, and IT departments everywhere were rediscovering the timeless beauty of safe mode. The irony was almost poetic: a tool designed to prevent global cyberattacks had, through a single faulty update, achieved what most hackers could only dream of — bringing down millions of systems simultaneously.

In the aftermath, CrowdStrike's engineers moved quickly to issue a fix, but recovery required manual intervention across fleets of machines. Systems without direct human oversight — kiosks, ATMs, medical terminals — remained frozen for days.

Then came the PR aftershock. In an attempt to thank its overworked support staff, CrowdStrike issued *$10 UberEats vouchers* (about £7.75 in the UK) accompanied by a cheerful note: "We appreciate the extra effort caused by the July 19 incident. Your next cup of coffee or late-night snack is on us!" The gesture backfired spectacularly when UberEats' own fraud-prevention system started blocking mass-activated coupons. Engineers ended up wrestling not only with unresponsive systems but also with denied lunch orders — a moment many dubbed "the worst apology ever."

LESSON LEARNED

- Kernel-level software leaves zero margin for error — one stray bit can take down millions of systems.

- Automation without staged rollout is a loaded gun pointed at your own infrastructure.
- Rollback mechanisms matter as much as deployment speed.
- Good intentions don't fix bad optics — especially when your apology arrives via a blocked coupon.
- When your protection stack outruns its own testing, your uptime becomes the sacrifice.

The CrowdStrike panic showed how fragile "secure by design" becomes when design forgets humility. One line of code, one missing slot, one global push — and the world's shield briefly became its sword.

SentinelOne Outage

Date: May 29, 2025

Impact: Global outage disrupted threat detection and response for over 11,000 organizations — from Fortune 500 giants to hospitals. Estimated cost: **$100M+** in productivity loss and incident delays.

Root Cause: A backend configuration error cascaded through SentinelOne's infrastructure after an unvetted update was deployed globally.

SentinelOne markets itself as an "autonomous protection platform," which is a poetic way of saying "trust us, we automated everything." On May 29, 2025, that promise aged like milk. For seven hours, one of the world's leading EDR vendors accidentally demonstrated what happens when a security platform becomes the incident.

It started with a migration to a shiny new Infrastructure-as-Code stack. Somewhere inside that machinery, a long-forgotten script — a fossil from old deployments — woke up and began deleting critical network routes and DNS resolvers across regions. Imagine an intern with root access and no adult supervision, except the intern is cron.

Within minutes, SentinelOne's cloud lost the plot. Dashboards froze on "Connection Lost." The management console went dark. Detection pipelines stopped moving. Support queues detonated across every timezone. Reddit lit up with screenshots, swearing, and disbelief. Global security teams were suddenly forced back to stone tools: spreadsheets, Slack channels, improvised playbooks, and the ancient ritual of "refresh the page again, maybe this time it works."

Not everything died, though. Endpoint agents kept patrolling on cached rules like bouncers with no radio but a good memory. They blocked known threats but had nowhere to send alerts, so those piled up like uncollected mail.

Engineers eventually tracked the chaos to a rogue backend config sync. Redeploying gateway configs brought the platform back to consciousness, followed by a Niagara Falls of delayed alerts catching up all at once. Days later, SentinelOne published its post-mortem: no hackers, no sabotage — just automation sprinting past its own guardrails. The company promised audits, cleanup of legacy triggers, and a safer IaC rollout. Amusingly, the failed migration *was* the safer IaC rollout.

This wasn't an isolated blip. By mid-2025, SentinelOne's track record looked like a highlight reel of configuration self-harm: the February access-block fiasco, the June 2024 false-positive meltdown that crippled hospitals, the November 2024 datacenter outage, and the August 2025 reporting freeze. Different symptoms, identical diagnosis: automation moving faster than validation.

When a platform built on "autonomous protection" stops validating its own changes, it stops being protection at all. It becomes the threat.

LESSON LEARNED

- Infrastructure-as-Code without testing is just code waiting to explode.
- Cloud automation needs brakes as much as it needs speed.
- AI-driven security is only as trustworthy as its configuration files.
- Recurring configuration arrogance turns reliability into roulette — leaving manual competence as your last line of defense.

SentinelOne's May outage reminded the industry that no matter how advanced your defenses, one unchecked line of code can still do what thousands of hackers can't — take down your own system from the inside.

Explainer:
From Fortresses to Paranoia — VPNs, Zero Trust, and the Art of Not Getting Owned

One of the simplest ways to protect company data is to lock it behind an internal network — accessible only from inside the office. Think of it as having a company-only phone number: just like the internal extensions mentioned in the DNS explainer back in Part II, the outside world can't dial in directly. In the age of cubicles and coffee machines, that was enough: a laptop plugged into the office network had access to sensitive systems, while the same device connected to home Wi-Fi did not.

The problem? Companies rarely fit into one building. Different offices — or remote workers — still need to connect securely. That's where **VPN (Virtual Private Network)** comes in. A VPN is essentially a private lane through the public internet. It lets computers in different places behave as if they were all inside one private network. The data still travels through the internet, but it's encrypted — only the trusted devices inside that virtual bubble can read it.

The side effect of this setup is that all decrypted traffic can exit through a single point. For companies, this is a blessing: they can monitor what enter and leaves their network. For ordinary users, it's the same mechanism that makes those "watch Netflix from anywhere" ads possible — by routing traffic through a remote gateway, you can appear to be somewhere else entirely.

In short, a VPN is like a virtual military base. Everything happening inside is strictly confidential, and everyone entering or leaving is checked at the gate.

But there's a flaw in that logic. What if, despite all precautions, an impostor makes it inside? Maybe someone stuck on a fake mustache, fooled a distracted guard, or found a side door nobody watched. Once they're in, the system assumes they belong — and that's where things start to fall apart.

Enter **Zero Trust**. For once, the name actually says what it means: trust no one. Not even those already inside the fortress.

If a VPN is about checking IDs at the gate, Zero Trust is about checking them at every interaction. Want to ask a colleague how their weekend was? Show your ID — and ask for theirs. Buying a sandwich in the canteen? Scan your badge; the cashier must do the same, just in case he's a spy adding laxatives to the mayonnaise. Even heading to the restroom requires a quick verification at the door.

This may sound excessive, but that's the point. Zero Trust assumes that breaches are inevitable and builds security around continuous verification. Every access request is checked, every connection re-authenticated, and nothing is taken at face value — no matter how familiar it looks.

The concept exploded in popularity after 2020, when COVID-19 forced companies to embrace remote work overnight. With employees scattered across the world and sensitive data moving through home routers and coffee shop Wi-Fi, the old idea of "inside the office = safe" collapsed. Zero Trust offered a new philosophy: assume compromise, verify everything. Vendors like Zscaler turned it into a billion-dollar industry, selling the promise of safety through perpetual suspicion.

It's a brilliant idea. But here's the quiet irony: Zero Trust boldly declares "trust no one"... then adds, in much smaller print, "except the pass controller." The trouble starts when that controller has a bad day — because in a world where nobody's trusted, that one failure means *everybody* gets locked outside.

Zscaler "Reboot Loop" Outage

Date: May 8, 2023

Impact: Global instability in Zscaler Internet Access (ZIA); half-loaded webpages, broken sessions, mass "Connection Reset" errors

Root Cause: Faulty software update deployed across Public Service Edge nodes, triggering a global crash-restart loop

---

DISCLAIMER

Zscaler talks about trust a lot. Their public Trust Portal lists incidents affecting the platform — but only within a rolling three-month window. For a company whose product is literally built around the concept of trust, that horizon feels... brief. Their public incident record tends to disappear faster than election promises.

Some other companies use similar rolling logs, but older incidents usually remain documented elsewhere — in engineering blogs, retrospectives, conference talks, or technical write-ups. In Zscaler's case, the official memory tends to be noticeably shorter.

Because of this unusually brief memory, the case below is reconstructed from contemporary reporting, archived incident discussions, and the collective troubleshooting efforts of the IT industry.

On May 8, 2023, Zscaler proved a timeless truth: the only thing more dangerous than trusting strangers is trusting your own deployment pipeline.

The day began with a routine push of new software to Zscaler's Public Service Edge nodes - the machines responsible for inspecting and forwarding global enterprise traffic. "Routine" in this context meaning "no one expects anything to explode." Unfortunately, the code had other plans.

Within minutes, the internet developed what can best be described as chronic hiccups. Webpages loaded halfway before giving up on life. Teams and Slack behaved like they had accepted their fate. Authentication pages spun like slot machines. And browsers around the world displayed "Connection Reset" with the smug certainty of a parking inspector writing a ticket.

Behind all this was a single, beautifully stupid logic bug: when encountering certain HTTP headers, the proxy crashed. Not slowed. Not degraded. Crashed.

Enter the watchdog - Zscaler's automated babysitter whose job is to restart anything that looks sleepy. It kicked the process back up, cheerfully shouting "Rise and shine!" The process rose, touched the same cursed packet as before, and immediately died again.

The watchdog tried again. And again. And again. Meanwhile, globally distributed proxy nodes slipped into synchronized crash loops - a zombie ballet of failure choreographed entirely by accident.

To users, this was not a traditional outage. A clean outage has dignity. This was a half-working, half-broken purgatory where nothing behaved predictably. Sessions died at random. Traffic stuttered like a dial-up modem having an existential crisis. Helpdesks worldwide became involuntary therapy centers.

Redundancy didn't save anyone because the buggy update rolled out to *every* node. In the cloud, a single bad line of code can take down more machines in ten minutes than a power grid failure could in a month.

Eventually, Zscaler pushed a fixed build, reboot loops calmed down, and the world pretended everything was normal again. From the outside it looked like an internet glitch. From the inside, it was a masterclass in how not to run global infrastructure.

If you go searching for Zscaler's transparency about the incident, pack a lunch. While researching this chapter, you'll inevitably stumble across several other Zscaler events that mysteriously lack official documentation:

- Zscaler Multi-Service Outage (January 19, 2025)
- ZIdentity Global Outage (October 6, 2024)
- "SharePoint Selective Blindness" (January 4, 2024)
- Zscaler "Thundering Herd" Blackout (October 25, 2022)

All public. All impactful. All strangely absent from Zscaler's own trust pages - proof that the internet never forgets, no matter how hard a vendor might hope otherwise. Relevant media links are, of course, listed in the bibliography.

A transparency model based on what can only be described as goldfish memory is difficult to applaud. Evaluating and deploying a platform like this often takes longer than three months — longer than the period their public incident history remembers. In a book dedicated to learning from real failures, that kind of short institutional memory is difficult to applaud.

LESSON LEARNED

- Redundancy is meaningless when every redundant node is running the same ticking time bomb.
- Watchdogs are great - until they start reviving something that should stay very, very dead.

> - In distributed systems, bad code scales faster than good architecture.
> - A half-functional internet hurts more people than a full outage.

Zscaler builds its brand on the slogan "Trust No One." Looking at their Trust Portal, a more accurate motto might be: "Remember Nothing."

 **Explainer:**
The Value of SSO — One Key To Rule Them All

To truly appreciate the chaos of SSO, we need to take two quick detours. Yes, we are stepping away from the main topic for a moment, but trust me—it's worth the scenic route to clear up the mess of passwords and acronyms first.

Detour #1: Passwords — Humanity's Most Commonly Forgotten Invention

Detailed password security guidelines are way beyond this book's scope — and, frankly, the internet is already full of them, most either outdated, wrong, or written by people who forgot that passwords are used by *humans*. Real, busy, distracted humans. The kind who open a password reset email with the same level of existential dread as a dentist appointment reminder.

Still, here's a condensed, no-nonsense version of a sane password policy:

1. **Use a password manager.** It's an app that securely stores all your passwords — think of it as a safe that actually remembers its own combination.

2. **Create one strong master password** (16+ characters, something only you know) and protect the manager with it. Also, **enable MFA** — multi-factor authentication.

3. **From now on, generate unique, random passwords** for every service and let the manager remember them for you.

4. **Never, ever share your master password.** Not with your partner, not with your boss, and definitely not with the "IT guy" who looks suspiciously like a Nigerian prince.

That's it — enough to sleep well at night. Now, onto the next detour.

Detour #2: Authn vs. Authz — The Alphabet Soup of Access

Off-topic but useful: there's often confusion between **authentication** and **authorization**. Authentication (*authn*, or occasionally *a12n*) is about verifying *who you are*. Authorization (*authz*, or *a11n*) is about checking *what you're allowed to do*. In simpler terms: authentication gets you into the building; authorization decides which rooms you can enter — and whether there's free coffee in any of them.

Now, onto the real prize

Every company today runs on dozens of apps: email, chat, HR portals, expense trackers, dashboards, and tools built specifically to ensure everyone looks busy. Each one wants its own login. Each one is a new place to forget your password or reuse a bad one.

So what if you could secure all those applications with one authentication system? Even better—what if you could control, from a single place, who in the company has access to what? A central control tower not just for hiring, but also for the 2023/24 layoff peak's particularly fashionable "human resources optimization."

Enter **SSO—Single Sign-On.** As the name suggests, it's a system that promises one login for everything in your company. In practice, when you try to log into your corporate email, calendar, or Slack, you get redirected to a central service that handles your credentials. Once you authenticate there, that system vouches for you everywhere else.

Think of it like having professional security guards who check every badge. In our digital fortress, we don't teach every receptionist how to recognize every employee—we just ask Bob from Security: "Hey, can we trust this guy?" Bob nods, and the gates open.

SSO makes life easier for everyone. IT teams don't have to enforce complex password policies across every service. Employees don't have to remember twenty different logins. They just know one password—their key to the kingdom.

That convenience, however, needs a bit of adult supervision. That's why mature setups pair SSO with multi-factor authentication (a keycard needing your fingerprint and a timed QR ping), device checks, and strict session lifetimes—turning the master key into a controlled access tool.

The rise of cloud apps made SSO nearly unavoidable, and it's one of those rare cases where convenience and security can align—if done right.

But every fortress has its siege engine, and history loves a siege.

That convenience comes with a catch: what if a hacker slips past Bob with a forged badge or jams the central lock with a blob of interdimensional sludge, blocking everyone from entering at all? A breach in one central identity provider can cascade into dozens of systems instantly.

Like everything else in this book, the real problem isn't the technology itself. It's what happens when people start believing it's infallible—or when Bob from Security takes a lunch break at exactly the wrong time. When Bob naps, the fortress crumbles—and the next story proves it.

Okta Breach

Date: January 16–21, 2022 (disclosed March 22, 2022)

Impact: LAPSUS$ hackers accessed Okta's internal SuperUser tools via contractor Sitel, exposing roughly 450 customers and tens of thousands of logins across affected clients.

Root Cause: Compromised vendor laptop, weak oversight, delayed disclosure.

In January 2022, Okta — the company that built its name on managing everyone's logins — learned the hard way what happens when you outsource the keys to your own kingdom.

The breach began not inside Okta's servers but inside Sitel, a third-party support provider hired to handle customer requests. LAPSUS$, a hacking collective with a reputation for teenage-level bravado and surprisingly adult-level success, managed to infiltrate Sitel's systems by compromising one of its laptops. The attackers didn't need to hack Okta directly — they simply walked in through the side door, carrying a legitimate employee's credentials and a backpack full of digital confetti. With that single move, they inherited access to Okta's SuperUser tools — software designed to reset passwords and multi-factor authentication tokens across customer accounts.

In other words, the intruders didn't just steal keys — they got the locksmith's master set.

According to Okta's timeline, the attackers lurked undetected for five days — not rampaging, but quietly observing and documenting their access. Then, two months later, they posted screenshots of their exploits online on March 21st — forcing Okta to admit what had happened only after the internet had already finished the popcorn. By the time the company issued its statement, customers were already asking how their "identity provider" had managed to lose its own identity.

The real damage wasn't in the data exfiltrated — it was in trust. Okta's entire business rests on being the digital gatekeeper for tens of thousands of logins across affected clients. The breach revealed that even the gatekeeper had given a spare key to a contractor and never bothered to check if they locked their office.

Investigations showed predictable sins: overprivileged vendor access, limited network segmentation, and a monitoring system that dutifully reported anomalies — which no one read. It was a familiar symphony of human oversight failing beneath the rhythm of automation.

Okta insisted that the attackers' reach was "limited in scope," a phrase that in PR translates to "we're still counting." The truth was more embarrassing than catastrophic, but the optics were brutal: a company selling peace of mind had just demonstrated how easily peace can be misplaced.

LESSON LEARNED

- Don't outsource your master keys — or at least, check who's cleaning the locksmith's desk.
- Vendor trust should be earned, not inherited.
- Alerts mean nothing if no one reads them.
- Disclosure delays always make the fire look bigger.

Okta forgot its combo — proving that even gatekeepers need a password reminder app.

—— When Windows Defender Fought Chrome ——
(And Maybe Linux Too)

Date: 2020 (with an anecdotal callback to ~2010)

Impact: Chrome updates blocked, users confused, Edge marketing thrilled, and one antivirus team in need of a group therapy session.

Root Cause: Heuristic overreach colliding with corporate timing.

DISCLAIMER

Around 2010, Windows Defender (and its predecessor, Microsoft Security Essentials) had a habit of flagging Ubuntu installers as potential malware. I remember this vividly — but durable, authoritative sources have largely vanished from the internet. Treat that part as an anecdote from someone who lived through it. The documented, verifiable case below focuses on Chrome.

In early 2020, Microsoft was on a mission. A loud, sparkly, omnipresent mission: convince the world that the new Chromium-based Edge was the browser of the future. Pop-ups suggested it. Ads hinted at it. System notifications all but begged for it.

And then Windows Defender joined the campaign. It began quietly. Chrome users noticed their browser refusing to update. No warnings, no polite explanations — just update errors that smelled less like malware and more like corporate rivalry wearing a trench coat.

Under the hood, Defender's heuristic engine had decided that Chrome's updater looked a little too much like a malware dropper. It downloaded an executable from the internet, placed it in a temp directory, and ran it. In fairness to Defender: this *is* exactly how many infections begin.

In fairness to everyone else: this is also how Chrome has updated itself since the Pleistocene.

The timing could not have been worse. Edge marketing was firing on all cylinders — the built-in Browser Choice prompts, the "Try Edge, it's better for battery life!" pop-ups, the full-page Windows welcome screens desperately trying to shepherd users away from Chrome.

So when Defender suddenly started flagging Chrome updates as "potentially harmful," the internet didn't see heuristics. It saw sabotage — a conclusion helped along by the timing and the already-noisy browser war unfolding on every Windows desktop.

Official Microsoft messaging called it "a false positive triggered by heuristic analysis." Which, translated into plain English, means: "Oops, our security guard tackled the wrong guy again."

Unofficially, the joke wrote itself: Defender had finally stopped malware... by stopping Google, turning a routine update into an unintentional act of corporate comedy.

Once Microsoft issued fresh signatures, Chrome updates began working again. Everything returned to normal — or at least as normal as things get when two trillion-dollar companies passive-aggressively fight over who gets to render your cat videos.

As for the Ubuntu saga: yes, I distinctly remember Windows Defender flagging Ubuntu installation media itself as a threat around 2010 — treating a perfectly innocent Linux installer CD as if it were plotting a coup. But since durable sources from that era have evaporated, treat this as an anecdote rather than a formally documented incident, and a reminder that even security history suffers from data decay.

> **LESSON LEARNED**
>
> - Heuristics are great until they start defending your market share instead of your system.
> - Updaters behave like malware because malware behaves like updaters — and your antivirus doesn't always know the difference.
> - Timing matters: a false positive during a marketing push looks a lot like intent.
> - Overprotective security tools can break trust faster than actual threats.
> - When your antivirus starts playing politics, it might need boundaries.

Defender vs. Chrome: a browser war disguised as a safety feature — and Edge somehow walks away looking like the hero.

PART IV: SUMMARY
THE ILLUSION OF SAFETY

This part wasn't about villains or victims—it was about misplaced trust. The modern internet runs on systems that promise protection, automation, and peace of mind, yet every promise comes with fine print. We built tools to defend us from failure and ended up building new ways to fail. The illusion of safety thrives not in our ignorance, but in our confidence that someone—or something—else has it covered.

Here, we saw storage systems turned into billboards, billing engines behaving like slot machines, and security platforms crashing the very machines they were meant to protect. None of these incidents started with bad intentions. They started with convenience: a checkbox left on default, an API key forgotten, an update deployed without human eyes on the logs. Automation didn't just accelerate our workflows—it accelerated our mistakes.

The recurring theme across all three chapters was simple: the stronger our defenses, the more spectacularly they collapse when they fail. From CrowdStrike's kernel panic to Zscaler's cascading outages and Okta's contractor debacle, each case showed what happens when trust chains grow longer than our ability to oversee them. The very systems built to secure the cloud became the cloud's weakest links.

But these stories also serve as calibration points, not just cautionary tales. They remind us that safety isn't a feature—it's a process. True security comes not from removing humans from the loop but from designing systems that expect them to be imperfect. The goal isn't to eliminate failure; it's to make failure survivable.

Part V, *The Illusion of Resilience — Backups & Redundancy,* continues this exploration. Having seen how our shields can betray us, we now turn to the nets we trust to catch us when they do. From backup systems that vanish when needed most to redundant setups that fail in unison, we'll learn why resilience isn't about having duplicates—it's about understanding dependencies. And as the line between digital and physical failures begins to blur, we'll take our first steps beyond the screen, into the real-world consequences of believing that safety is ever guaranteed.

V. THE ILLUSION OF RESILIENCE

PART V:
THE ILLUSION OF RESILIENCE – DISASTER RECOVERY AND OTHER OPTIMISTIC PLANS

So far, we've toured the digital underworld of arithmetic betrayals, temporal black holes, security tools that accidentally set the house on fire, and storage systems that forgot what they were storing. In short: we've seen how things can go spectacularly wrong. But now, for a change of pace, let's talk about the times when people actually tried to prepare for disaster — and failed anyway.

This part is about the illusion of safety. About the organizations that knew something might break and proudly declared, "We've got a disaster recovery plan!" only for that plan to collapse in perfect synchronization with the primary system. It's the story of failover mechanisms that heroically jumped straight into the same hole, redundant infrastructure that amplified rather than absorbed failures, and recovery procedures tested in lab conditions that dissolved under real-world chaos.

Humans love the idea of resilience — it feels comforting. Two data centers, automated failovers, rehearsed recovery playbooks. But resilience without independence is just synchronized failure. Redundancy without testing is theater. We'll meet teams whose failover triggered the outage, operators who activated disaster recovery only to discover it didn't work, and systems that collapsed not from lack of preparation, but from overconfidence in untested safety nets.

If the earlier parts showed us how chaos emerges from tiny cracks in logic, time, trust, and memory, this one explores how we try — and often fail — to contain that chaos. The real enemy here isn't ignorance, but the comforting belief that having a plan means being prepared. Each story ahead starts with good intentions: redundancy, failovers, disaster recovery protocols. And each ends with a reminder that "resilient" doesn't always mean "safe." Sometimes it just means "takes longer to die."

And here's where things start to shift. For the first time, we'll step beyond purely digital failures. Not every fuckup hides in code or cloud infrastructure. Some live in reinforced concrete, metal, and split-second human decisions — where the cost of failure isn't downtime or lost revenue, but lives.

We'll encounter cases involving critical infrastructure, physical systems, and disasters whose consequences proved far too grave for wry humor. That's why certain chapters in this part will briefly set aside the usual tone — because some failures demand respect more than punchlines.

It won't all be somber. There's still room for dark humor when systems fail in absurd ways. But as we move through this final part, the stakes rise. The patterns remain familiar — overconfidence, untested assumptions, synchronized failures — but the consequences become impossible to laugh away.

So buckle up (redundantly, if you like) and prepare to discover that sometimes the scariest thing isn't the absence of a safety net. It's the moment you realize the net was never tested, or worse — that everyone's falling into it at once.

CHAPTER 19:
REDUNDANCY IS NOT RESILIENCE

In Part III, we explored what happens when backups fail — or never existed in the first place. Along the way, one term kept popping up like a background character waiting for its spotlight: redundancy.

For the average person, the word might sound like some sort of sci-fi gadget — a discombobulator, perhaps. For the IT crowd, though, it translates to something much more specific (and deceptively comforting): multiple copies! Extra systems! Safety in numbers! But as you'll see, redundancy isn't the same as resilience. The former means you've duplicated something; the latter means those duplicates actually work when you need them.

This chapter takes a closer look at how redundancy can lull people into a false sense of security — especially when all those "independent" systems depend on the same power source, the same data center, or the same human assumptions. Because nothing says "robust infrastructure" like discovering your backups, replicas, and failovers all fail in perfect synchrony.

 **Explainer:**
Redundancy Explained – What It Is and How to Break It

As you already know, engineers love inventing new words for things that already exist. A week without creating a new term feels wasted. This time, however, instead of coining a new term, an existing word was hijacked and its interpretation flipped. Suddenly, a synonym for waste became a desired state and industry gospel.

Put simply, redundancy is about having spare copies—multiple systems, backup plans, safety in numbers. At its core, it's simple: when Plan A catches fire (sometimes literally), Plan B takes over.

Redundancy looks elegant on PowerPoint slides—just add an extra copy, sprinkle in some automation, and voilà, instant immortality! In reality, it's more like building a Rube Goldberg machine out of duct tape, crossed fingers, and whatever was left in this quarter's budget.

The catch? Redundancy isn't the same as resilience. Having duplicates means you copied something; having resilience means those duplicates actually work independently. And as you'll see, there are countless ways to have "multiple systems" that all fail together in perfect harmony.

So let's go through the greatest hits—the myths that keep turning "highly available" systems into synchronized explosions.

1. N+1: When Math Meets Murphy's Law

Ah yes, the mathematical lullaby of engineering — N+1. Sounds clever, doesn't it? Like something you'd scribble on a napkin and call a design. The idea: if you need N components to work, adding one more magically saves the day. Easy. Elegant. Wrong.

Picture this: your car needs four tires, so you toss a fifth one in the trunk. Redundancy achieved! Until winter hits and all five turn out to be summer tires. Or your airplane can stay in the air with two engines, so you add two more — one on each wing. Great plan, until you run out of fuel. Redundancy doesn't beat physics, and it sure doesn't beat shared failure.

So yes, the math looks right — but reality never signed that equation.

2. Common Mode Failure: The Art of Failing in Unison

By now, you can probably guess the punchline: adding more of the same crap doesn't help if all copies share the same flaw. Common Mode Failure is where optimism meets symmetry — everything fails together, just beautifully.

Maybe all your systems depend on the same dodgy assumption. Maybe they share the same power line, internet provider, or intern. Or maybe, like our good friend Ariane 5 from chapter 1, they're running the same buggy code that cost $380 million to rediscover in stereo.

The rocket was built to handle a hardware failure — but both flight computers crashed just a few milliseconds apart because they shared the same software brain fart. Two perfect clones, failing in unison. Efficiency!

Redundancy without diversity is just synchronized disaster.

3. SPOF: The Single Point of 'Oh Fuck

No, this isn't about hacking. (That's *spoofing* — different rabbit hole entirely.) But since engineers have an incurable love of acronyms, sitting through their meetings feels like watching Wheel of Fortune on mute — you're half-tempted to buy a vowel just to understand what they're saying.

SPOF stands for Single Point of Failure — that one thing that, when it dies, takes everything with it.

Imagine a plane with 20 passengers and 100 parachutes. Safe, right? Except all the parachutes are locked in a cabinet, and the captain left the key on his nightstand. That's your single point of failure.

And these things love hiding in plain sight: one power switch, one database, one person named Bob who's the only one who knows where the backups are.

That last one's so common it even got its own morbid nickname — Bus Hit Syndrome. As in, "What happens if Bob gets hit by a bus on the way to the office?" (Hint: you find out how much you didn't know.)

4. Automatic Failover: Never Tested, Always Trusted

Ah, the sweet lie of "it's been running for years and never caused a problem." Translation: we've never actually tested it, and we're terrified to try.

Automatic failover sounds like magic — until it fails automatically. If you've never forced your backup system to take over, you have no idea whether it works. Maybe your "redundant parachute" is just a bag of laundry. Or worse — maybe your intern packed it with white phosphorus instead, and your shiny automation happily deploys it mid-flight, setting everything ablaze.

Absurd? Sure. But digital equivalents happen all the time. Just ask AT&T's network engineers from Chapter 5 — their recovery logic spread failure faster than the actual bug. And trust me, an even nastier example is coming soon.

5. Geographic Redundancy: Same Failure, Longer Cable

For the past decade, "spread it across regions" has been the go-to mantra of every architect trying to sound clever. And fair enough — it's the right instinct. In fact, in Chapter 21 you'll find out exactly what kind of catastrophe forced the industry to learn that lesson the hard way. But like most good ideas, it tends to stop halfway.

As you already know from our old friends SPOF and Common Mode Failure, distance doesn't equal safety. Two systems an ocean apart can still share the same weak point, just on a longer cable.

You can run your app in both Tokyo and New York and feel smugly invincible. But as you learned from the AWS outage in Chapter 10, there are services everything depends on — and if one of those sneezes in Virginia, the whole internet catches a cold. Distance is great for latency bragging rights, not for immunity.

6. The Cloud Is Not Your Safety Net (It's Your Landlord)

Ah, the cloud — the universal bandage for all sins. We've collectively convinced ourselves that if a trillion-dollar company hosts our mess, it somehow becomes less messy. Spoiler: it doesn't.

Cloud providers give you tools, not salvation. They'll keep the lights on, but you still have to wire them properly — and pay the electric bill. Remember that Shared Responsibility Model from part III? Yeah, the "shared" part means you still have homework.

And as you'll soon see, some aspects of that wiring can be more surprising than you'd expect.

Those were the fan favorites — the greatest hits of misplaced confidence. In practice, human creativity in finding new ways to screw up redundancy is endless: circular failovers, shared "independent" networks, and chaos as a service.

Now you know what redundancy is and the six most popular ways to break it. There's just one more thing: the language engineers use to measure these disasters. Because when systems fail, people don't just say "it broke"—they also measure how often.

 **Explainer:**
Reliability and the Magic Nines

Back in Part III we talked about availability — how often your system picks up the phone when you call — and durability — whether it still remembers who you are after the fire.

But even if both check out, there's one more layer of self-delusion left: reliability.

Reliability isn't about uptime or backups. It's about whether the damn thing actually behaves as promised once it's awake. It's the friend who not only answers the call and remembers your name, but also manages to show up roughly on time and without creating a new crisis on the way.

Engineers, of course, couldn't resist quantifying that, so they came up with the **"number of nines"** — a metric so catchy it sounds like a pop band.

Each extra nine is a badge of honor, a corporate flex, and a budgeting nightmare rolled into one.

- **99% ("two nines")** → about **87.7 hours** of downtime per year.

- **99.5% ("two and a half nines")** → around **43.8** hours.

- **99.9% ("three nines")** → roughly **8.8 hours.**

- **99.99% ("four nines")** → just **52.6 minutes** of downtime per year.

These values are approximate — availability is often measured over shorter windows (months, quarters, or individual services). But they illustrate the principle: every extra "9" costs exponentially more to achieve.

That's where the law of diminishing returns kicks in (we already met this old friend back in Part I, Chapter 1). The closer you get to perfection, the more each improvement drains your wallet and sanity. Achieving 50% availability isn't impressive (you'd almost have to try to be worse). One "9" is trivial. Even 95% is achievable on a home PC while you're making coffee. But push beyond that, and the curve turns vertical. In practice, even the biggest players like AWS or Microsoft rarely promise more than three nines — because the fourth one costs real money. Millions, in fact.

Long story short, the first "9" of reliability is easy, the second still cheap, but the fourth? That's where budgets cry and engineers start bargaining with deities.

The law of diminishing returns is a favorite buzzword in IT circles. But it actually applies to nearly every aspect of life.

Think about running: it's easy to improve your one-kilometer time (roughly 0.6 mile) from an hour to twenty minutes (mostly by not falling asleep midway). Dropping from twenty to twelve minutes isn't too bad — the average adult can walk that distance in about 12.5 minutes. Hitting ten minutes? A brisk walk. A slow jog? Around six and a half. A fit amateur might hit five minutes. But an Olympian? Roughly three minutes — and every extra second shaved off takes years of training, nutrition plans, and entire coaching teams.

Each improvement gets exponentially harder and more expensive. For reference, the men's world record for one kilometer is **2:11.96**, set by Noah Ngeny of Kenya in September 1999 (about **27.1 km/h**). The women's record stands at **2:28.98**, achieved by Svetlana Masterkova of Russia in August 1996 (roughly **24.2 km/h**). And yes, those times are measured down to hundredths of a second for a reason — at that level, every fraction counts.

The same principle applies everywhere. It's true for learning new words in a foreign language, typing faster on a keyboard, or even mastering the delicate art of competitive cheese rolling — the first gains come easy, the later ones cost you your sanity.

In short: reliability is the ideal, availability is the goal, and durability is what saves you when both of those fail.

Armenian Internet vs. Georgian Scrap Hunter With A Shovel

Date: March 28, 2011
Impact: Up to 90% of Armenia offline for hours; partial outages in Georgia and Azerbaijan
Root Cause: A single unprotected fibre route; physical redundancy existing only on PowerPoint

Network engineers love drawing redundant paths. Two lines, maybe three. Lots of arrows. A reassuring amount of symmetry. It all looks very "carrier-grade" — right up until reality shows up with a shovel.

In 2011, Armenia's internet relied on a major fibre link running north through Georgia into Europe. In theory, alternative paths existed. In practice, almost all traffic flowed through a single physical conduit: one buried line that passed, somewhat unfortunately, through an area frequented by scrap metal scavengers.

Enter a 75-year-old Georgian woman searching for copper.

While digging for metal near the village of Ksani, she struck the fibre backbone and sliced straight through it. One motion, one shovel, one accidental backhoe-in-human-form — and Armenia lost **up to 90% of its internet connectivity**. Georgia and parts of Azerbaijan experienced outages too. The culprit? Not hackers. Not foreign adversaries. Not sophisticated cable-cutting operations. Just a pensioner with excellent aim.

The incident would be funny if it weren't so on-brand for how fragile "redundant" systems often are. ISPs had assured regulators that failover paths existed. And they did — on paper. But commercial routing policies, cost optimization, and "temporary" capacity limitations had quietly funnelled nearly all traffic into the one link a determined grandmother could reach with a shovel.

The repair took hours. The memes lasted years. The lesson will outlive us all.

Redundancy diagrams don't matter. Physical paths do. And unless your backup route is actually built, actually provisioned, and actually carrying traffic, you're one enthusiastic metal hunter away from watching an entire country fall offline.

LESSON LEARNED

- Redundancy that exists only in documentation does not exist at all.
- Physical layer failures are the most democratic: anyone with a shovel can participate
- Cost-optimized routing quietly erodes resilience until one cut becomes a nationwide outage.
- The universe does not need cyberwar when it has pensioners and copper prices.

If something is considered impossible, find someone who doesn't know that — they'll go out and do it. A Georgian scrap hunter took down a country's internet; CIA and FSB may want to take notes.

Knight Capital
The One-Server Suicide Note

Date: August 1, 2012

Impact: $440 million lost in 45 minutes; 75% market value wiped overnight

Root Cause: One SMARS server left running test code while the load balancer treated it like a productive member of society.

If you ever need a story that explains why "move fast and break things" should never apply to financial markets, Knight Capital is your patron saint. In August 2012, a routine deployment turned into the financial equivalent of firing a starting pistol at a demolition derby. Half a billion dollars evaporated before lunch – not because of a sophisticated hack, a cascading automation failure, or a malevolent AI uprising. No. It all came down to one box. One lonely, forgotten, obsolete box.

Every engineer knows the phrase "It's just a small update." That's how tech haunts begin. Knight pushed 26 code changes, forgot to disable an old feature flag, skipped anything resembling end-to-end testing, and marched confidently into production. Seven of their SMARS servers picked up the new release. One didn't. Normally that's a footnote. At Knight Capital, it became the plot.

The architecture was deceptively neat: eight identical SMARS nodes behind a load balancer, all meant to run the same routing logic. Except they didn't. The LB did what LBs do: it checked if the server was alive, not if it was sane. All eight answered health checks, so all eight got work. The result? Imagine hiring seven sober traders and one sleep-deprived intern hallucinating colors, then giving them equal control over billions of dollars. That's what went live at 9:30 AM.

And live it was. The outdated server began executing an old internal test routine that sprayed orders into the market like a fire hose with a grudge. Buy, sell, reverse, repeat – financial chaos on fast-forward. At one point, Knight accounted for nearly 97% of NYSE market volume. Statistically breathtaking. Economically suicidal.

The beauty – or horror – of this case is its simplicity. Unlike so many disasters in this book, nothing propagated automatically. No tooling replicated the bug. No script spread corruption to the cluster. Reality was far more banal: the system assumed homogeneity. It never occurred to anyone that a single server could be wrong. That assumption cost them $10 million per minute.

By 9:35 AM, Knight had accidentally bought roughly $7 billion worth of positions it neither wanted nor could fund. Exchanges halted 148 stocks in sheer self-defense. Knight's losses hit $440 million in 45 minutes. That's not failure – that's speedrunning bankruptcy.

To make matters worse, Knight's market footprint magnified everything. Handling nearly a fifth of all U.S.

equity trades on a normal day meant their bug didn't just torch their own shop; it sprayed shrapnel into everyone else's algorithms. Other trading systems interpreted the insanity as opportunity, dutifully piling into the madness like lemmings with MBAs. A small glitch became a market-wide carnival of terrible decisions.

Knight technically survived – the same way a patient "survives" after being revived with donor organs from rivals. A $400 million bailout kept the lights on; months later, the company was absorbed into another firm. Regulators fined them $12 million, which is adorable compared to the crater left in their credibility.

One executive later summed it up: "We built for speed, not stupidity." Unfortunately, stupidity is exactly what outruns you when you build for speed.

LESSON LEARNED

- If you want N+1, make damn sure all N+1 copies agree on what their job is – otherwise you're scaling inconsistency, not resilience.
- Load balancers aren't moral arbiters; they'll happily route traffic into a blender if it returns 200 OK.
- Deployment tools that verify liveness but not correctness are security blankets, not safeguards.
- In high-speed systems, tiny inconsistencies become financial Chernobyls.
- Speed isn't a virtue when your release process assumes infallibility.

Knight Capital didn't fall off a cliff. It sprinted. And it only took one server to hand it the shove.

AWS US-EAST-1
Black Friday Massacre

Date: November 25, 2020 (Black Friday Eve)

Impact: Thousands of services down for ~11 hours; major platforms (Reddit, Roku, Flickr, Twilio, Capital One) affected; no data loss, but widespread paralysis

Root Cause: A scaling bug in Kinesis caused internal overload that throttled AWS's shared control plane — proving that even "independent" Availability Zones share a single throat to choke.

If Knight Capital showed us how automated failover can amplify disaster, AWS's 2020 US-EAST-1 outage taught a different lesson: even "independent" zones share a throat to choke. It happened, fittingly, on the eve of Black Friday — the most expensive possible moment to discover that your "redundant" systems all breathe through the same straw.

Before we dive in, it's worth understanding what those "Availability Zones" actually are. They're the backbone of geographic redundancy in cloud computing — separate data centers spaced a "meaningful distance" apart — far enough that a fire won't take them all out, close enough that data can sync without lag. Think 1-6 miles typically, though AWS has hinted they can stretch up to 60 miles when needed. The sweet spot: distant enough to survive, close enough to feel connected — like a relationship status on Facebook: in private messages, "connected"; on your public profile, "it's complicated."

It started with Amazon Kinesis, the data stream service used for everything from analytics to security monitoring. A well-meaning scaling event added servers too aggressively, overloading the internal front-end fleet. That congestion rippled through AWS's internal network like cholesterol through an artery. Soon, a shared metadata service — the quiet librarian that keeps the entire ecosystem talking — started choking. The result: healthy servers in other Availability Zones couldn't get updates, couldn't launch, couldn't authenticate. Multi-AZ apps, supposedly immune to failure, suddenly forgot who they were.

The irony was delicious: the world's largest distributed system was brought to its knees not by a hardware failure, but by software doing exactly what it was told to do. The system tried to scale — and succeeded, until it throttled itself into silence. Engineers described it later as a "congestion loop," which is a polite way of saying the cloud tripped over its own shoelaces.

That day exposed the myth of "independent Availability Zones." On paper, each AZ is its own island. In practice, they all depend on shared services like the control plane, internal DNS, and metadata APIs. When that layer hiccups, the islands sink together. What was marketed as multi-zone resilience turned out to be multi-zone synchronization of pain.

Recovery was a slow, manual dance: throttling scaling operations, clearing backlogs, restarting subsystems, and probably brewing several gallons of coffee. By late afternoon, the storm cleared. Customers got their dashboards back; Amazon got a reminder that "high availability" and "infinite availability" are not synonyms.

AWS later added circuit breakers, improved observability, and a few paragraphs of humble pie to its postmortem. But the incident left a mark: even the mightiest clouds have single points of failure, just well-camouflaged ones.

LESSON LEARNED

- Independence is a comforting illusion — shared control planes make even clouds codependent.
- Over-scaling is still failure, just faster and with more confidence.
- Multi-AZ is not multi-brain; one bad signal can sink the whole fleet.
- Test your "independence" like you test your backups: by breaking things on purpose.
- Cloud marketing promises elasticity; reality delivers entanglement.

On paper, AWS had N+1 zones. In practice, it had N+1 ways to fail together — and learned it the hard way on Black Friday.

OVHcloud
The Fire That Burned Every Backup

Date: March 10, 2021

Impact: One data center destroyed, another severely damaged, two more shut down, thousands of businesses offline — many permanently.

Root Cause: Physical fire cascaded through shared infrastructure, revealing that OVH's "redundancy" was more philosophical than architectural.

OVHcloud isn't a household name like AWS, Azure, or Google Cloud, but in Europe it's the scrappy cousin — born in a family garage in Roubaix in 1999, proudly independent, and famous for offering "cloud" at a fraction of the Big Three's prices. For years, the company's Strasbourg campus was its crown jewel: four data centers (SBG1–SBG4) humming in harmony, supposedly providing safe, regional redundancy.

Until one night in March 2021, when harmony turned to barbecue.

A fire broke out in SBG2 around midnight. Within hours, it burned to the ground. Its neighbor, SBG1, was gutted by heat and smoke. The other two — SBG3 and SBG4 — technically survived, but went dark anyway. Why? Because all four buildings, in a stunning display of optimism, shared the same power, network uplinks, and other critical infrastructure. Physically separate, logically married. In theory, these buildings were OVH's version of Availability Zones — like the ones in the previous AWS story — designed to ensure service continuity across failures. In practice, they were neighboring houses connected by extension cords — great until one catches fire.

The result: one regional campus, four data centers, zero functioning systems.

Firefighters did their best, but the setup was doomed from the start. OVH didn't use a gas-based fire suppression system — the industry standard for data centers. Their backup plan? Handheld extinguishers. Yes, really. The kind you'd find under your kitchen sink. By the time crews arrived, the blaze was so intense that even the metal racks inside SBG2 had melted. Backup generators, cables, and routing equipment linking the buildings were either fried or flooded. Every customer hosted there woke up to the same message: "Please restore your backups."

That message aged poorly when many replied: "What backups?" Many customers had bought into the dream of cloud resiliency — trusting that the word "cloud" implied safety. Drawn by OVH's lower prices compared to the Big Three, they'd cut costs further by skipping offsite backups and keeping everything in one data center. I personally know a few people who lost everything that day. OVH's response was brutally honest: according to their own Shared Responsibility Model, customers were expected to store backups in other facilities. In short — the fine print was right, even if the marketing wasn't.

Not every data loss was the customer's fault. Some had followed best practices — storing backups in SBG1 as OVH recommended — only to watch that building burn too. OVH acknowledged responsibility in those cases and covered losses, admitting their physical layout turned one fire into a campus-wide disaster.

OVH was remarkably transparent throughout, posting updates in real time and even livestreaming parts of the recovery. It didn't help that the recovery involved finding replacement cables that hadn't liquefied. In the official postmortem, they wrote: "We are working hard to bring SBG3 and SBG4 back online. No ETA yet." Translation: we're trying to find something that still conducts electricity.

Beyond the charred remains lay a painful truth: redundancy on paper doesn't mean resilience in practice. The entire Strasbourg region functioned as a single failure domain. When one building caught fire, the others followed — not in flames, but in silence.

LESSON LEARNED

- Firewalls don't stop actual fires.
- "Multi-AZ" means nothing if all AZs share the same cables and parking lot.

- Handheld extinguishers are not a disaster recovery plan.
- Transparency after disaster is noble; fire suppression before disaster is smarter.
- Backups stored in the same region are just souvenirs waiting to burn.

OVHcloud promised the safety of four data centers. The fire proved they had one — four times.

The 2003 Northeast Blackout
The Cascade Nobody Saw Coming

Date: August 14, 2003

Impact: 50 million people across 8 U.S. states and Ontario left in the dark; 11 indirect deaths (heat/accidents); $6–13 billion in losses

Root Cause: A software bug, untrimmed trees, and human overconfidence created a cascading failure that exposed how fragile "redundancy" can be when everyone shares the same blind spot.

By the summer of 2003, the U.S. power grid was a modern marvel — a vast, interconnected web designed to handle any single failure. Engineers proudly called it N-1 compliant: if one part failed, the rest would pick up the slack. That confidence lasted right up until 3:06 PM on August 14th, when a few overgrown trees in Ohio decided to play their part in electrical history.

At first, three high-voltage lines sagged into the trees and tripped offline — nothing unusual. Normally, alarms would blare and operators would reroute power. But that day, the alarm system at FirstEnergy's control center crashed due to a software race condition — the same timing bug we explored back in Chapter 3, when two actions happen just slightly out of sync and chaos quietly slips in. Different system, same flavor of disaster. No alerts, no warnings. Operators thought everything was fine and carried on with their day while the grid quietly began to unravel.

As more lines overloaded, power automatically rerouted through neighboring states. Without visibility, operators didn't shed load or isolate the fault — they simply assumed it was a local issue. The grid, following physics rather than policy, kept trying to balance itself until it couldn't.

Then physics took over. In just seven seconds, over 100 power plants tripped offline — a continental-scale domino effect faster than most people could process what was happening. The lights went out from Michigan to New York, from Toronto to New Jersey.

The grid was built with redundancy — but redundancy isn't magic. It relied on shared control systems and a shared assumption: that someone, somewhere, was watching the dashboard. When the alarms died, everyone assumed their neighbor had it covered. Nobody did. This was every redundancy myth in one package: N-1 that failed because everyone shared the same blind spot, geographic separation that meant nothing when the cascade crossed borders, and automatic systems that amplified disaster because nobody tested what happens when the monitoring goes dark.

Cascading failures don't politely stop at borders — they just collect frequent-flyer miles. Traffic lights froze mid-cycle. Water treatment plants stalled. Subway passengers sat in darkness while control rooms scrambled to understand what had happened. Airports shut down. Cell towers drained their batteries. All because of a handful of trees, a failed alarm system, and a few fatal assumptions.

Restoration took days. Some areas had power back within 24 hours; others waited four. Black-start generators — diesel units designed to jumpstart dead grids — became the unsung heroes. Engineers spent the weekend manually reassembling the electrical puzzle they thought could never fall apart.

The incident became a global case study in systems thinking: a perfect storm of N+1 logic, common-mode dependencies, and human complacency. It showed that even when every component does what it's supposed to, the system as a whole can still find brand-new ways to fail — Murphy's Law at continental scale.

LESSON LEARNED

- Redundancy doesn't matter if everyone shares the same failure path.
- N+1 compliance is not a personality trait — it won't save you from physics.
- Human optimism is the most common single point of failure.
- Alarm systems need backups too — especially the ones that tell you the backups are down.
- Never underestimate the destructive potential of trees.

The grid was built for every failure except the one that happened — and reality doesn't offer do-overs.

The 2003 Italy Blackout
When Europe Hit Snooze

Date: September 28, 2003

Impact: 56 million people without power; 3 indirect deaths (accidents/medical); trains and airports halted; telecom and water systems down; ~€1 billion economic loss

Root Cause: Tree flashover in Switzerland, cross-border miscommunication, and delayed load-shedding cascaded into a nationwide blackout — proving that N-1 redundancy fails when operators speak different languages.

2003 was not a great year to be an electrical engineer. Barely six weeks after the U.S. and Canada plunged into darkness, Europe decided to try its own version. This time, the lights went out over an entire country — and not just any country, but Italy, home of espresso machines, high-speed trains, and people who really don't like it when the air conditioning stops working.

It started at 3:01 a.m., when a tree in Switzerland brushed against a 380 kV power line near Lukmanier Pass. The line tripped, as designed. No panic. A single fault, N-1 compliant — everything should've been fine. But 24 minutes later, a second Swiss line tripped under load, and that's when the fun began. The Italian grid, now isolated on just a few interconnects, started to wobble.

Operators on both sides of the border — Swiss and Italian — miscommunicated, partly due to language, partly due to overconfidence. Each assumed the other was handling the issue. Italy didn't shed load in time, believing the problem was remote. It wasn't. The growing imbalance caused the frequency to plummet. At 3:28 a.m., all remaining interconnects tripped. The Italian grid went dark, taking 110 power plants with it in a synchronized shutdown that would've made a ballet choreographer proud. So much for "independent" national grids — when the physics said die, they all died together.

The blackout lasted roughly 12 hours for most of the mainland, longer for Sardinia and smaller islands. Black-start generators in France and Slovenia eventually jump-started the recovery. By dinner time, power was mostly back — and so were the debates over what, exactly, went wrong.

The post-mortem revealed the communication gaps were deeper than just technical jargon. The Swiss and Italians literally weren't speaking the same language — and neither side wanted to admit they didn't fully understand what the other was saying. It's like asking an Italian waiter why there's no cream in carbonara. (I once did that on purpose in Calabria. I had a great time; my Italian friend who had to explain it, considerably less so.)

Technically, the grid had done what it was designed to do. The first Swiss line tripped? Fine, N-1 compliant. The second line tripped? That's when the assumptions collapsed. The grid was designed for equipment failure, not human miscommunication. The cascade wasn't just electrical — it was organizational. This was the geographic redundancy myth on display: separate countries, separate operators, separate grids — but shared physics and shared assumptions that synchronized the failure. Add language barriers and you get common-mode failure with an accent.

LESSON LEARNED

- N+1 logic doesn't translate well across borders — or languages.

- Common-mode failures aren't always mechanical; sometimes they speak with an accent.
- "Independent" national grids still share the same physics — and the same ability to fail together.
- Testing load-shed plans is cheaper than explaining why they didn't work.
- Trees are undefeated.

In 2003, America proved redundancy couldn't save one continent — and Italy immediately volunteered to prove it couldn't save another.

CHAPTER 20:
RESILIENCE THEATER – PRACTICING SAFETY WHILE EVERYTHING BURNS

If you've made it this far, you've already seen systems fail in every imaginable way. Numbers can lie, processors can stall, memory can eat its own tail, and networks can spontaneously decide they're on strike. Data corrupts itself, caches go feral, protocols fall apart, and sometimes the cloud just... forgets how to cloud. All of that is real, and all of that is normal.

Engineers eventually accepted a grim truth: you can't prevent every disaster. So we invented a discipline to cope with the inevitable. Disaster Recovery was supposed to be the adult in the room—the handbook for what to do when the universe kicks your infrastructure in the teeth. If failure is guaranteed, the least we can do is fail with dignity.

But humans being humans, we found wonderfully creative ways to screw up even *that*. Instead of resilience, we got rituals. Instead of preparedness, we got theater. And instead of real recovery, we got disaster plans that work perfectly—as long as nothing actually goes wrong.

As you'll soon see, DR failures come in two flavors: there's the kind where you make things actively worse (pouring gasoline on fires), and the kind where you practice religiously with toy hoses and wonder why nothing works when real flames arrive. Fake failovers, tabletop exercises that test precisely nothing, pandemic continuity plans that never left Excel—it's all here.

As usual, let's establish the basics first. What does real DR planning actually require? And why does missing even one piece turn a safety net into a decorative napkin? That's where our next explainer begins...

Explainer:
The Parachute Principle: What to Do When It All Falls Apart

Redundancy, as you've just seen, isn't a silver bullet—it's spare copies with attitude. But having duplicates is only the first move. The second? Figuring out what happens when everything goes south.

That's where Disaster Recovery comes in—the less sexy sibling of redundancy. DR doesn't prevent failure; it answers the follow-up question: "Okay, everything's on fire. Now what?" And like most survival plans, it's a careful balance between our familiar tradeoffs: **RTO** (how fast can you recover?), **RPO** (how much data can you lose?), **cost** (how much pain can your budget take?), and **complexity** (how many exciting new failure modes you just introduced).

Engineers also love assigning temperatures to things, and DR strategies are no exception. So, let's walk from the coldest to the hottest — or from "we'll rebuild it eventually" to "we're running two internets just to be sure."

Backup & Restore — The Blueprint Approach

RPO	RTO	Cost	Complexity
hours to days	hours to days	low	low

Imagine having exact architectural plans for your house, down to the brand of every lightbulb and the color of every wall. When the house burns down, you can rebuild it brick by brick. It'll take time — weeks, maybe months — but the cost of storing a blueprint is basically a rounding error.

In IT terms: you have backups stored somewhere safe (often offsite, sometimes even on tape). When disaster strikes, you spin up new infrastructure and restore everything from scratch. Cheapest option, slowest recovery. Great if your business can survive days of downtime. Terrible if you're running an e-commerce site during Black Friday.

Pilot Light — The Spark Before the Fire

RPO	RTO	Cost	Complexity
minutes	minutes to hours	low to medium	medium

It's like a spare tire in your car's trunk. Not glamorous, but when the wheel explodes, you at least have something round enough to get you moving. You still need to stop, replace, and inflate it — but you won't be calling for a tow truck.

The name comes from that tiny flame in gas furnaces that's always burning — small, cheap, and ready to ignite the full blast at a moment's notice. Here, you keep the bare minimum of your system permanently running — a skeleton setup that can be expanded into a full environment when disaster hits. Think of it as leaving a small flame alive so the restart doesn't take forever.

Warm Standby — The Backup Parachute

RPO	RTO	Cost	Complexity
seconds to minutes	seconds to minutes	medium to high	high

A warm standby is a full system replica, already configured and syncing with production data, but not yet handling real traffic.

Like the reserve parachute you hope to never touch. It's fully packed, tested, and ready — but you only pull it when the main one fails. In the air, you can't stop to rebuild it or inflate it; you just switch and pray everything opens properly.

It's faster than a Pilot Light and far safer than a "let's rebuild it from scratch" plan. Still, it costs more and needs regular testing — because nothing's worse than discovering your backup parachute was repacked wrong *months ago.*

Hot Standby (Active-Active) — Two Ovens, One Kitchen

RPO	RTO	Cost	Complexity
near-zero	sub-second	high	astronomical

This is the holy grail — running two complete systems side by side, both handling live traffic simultaneously.

It's like a restaurant with two ovens. When one breaks, the kitchen slows down but doesn't stop. Orders still go out, and customers barely notice. But keeping both ovens hot and synchronized doubles your fuel bill and your stress level.

In IT: two fully operational environments in sync, balancing requests in real time. No downtime, but debugging becomes a philosophical exercise.

Putting It All Together — The Parachute Test

Now let's tie these approaches together with a single, dramatic metaphor — skydiving.

In the *Backup & Restore* scenario, all the materials and blueprints for a new parachute are neatly stored back at the airport. You've got everything you need to make a perfect one, complete with sewing patterns and fabric rolls. The problem? You're already mid-air. Good luck stitching it together before you hit the ground.

With *Pilot Light*, things get slightly better. The plane carries a few extra parachutes. That's comforting — as long as you notice the problem before jumping. But once you're out the door and falling, you won't exactly circle back to grab one, like going home for a forgotten phone.

A *Warm Standby* is the sensible approach. You're wearing a backup chute. It's packed, tested, and ready to deploy if the main one refuses to open. When everything goes wrong, you just pull the second handle and hope for a soft landing.

And *Hot Standby / Active-Active*? That's the daredevil move — you're diving with both parachutes open at once. It looks impressive and feels safe, but coordinating two canopies mid-air will drive you absolutely bananas. One gust of wind, one misstep, and suddenly you're wrapped in a death burrito of tangled lines. Maximum safety, maximum paranoia.

In Real Infrastructure Terms

- **Backup & Restore:** Incremental data backups + full Infrastructure-as-Code templates to rebuild everything from scratch (as we already saw back in Chapter 18).

- **Pilot Light:** Pre-provisioned replicas of key services (databases, configs, DNS) — quick to ignite, slow to perfect.

- **Warm Standby:** A complete but downscaled copy of production, ready to autoscale up when needed.

- **Hot Standby / Active-Active:** Two (or more) data centers, each running the full stack and splitting live traffic.

Moral of the Story

In the end, redundancy isn't really about having duplicates — it's about *independence.* Two systems that share the same assumptions will fail together in perfect harmony. The trick isn't to double everything, but to make sure your Plan B doesn't trip over the same banana peel as Plan A.

And of course, every strategy hides its own set of traps — design flaws, cost surprises, or plain human laziness. We'll get to those soon enough. But before we do, let's clear up what engineers actually mean when they throw around terms like *reliability*, *durability*, and *availability.*

THE PARACHUTE PRINCIPLE™

Too few chutes and you're dead; too many and you wish you were.

That's the redundancy paradox in one sentence. Not enough safety nets and you hit the ground. Too many and you're wrapped in a death burrito of tangled lines, wishing for the simpler death.

Delta Airlines
The Cold-Start Carnival

Date: August 8, 2016

Impact: ~2,300 flights canceled; ~$150 million in losses

Root Cause: Failed power-control module (commonly referred to as a Static Transfer Switch, though Delta publicly labeled it "switchgear") + no application dependency map during restart

If you ever needed proof that "just turn it off and on again" stops working once an airline hits Fortune-500 scale, Delta's 2016 meltdown is your exhibit A. Cold-start recovery is supposed to be the simplest form of resilience: power dies, power returns, systems boot, life goes on. It's the bargain-bin strategy of disaster recovery — the IKEA desk of enterprise continuity. Cheap, minimalistic, and guaranteed to wobble the moment you put anything important on it.

Delta found out exactly how wobbly.

It all began with something small — insultingly small — in their Atlanta data center. A piece of switchgear hiccupped, an STS (power-control module (commonly referred to as a Static Transfer Switch, though Delta publicly labeled it "switchgear")) failed to transfer power, and suddenly the "backup" in "backup generators" became more of a suggestion than a fact. The generators spun up as designed, but the failed switch meant a chunk of critical servers remained silently, stubbornly dark.

What followed was a kind of electrical split-brain: half the data center alive and blinking, the other half in an unplanned power nap. In a hospital, this is where a surgeon yells for a crash cart. In a hyperscale airline? This is where 300 interdependent applications begin a synchronized breakdown.

When power was finally restored, every system — all 300+ of them — woke up at once and sprinted for the starting line like a Black Friday sale for CPUs. And that's when Delta discovered a truth older than aviation itself: if you don't control the order in which your systems wake up, they will invent their own, and it will be stupid.

The results were biblical. Databases waited on authentication. Authentication waited on networking. Networking wanted DNS. DNS wanted storage. Storage needed the database. It was a technological ouroboros — a serpent eating its own tail, except the tail was boarding passes, pilot rosters, and passenger itineraries.

The crew-tracking system — the software responsible for knowing where pilots and flight attendants are — couldn't sync with the operations system. So from the airline's perspective, thousands of employees simply vanished from reality. Planes sat on the tarmac fully fueled and ready, but legally uncrewable. Meanwhile, passengers slept on floors in airports worldwide because Delta's printers couldn't even generate hotel vouchers.

And all of it because the architecture was too tangled to reboot.

Delta had backup generators. They had documentation. They had DR procedures. They had everything except the one thing that mattered: a tested, validated, end-to-end restart plan.

They assumed that when the lights came back on, the systems would obediently rise from the dead in the correct order, like well-trained zombies. Instead, they got a stampede of undead applications trampling each other for access to resources.

Cold-start resiliency sounds elegant — until you realize it depends entirely on implicit assumptions about boot sequence, service dependencies, and how tightly coupled your ecosystem has secretly become. Delta assumed simplicity. They had complexity.

And complexity always collects its debts.

LESSON LEARNED

- Critical systems need explicit dependency maps — not tribal knowledge and crossed fingers.

- Tiering matters: bring up the spine first, bells and whistles later.

- If you never test full power-off recovery, your systems don't have resilience — they have faith.

- A power-control module (commonly referred to as a Static Transfer Switch, though Delta publicly labeled it "switchgear") is a single point of failure wearing a fake mustache.

Delta accidentally ran a full-scale clearance-sale simulation: every system sprinting for a scarce resource, tripping over each other in the rush — only to discover at checkout that they'd knocked out the cashier halfway through the stampede.

T-Mobile
Tabletop Resilience Without The Table

Date: June 15, 2020

Impact: 15-hour nationwide outage; 23.000 911 call failures; >100M customers affected

Root Cause: failure of a leased fiber circuit + routing software bug that funneled massive traffic into a single undersized node, triggering network-wide routing loops

T-Mobile entered June 15, 2020 with confidence. Not because their network was flawless, but because on paper it looked flawless. Somewhere in a SharePoint folder lived a glossy disaster-recovery plan: all arrows straight, all boxes aligned, all failure scenarios resolved through the magic of PowerPoint optimism. Years of tabletop exercises had produced a cast-iron belief that resilience was something you could rehearse while seated.

Reality, unfortunately, does not attend tabletop meetings.

At around 6:30 p.m. ET, voice and data traffic across the U.S. network collapsed. Not a wobble, not a hiccup — a nation-scale faceplant. Calls failed at a rate of over 100,000 per minute. SMS vanished. LTE and VoLTE connections fell over like damp cardboard. Even worse, over a million 911 calls failed to connect, instantly elevating the incident from operational problem to public safety crisis.

The technical trigger wasn't a botched upgrade — it was far more embarrassing. A leased fiber circuit failed, shunting a surge of traffic onto a backup path. Under normal conditions, the routing layer should have absorbed the change smoothly. Instead, a lurking software bug in T-Mobile's routing logic funneled the sudden traffic spike into a single, painfully underpowered server. One node became the choke point for an entire national network. The result: a self-feeding routing storm where packets looped endlessly rather than reaching their destination. Under normal circumstances, redundant systems should have caught this immediately and rerouted traffic around the problem.

They didn't. Because "normal circumstances" assumed those systems had been tested.

They hadn't.

When investigators dug into T-Mobile's continuity practices, they discovered that most "tests" weren't tests at all. They were tabletop walkthroughs — the corporate equivalent of children playing "house." No simulated traffic. No synthetic loads. No live failover. Just teams sitting around a table saying things like, "If the router fails, we'll reroute the traffic," and everyone nodding approvingly as if the universe were obligated to follow the script.

When the real outage hit, the system behaved exactly like a plan that had never been tested: it panicked. Routing loops intensified. Monitoring dashboards lagged behind reality. Automated systems waited for conditions they had never been instructed to look for. Engineers were forced into manual rerouting under fire, reconstructing a failover strategy that should have existed long before the crisis.

Fifteen hours later, the network staggered back to life. What had begun as a simple maintenance window metastasized into the worst outage in company history. The FCC later fined T-Mobile $19.5 million, which is basically the government's way of saying, "Next time, please test your stuff." The public delivered its own verdict in the form of memes, nicknames, and a brief rebranding to T-Outage.

One unexpected positive came out of the fiasco: T-Mobile finally got serious. Live DR drills. Synthetic traffic. Automated failover validation. Real chaos engineering, not conference room theater. The exact financial losses were never disclosed, but between lost revenue, FCC fines, and reputational damage, it's safe to assume the lesson cost millions. Management finally understood that resilience isn't a meeting — it's a muscle.

LESSON LEARNED

- Slides ≠ resilience.
- A plan untested is a plan untrusted.
- Practice failure under load, not under fluorescent conference-room lights.
- DR without chaos engineering isn't preparedness — it's delusion.

Practicing disaster recovery in PowerPoint is like practicing swimming on a couch: you'll look confident right up until the moment you hit the water.

Cloudflare
When A Permission Change Became A Planet-Sized Brick

Date: November 18, 2025

Impact: Global traffic degradation, outages across multiple services; customers unable to reach sites routed through Cloudflare's edge

Root Cause: A routine database permission fix caused the control-plane storage layer to generate an oversized metadata file, overwhelming critical systems and cascading into global routing failures

Cloudflare's edge network usually behaves like a well-trained hive mind: thousands of machines scattered across the planet, all politely agreeing on a shared definition of reality. On November 18, 2025, that reality arrived in the form of a metadata file so large it could have been registered with the Library of Congress—and the hive mind promptly suffered a philosophical crisis.

The chaos began with a routine database permission change, the kind of maintenance task engineers perform between sips of coffee. But Cloudflare's control-plane database regenerates metadata whenever permissions shift, and this time it produced something less like a metadata file and more like a PDF bundle of every tax document filed since 1974.

Downstream systems reacted with the appropriate level of horror. Some PoPs stared at the behemoth and froze. Others parsed a few kilobytes, reconsidered their life choices, and quietly refused to continue. A handful pretended the file did not exist, like cats who believe that if they maintain eye contact with nothing, nothing can hurt them.

Unfortunately, Cloudflare's control plane is built around the noble ideal of global consistency—which, in this moment, translated to "replicate the problem everywhere, immediately." And so the metadata brick propagated across continents with the mechanical cheerfulness of a vending machine dispensing bricks instead of snacks.

Once the file reached critical mass, the symptoms escalated. Latency skyrocketed. Routes flapped. Packets drifted aimlessly across the network like backpackers who ditched the map because "getting lost is part of the experience." Rollback attempts failed because validating old snapshots required consulting the same bloated metadata, and the validator had already thrown up its metaphysical hands.

Automation attempted a self-heal, which mostly meant downloading the enormous file again and insisting, loudly, that this time it would definitely work. It was disaster recovery by ritual: a system performing the same steps over and over in the desperate hope the universe might behave differently on the next try.

Human engineers eventually stepped in, herding clusters into isolation, unwinding the propagation, and regenerating the metadata at a size that didn't risk orbital decay. Gradually, routing stabilized. Latency subsided. The global brain stopped hallucinating.

Nothing permanent was lost—except perhaps the illusion that "routine permission updates" are inherently harmless. As it turns out, the quickest way to humble a planet-scale edge network is not with hackers, or fires, or BGP leaks, but with a single file that grows so large it begins radiating ambition.

LESSON LEARNED

- A global configuration system will happily propagate correctness—or catastrophe—with the same enthusiasm.
- Automation is only as safe as the assumptions baked into its defaults.
- Distributed systems don't fail one node at a time; they fail in beautifully coordinated herds.
- A "harmless" empty value is still a value, and sometimes the most dangerous kind.
- Resilience isn't about faster recovery; it's about preventing your safeguards from becoming amplifiers.

In the end, the outage wasn't dramatic at all—just a humble metadata file that briefly aspired to become the longest book ever written, and a global network polite enough to read it cover to cover.

Atlassian
The DR That Caused The Disaster

Date: April 5–18, 2022

Impact: hundreds of sites deleted across 400+ customers affected; up to 13 days downtime

Root Cause: Misconfigured maintenance script + untested end-to-end backup restoration

Atlassian is one of those companies most people outside tech have never heard of — and everyone *inside* tech has heard of far too much. Their tools (Jira, Confluence,

Bitbucket, Opsgenie) run half the world's software development. They are the digital glue of the industry, the backbone of project management, and, for many engineers, the reason their therapist insists on weekly visits. If you've ever filed a Jira ticket and thought, "This is psychological warfare," congratulations: you are part of their target audience. And if you haven't — bless your career choices.

Which makes what happened in April 2022 even more impressive.

It started as a routine cleanup. Atlassian was retiring a legacy app ("Insight"), and a maintenance script was prepared to delete old, unused data. Simple idea. Straightforward job. What could possibly go wrong? Well, everything — immediately.

The script ran in **permanent delete** mode. Not the safe "soft delete" that leaves data recoverable, not the "quarantine" mode engineers love as a safety net. No. Full obliteration.

The script was supposed to delete old Insight app data. Instead, the customer IDs it was fed pointed to active, production sites across Jira and Confluence. In a multi-tenant platform where one database hosts hundreds of separate customers, mixing up those IDs is the digital equivalent of confusing a recycling bin with a woodchipper.

Within minutes, 883 production sites vanished.

Atlassian quickly discovered that while they *did* have backups, they had never tested restoring them at this scale. Backup pipelines existed, but only in the same sense Schrödinger's cat existed — theoretically. The company had never attempted a full end-to-end recovery of live, multi-tenant customer workloads. This is how you learn that "we have backups" is not the same sentence as "our backups work."

What followed was nearly two weeks of handcrafted disaster recovery. Engineers manually restored sites in batches of 50–60 tenants at a time, cross-checking IDs, dependencies, and auth layers. Deleted support contact records broke internal workflows. Missing site metadata triggered cascading failures. Every day brought the same grim update: "We recovered more customers, but not all."

No cyberattack. No sabotage. No exotic cloud meltdown. Just a script that wasn't dry-run, a process that wasn't validated, and backups that weren't tested.

By April 18, the last customers were finally back online — thirteen days after the outage began. Atlassian issued multiple apologies, acknowledged human error, and announced new safeguards: soft-delete defaults, mandatory dry-runs for destructive scripts, multi-stage validation gates, and real end-to-end disaster-recovery tests.

The incident became a case study in multi-tenant risk: one tiny command, one flawed assumption, and thousands of people across hundreds of companies suddenly couldn't access their project plans, documents, or workflows. For a company that sells productivity tools, the irony was almost poetic — if you ignore the million-dollar productivity loss it caused.

LESSON LEARNED

- Untested backups are placebo — they comfort you without helping you.
- Every destructive script deserves a soft-delete mode and multiple gates.

> - Multi-tenant systems amplify human error into company-scale disasters.
> - Cleanup scripts deserve the same care as production code.

Atlassian didn't just fail to prevent a disaster — they accidentally *ran* one. And it only took a single script to turn housekeeping into a two-week resurrection marathon.

CHAPTER 21:
WHERE OUTAGES BECOME FATAL 🎗

After a long tour through the digital world — where outages mostly cost money, time, or professional dignity — it's time to lift our eyes from servers and cables and look outward. Everything you've seen so far, especially in Part V on redundancy, applies just as sharply beyond IT. The same misplaced confidence, the same fragile assumptions, and the same "it'll never happen" thinking show up in power grids, transport systems, industrial facilities, and the engineered structures we trust with our lives.

This chapter steps fully outside the datacenter. Here, failures are not about SLAs, angry customers, or a day of degraded service. They are about irreversible consequences. When redundancy collapses in the physical world, it doesn't produce a status page — it produces casualties. Because of that, we'll drop the irony and focus strictly on the chain reactions, the decisions, and the lessons written in hard data.

That's why, in the final chapter of this volume, the tone changes. Every incident described here was too tragic for punchlines. Redundancy in the physical world isn't a comfort blanket or a checkbox. It's the thin line between routine and catastrophe — and sometimes, it's the last thing that fails.

September 11, 2001
When "Two Buildings" Wasn't Redundancy

Date: September 11, 2001

Impact: Destruction of primary and backup data centers; collapse of co-located business infrastructure; long-term disruption across global finance sector.

Root Cause: Redundant systems placed within the same physical hazard zone, providing the illusion of resilience without true separation.

The tragedy of September 11th is beyond measure—both in human lives and in its global consequences. This case focuses strictly on the business continuity lessons that emerged. Not to diminish the human cost, but because the technical and organizational failures exposed that day reshaped an entire industry, and the lessons—paid for at an unbearable price—must not be forgotten.

When the Twin Towers fell, the world witnessed horror at a scale few could comprehend. But alongside the human catastrophe, an enormous and largely invisible failure unfolded: the collapse of two buildings simultaneously eliminated the primary *and* secondary operational footprints of hundreds of companies. Trading floors, data centers, recovery sites, voice communication hubs—all erased in the span of half an hour.

And the companies that believed they had planned for disaster discovered they had not planned for *this* disaster.

After the 1993 bombing of the World Trade Center, many financial institutions revised their continuity strategies — or believed they had. The prevailing model became to split critical operations between the two towers, treating them as if they were independent structures rather than adjacent components of a single target. Proximity was mistaken for diversity. On

September 11th, that illusion ended. When one tower fell, the fate of the other was never in question, and with it went every system that had been entrusted to a redundancy based on geography measured in meters rather than miles.

One of the clearest examples of this architectural blind spot was Cantor Fitzgerald. Their primary data center and headquarters operated in the North Tower (1 WTC), with designated backup and critical voice infrastructure hosted in the South Tower (2 WTC). When 2 WTC collapsed at 9:59 a.m., their backup systems were obliterated instantly. Twenty-nine minutes later, the fall of 1 WTC eliminated their primary site as well.

Cantor's experience was not unique. Several firms had adopted cross-tower redundancy after the 1993 bombing, believing that physical proximity still granted independence. The events of 9/11 turned that assumption into ash.

Other companies fared marginally better only because their true primary data centers lived outside Manhattan. Empire Blue Cross Blue Shield, for instance, maintained its main data center in Albany, which allowed it to restore core operations within days. Yet even these organizations faced severe delays: offsite tape archives stored in or near the WTC complex were inaccessible for months due to debris, forensic holds, and physical damage. Some tapes were eventually recovered, though many were rendered unusable by heat, water, or impact. Claims processing backlogs lasted weeks to months—not because the data didn't exist, but because the systems that housed it had been physically annihilated.

Empire was not alone. Over 430 companies lost operational records outright. Twenty-one corporate libraries vanished. Legal, medical, and financial archives disappeared into debris fields. Even materials that physically survived faced long delays: many tapes were waterlogged, heat-damaged, or held as forensic evidence by authorities.

The lesson was brutal and simple: redundancy is meaningless if all copies share the same blast radius.

In the aftermath, business continuity across the financial sector underwent a complete paradigm shift. Geographic separation became the new doctrine: backups must exist in different states, not different floors. True high availability required independent power, independent connectivity, independent physical access, and true infrastructural isolation. This thinking eventually crystallized into the modern concepts of multi-region design and Availability Zones—the cloud-native descendants of the hard lessons carved into the skyline that morning.

Today, most major institutions in Manhattan place critical data centers across the Hudson River in New Jersey, with long-distance failovers far outside the metro area. The skyscrapers that once stood as monuments to ambition now serve as a solemn reminder: height offers visibility, not safety; proximity offers convenience, not resilience.

LESSON LEARNED

- Redundancy without distance is synchronization of failure.

- Physical separation must account for shared dependencies—power, network, and human access.

- Recovery planning must consider not just hardware loss, but access restrictions and legal seizure.

- True business continuity begins where comfort ends: outside the same skyline.

- The cost of resilience is small compared to the cost of rebuilding from dust.
- Testing disaster recovery plans means testing worst-case scenarios, even the ones hard to imagine.

Japan Airlines Flight 123
When Redundancy Shared One Weak Point

Date: August 12, 1985

Impact: Loss of control of Boeing 747SR-46; 520 fatalities; deadliest single-aircraft accident in aviation history.

Root Cause: Improper bulkhead repair following a 1978 tailstrike led to structural failure and explosive decompression, severing all four hydraulic systems routed through the same aft fuselage section.

The Boeing 747 was designed around a powerful promise: no single failure could bring it down. Its four hydraulic systems, each controlling critical flight surfaces, embodied the concept of redundancy that defined modern aviation. Each circuit was meant to operate independently —so that even a catastrophic failure in one would leave three to carry the aircraft safely home.

That principle met its tragic test seven years after a seemingly minor accident. In 1978, this same aircraft suffered a tailstrike on landing at Osaka. Boeing engineers repaired the aft pressure bulkhead but deviated from the prescribed method, using a single row of rivets instead of two. Over years of pressurization cycles, the improperly repaired splice plate fatigued until it finally tore apart.

At 6:24 p.m. on August 12, 1985, during climb-out from Tokyo's Haneda Airport, the bulkhead ruptured. The sudden decompression—a catastrophic loss of cabin pressure where high-pressure air inside the fuselage explosively rushed outward—blew off the vertical stabilizer and shredded the tail section, severing all four hydraulic lines that ran through that confined area. Within seconds, the crew lost every control surface on the aircraft. The plane could no longer turn, climb, or descend through conventional means.

For the next 32 minutes, the pilots fought to keep the 747 aloft using differential engine thrust—a feat of skill and composure that remains extraordinary. But the loss of hydraulics left the aircraft at the mercy of aerodynamics. At 6:56 p.m., Japan Airlines Flight 123 struck Mount Takamagahara, killing 520 of the 524 people on board.

The investigation by Japan's Aircraft Accident Investigation Commission traced the cause to Boeing's improper repair and to inspection oversights that failed to catch it. The design itself—though redundant on paper—had hidden a deeper flaw: all four hydraulic systems were routed together through the same tail section. One structural failure disabled them all. What should have been four lines of defense had become a single point of collapse.

The aftermath reshaped both maintenance and design practices across the aviation industry. Boeing revised structural repair protocols, introduced secondary verification for critical repairs, and redesigned routing principles to ensure true physical separation of redundant systems. Regulatory authorities, including the FAA and Japan's Civil Aviation Bureau, incorporated new certification standards to prevent any one failure from disabling multiple redundant systems simultaneously.

> ## LESSON LEARNED
>
> - Redundancy that shares physical space is not redundancy—it is synchronized failure waiting to happen.
> - Independent systems must be separated not just functionally, but structurally and spatially.
> - Verification of repairs is as vital as the design itself; a single deviation can nullify every safeguard.
> - True resilience depends on both design integrity and long-term maintenance discipline.
> - The tragedy of JAL 123 remains a permanent reminder: redundancy must be built to survive its own failure.

Air France Flight 447
When Automation Met Its Limits

Date: June 1, 2009

Impact: Loss of Airbus A330 over the Atlantic Ocean; 228 fatalities; major shift in pilot training and automation philosophy.

Root Cause: Simultaneous icing of all three pitot tubes caused loss of reliable airspeed data, leading to autopilot disconnection and pilot disorientation amid cascading system warnings.

Air France Flight 447 from Rio de Janeiro to Paris began as a routine long-haul flight. The Airbus A330 was one of the most technologically advanced airliners of its time— fly-by-wire controls, layered redundancy, and automation designed to prevent pilots from ever exceeding the aircraft's flight envelope. But when all layers of automation depend on a shared data source, that sophistication can turn fragile.

At 2:10 a.m. UTC, while crossing the equatorial Atlantic, the aircraft encountered high-altitude thunderstorms. Supercooled water droplets began to freeze over the pitot tubes—the small sensors that measure airspeed. All three independent probes iced over within seconds, feeding the flight computers inconsistent data. The autopilot, detecting conflicting airspeed readings, disengaged as designed. Control instantly reverted to manual, but the pilots now faced contradictory warnings from systems no longer certain of their inputs.

Deprived of valid airspeed, the flight directors and autoprotection systems shut down. The crew saw speed indications fluctuate wildly—from overspeed to stall warnings in rapid succession. Without reliable feedback and amid severe turbulence, the pilots pulled the nose up to maintain altitude—an instinctive but fatal reaction. The aircraft entered an aerodynamic stall at 38,000 feet, descending for more than three minutes before impacting the ocean.

The investigation by France's BEA found that the immediate trigger—the icing of pitot probes—was well understood, but its systemic consequences were not. The triple redundancy of sensors had failed identically, producing the same wrong data. Automation, designed to guard against human error, withdrew precisely when it was needed most. And without clear sensory cues or stable references, the human crew could not diagnose the problem fast enough.

After the accident, Airbus replaced pitot tubes fleetwide with improved models resistant to icing. Airlines revised procedures for unreliable airspeed events and updated training to emphasize manual flying skills in high-altitude scenarios. Regulators introduced new guidelines for human–automation interaction, stressing that redundancy must include not only multiple sensors, but also diversity in failure modes and data sources.

LESSON LEARNED

- Redundancy that fails identically provides no safety margin—it only amplifies confusion.
- Automation is only as reliable as the data it receives; when inputs fail, so does trust.
- Pilots must retain proficiency in manual flight even in systems built to fly themselves.
- Design diversity—different sensor types, algorithms, or physical placements—is essential to true redundancy.
- The legacy of AF447 reframed aviation safety: independence of information is as vital as independence of systems.

Piper Alpha
When Safety Systems Shared A Single Oversight

Date: July 6, 1988

Impact: Explosive chain reaction on North Sea oil platform; 167 fatalities (out of 226 on board); total destruction of the $1 billion facility; sweeping reforms in offshore safety worldwide.

Root Cause: Common-mode failure in redundant fire suppression and shutdown systems, triggered by a mismatched permit-to-work process that allowed a gas pump to restart amid a live steam leak.

The Piper Alpha platform, operated by Occidental Petroleum in the North Sea, was a symbol of the era's offshore oil boom—producing 300,000 barrels daily with layered redundancies to prevent catastrophe. Dual fire pumps, automated shutdown valves, blast walls, and deluge systems were designed to isolate and suppress any ignition source. Each safeguard was meant to stand alone: if one failed, another would engage, buying time for evacuation. They all shared a single point of failure: the permit-to-work system.

That design faced its unraveling during a routine maintenance shift. A pressure safety valve on a gas compressor had been removed for repair, leaving a temporary blind flange exposed. A permit-to-work system —a safety protocol that tags equipment as under maintenance—confirmed the work was complete, but a shift change led to miscommunication. At approximately 10:00 p.m., the incoming crew, unaware the valve was still absent, restarted the pump. Pressurized gas leaked from the unprotected pipe, causing an explosion in the module's confined space.

The initial explosion should have been contained. But the redundant firewater pumps were in a separate module, isolated by blast walls—yet the deluge system failed to activate fully. One pump tripped offline due to low pressure; the backup engaged but was starved of power when the platform's electrical switchgear, shared across modules, shorted in the heat. Automated gas isolation valves, reliant on the same control room, remained open, feeding the blaze with massive volumes of hydrocarbons— enough to overwhelm any fire suppression system.

Within 20 minutes, a vapor cloud explosion breached the living quarters, where most workers were sleeping. For nearly two hours, the platform burned, its redundancies undone by shared dependencies: a single permit process for all systems, co-located controls vulnerable to blast overpressure, and no independent power for emergency shutdown. At 11:20 p.m., Piper Alpha collapsed into the sea, killing 167—nearly all in the control room and living quarters.

The Cullen Inquiry, led by Scotland's Lord Cullen, pinned the root cause on systemic flaws in safety culture, not individual error. Redundant systems had been engineered for isolation, but procedural silos and shared infrastructure turned them into amplifiers of failure. What was built as a fortress became a tinderbox.

In the aftermath, the UK mandated "safety cases" for all offshore platforms—comprehensive risk assessments requiring independent verification of redundancies. Operators like Occidental (now Oxy) adopted diverse fire suppression (e.g., separate seawater intakes, nitrogen inerting), segregated controls, and rigorous permit-to-work hierarchies. Globally, it birthed the Offshore Installations (Safety Case) Regulations, emphasizing that true resilience demands procedural diversity as much as mechanical duplication.

LESSON LEARNED

- Redundant systems tied to shared procedures fail in unison when communication breaks.
- Communication protocols and safety culture are part of the same infrastructure—when they fail, every safeguard fails with them.
- Physical and procedural separation must extend to operational silos—permits, shifts, and controls.
- Designing for worst-case isolation requires testing beyond isolated components.
- Safeguards concentrated in one hazard zone will fail together, regardless of their technical independence.

NHS Pandemic Continuity Plans
Theater On A National Scale

Date: March–December 2020

Impact: Nationwide system overload; severe shortages of ventilators, PPE, and staff; tens of thousands of deaths involving COVID-19

Root Cause: Continuity plans built on unimplemented lessons from prior testing (Operation Cygnus), assuming resources that did not exist and actions that were never taken

Across the United Kingdom, every NHS trust entered 2020 with thick binders labeled *Business Continuity Plan*. These documents described, in careful detail, how hospitals would rotate staff, expand ICU capacity, and manage prolonged disruption in the event of a pandemic. On paper, the system looked prepared: escalation charts, surge diagrams, staffing matrices, supply assumptions, and flowcharts outlining how each department would adapt under pressure.

When COVID-19 arrived, the binders stayed on the shelves.

The virus moved faster than any of the plans anticipated. Intensive care units filled in days, not weeks. Staff illness and burnout depleted the workforce at a rate no rotation protocol could compensate for. PPE stocks, assumed plentiful in continuity documents, evaporated as global supply chains faltered. Hospitals that were theoretically supposed to "absorb surge demand" instead found themselves improvising makeshift wards, reusing disposable equipment, and redeploying staff far outside their usual scope of practice.

The gap between documented plans and operational reality became impossible to ignore. Many continuity assumptions rested on resources that had never been stockpiled, supply chains that had never been reinforced, and staffing models that could not function under simultaneous nationwide stress. The continuity plans described strategy; what the system actually needed was capacity. When pressure rose, the latter was absent.

Public inquiries later described these plans as optimistic at best and "fantasy" at worst. Crucially, the UK *did* conduct a major pandemic simulation — Operation Cygnus in 2016 — which predicted many of the exact failures that unfolded in 2020: PPE shortages, overwhelmed ICUs, staff depletion, and insufficient surge capacity. The issue was not the absence of testing, but the absence of action. Cygnus produced clear recommendations, many of which were never implemented due to budget constraints, political hesitation, or misplaced confidence that such a scenario was unlikely.

Instead of treating Cygnus as a warning, the system treated it as an academic exercise. Subsequent continuity drills reverted to tabletop rehearsals — conversations rather than simulations. No large-scale tests verified whether ventilators could be relocated quickly enough, whether surge wards could be staffed, or whether procurement systems could scale under pressure. When the real crisis arrived, systems defaulted to the assumption of success precisely because no one had validated what failure looked like.

As the first wave peaked, the consequences were stark: cancelled operations, delayed diagnoses, overwhelmed ICUs, and elevated risk for both patients and clinical staff. The human toll was profound. Medical teams faced conditions that continuity binders never envisioned and were forced to innovate under crisis rather than operate under plan.

In the months that followed, the NHS initiated extensive reviews. Emergency procurement brought equipment in at unprecedented speed. Staff were redeployed across regions, temporary hospitals were established, and later reforms — such as the *NHS Resilience Framework (2023)* — introduced stockpiling requirements, clearer command structures, and mandatory live testing of critical pathways.

The pandemic exposed a truth extending far beyond healthcare: **preparedness is not a document.** It is the combined effect of planning, capacity, logistics, and practice. Without all four, continuity cannot survive real pressure.

In 2020, the NHS discovered that resilience is measured not by how detailed the plans are, but by how well a system performs when the plans fail.

LESSON LEARNED

- A continuity plan without resources is a plan in name only.
- Real preparedness requires testing under real constraints, not tabletop discussions.
- A test is only as valuable as the actions taken afterward — ignored findings guarantee repeated failure.
- Effective resilience depends on stockpiles, staffing depth, and supply security—not assumptions.
- National-scale crises demand systems able to fail safely, not simply documented procedures.

Fukushima
The One That Survived

Date: March 11, 2011

Impact: Level 7 Meltdown in Units 1-3; Successful Cold Shutdown in Units 5-6.

Root Cause: Common-mode failure due to flooding disabled 12 of 13 generators. However, design diversity (elevation and cooling type) allowed the 13th generator to survive and prevent total collapse.

The Fukushima Daiichi disaster is often cited as the ultimate failure of redundancy. And for Units 1 through 4, it was. Designers had stacked layers of backup systems—

diesel generators, batteries, pumps—believing that quantity equaled safety. But because these redundant layers shared the same physical location (basements) and the same environmental vulnerability (flooding), they didn't function as independent safeguards. They functioned as dominoes.

When the tsunami cleared the seawall, it flooded the lower levels of the plant. Within minutes, 12 of the 13 emergency diesel generators on site were submerged or lost cooling water intake. The "fortress" of redundancy collapsed because every backup had the exact same weakness: they were too low.

But the story doesn't end with total darkness.

Amidst the chaos, Units 5 and 6 managed to avoid the fate of their sister reactors. The reason wasn't luck—it was a deviation in design.

Unit 6 was equipped with one emergency diesel generator that was different from the others. Unlike its water-cooled counterparts in the basements, this unit was air-cooled and, crucially, installed inside a dedicated building closely adjacent to the reactor but at a higher elevation.

When the water rushed in, this single generator stayed dry. Because it didn't rely on seawater pumps (which had been destroyed), it kept running.

This solitary survivor didn't just save itself. Engineers managed to route its power to the adjacent Unit 5 as well. That one generator provided enough electricity to maintain cooling pumps and instrumentation for two reactors simultaneously. While Units 1, 2, and 3 spiraled into meltdown, Units 5 and 6 were brought to a stable "Cold Shutdown."

The tragedy of Fukushima remains enormous, but it could have been twice as devastating. The survival of

Units 5 and 6 proves the most critical lesson of this chapter: True redundancy requires diversity, not just duplication.

If you copy-paste a system five times, you replicate its flaws five times. But if you change the location, the technology, or the dependency chain, you create a legitimate safety net. In the face of overwhelming force, that one decision to build *differently*—higher up and air-cooled—was the only thing that stood between a manageable crisis and a doubled catastrophe.

LESSON LEARNED

- Reliability is measured by the diversity of your safeguards, not the quantity of your copies.

- Identical systems share identical vulnerabilities; true resilience requires a change in technology or location.

- When standard redundancies collapse in unison, the only thing that prevents total disaster is the one component that breaks the pattern.

- Designing for historical averages ignores the statistical tail—the events that truly test systems.

PART V: SUMMARY
THE ILLUSION OF RESILIENCE

Designing safeguards—whether for networks, data-centers, or nuclear plants—is an exercise in controlled paranoia. To make a system truly safe, one must first imagine every possible way it could fail. Every wire that might short, every valve that might jam, every failover that might trigger at the worst possible moment, every engineer who might misread a dashboard during a crisis. True resilience begins with the mindset of an ultimate fatalist: someone willing to picture not just the worst-case scenario, but the moment when all your safety nets fail simultaneously.

Then comes the second ingredient: the pragmatist with the spreadsheet, weighing catastrophic what-ifs against budget realities and operational constraints. It's an uncomfortable calculus—how much is "unlikely" worth? How many nines of uptime can you actually afford? How thoroughly should you test something that might never be needed?—but someone has to make those calls. Somewhere between the fatalist who imagines everything and the pragmatist who has to fund something, real engineering happens. It's rarely elegant, and the compromises are never comfortable.

And even when it's done right, even when smart people design thoughtful systems with genuine redundancy, the universe still finds creative ways to slip through the cracks.

Because redundancy, like trust, is never absolute. Systems can multiply their backups, distribute their infrastructure across continents, and still fail in perfect unison. Disaster recovery plans can fill binders and still evaporate the moment someone needs to execute them under pressure.

This part showed us what happens when that illusion shatters. We watched organizations confidently activate their disaster recovery plans only to discover they'd never been properly tested. We saw failover systems that amplified rather than absorbed failures. We encountered infrastructure designed with genuine redundancy that nonetheless collapsed because every backup depended on the same hidden assumption. And in the most sobering cases, we stepped beyond digital failures entirely—into aircraft cabins, reactor control rooms, and offshore platforms where the gap between "designed to be safe" and "actually safe" was measured in lives rather than downtime.

The common thread wasn't ignorance or malice. It was overconfidence. The comfortable belief that having a plan meant being prepared. That redundancy guaranteed survival. That resilience could be achieved through documentation rather than discipline. Every disaster in this part began with genuine attempts at safety—and ended with the discovery that theoretical resilience and operational resilience are very different things.

If there's a lesson woven through these chapters, it's this: resilience is a practice, not a feature. It requires constant testing, honest failure analysis, and the uncomfortable willingness to believe your safety nets might not work. The systems that survive aren't the ones with the most backup generators or the thickest disaster recovery binders. They're the ones whose operators never stopped asking, "What if this doesn't work the way we think it does?"

And even then, sometimes the answer is: it doesn't.

EPILOGUE:
EVERYTHING WORKED AS DESIGNED
(UNTIL IT DIDN'T)

We have reached the end of our tour through the foundations of the digital world-an expedition through the quiet machinery that runs our lives, and the equally quiet ways in which it can misfire. If you walked into this volume thinking of computers as obedient tools, you've probably left with a different impression: they are obedient, yes, but almost *dangerously* so. And obedience without understanding is its own kind of chaos.

Across these chapters, we traced the three great domains of computation: **compute, network, and storage:** the digital equivalents of muscle, voice, and memory. Each is indispensable. Each is intricate. And each, when pushed beyond the assumptions baked into it decades ago, reveals cracks that are as human as they are technical.

We began with the arithmetic itself, the most basic promise a computer ever makes: that numbers will add up and logic will behave. And yet even here, at ground zero, we found surprises-miscalculated trajectories, broken floating-point units, silent overflows, bugs hiding in bit patterns that seemed almost too small to matter. A reminder that in a universe built on absolutes, a single rounding error can still bend reality.

From there, we followed the threads outward into the global tangle of connectivity. Networks introduced a different flavor of fragility-the kind born not from math but from coordination. Here, the world is held together by protocols built on trust, conventions built on hope, and routing decisions that sometimes resemble gossip more than engineering. A typo in Pennsylvania slowed down half the Internet. A BGP withdrawal erased an entire corporation from the map. A misconfigured router in Canada became a national emergency. Suddenly, the abstractions we take for granted-"the Internet just works"-looked more like a high-wire act performed without a safety net.

Then came storage, where data rests, decays, corrupts, vanishes, or survives purely because someone remembered to check that the backups weren't also on fire. We've seen tapes rot quietly in basements, cloud buckets exposed like billboards, and corporate archives deleted in the name of convenience-or cost cutting. We've watched databases fail in ways both subtle and spectacular, from botched indexes to catastrophic migrations. Through all of it, one pattern held steady: information is more fragile than we care to admit, and more irreplaceable than we ever plan for.

And woven through all these layers was our exploration of **safety**—what it claims, what it delivers, and what it fails to account for. Redundancy that collapses in perfect synchrony. Backups that triumph only at the third attempt. Failover strategies that crumble at the exact moment they become necessary. Disaster recovery plans that looked excellent in spreadsheets and then disintegrated upon contact with reality. If there is a lesson here, it's that safety is not something you *declare*; it's something you *practice*, repeatedly, until the system itself begins to internalize caution.

It's worth pausing here-not to marvel at the failures, but to consider the strange symmetry beneath them. Whether it was a kernel bug, a timekeeping quirk, a misrouted prefix, a corrupted byte, or an operator clicking a button labeled a little too vaguely, each incident revealed the same truth: systems do not fail because they are poorly built. They fail because they are built by people. People with deadlines. People with assumptions. People with blind spots, ambitions, or a simple inability to imagine how creative failure can be.

If there is one invitation I want to leave you with, it is this: **reflect**. Let the stories settle. Think about the principles beneath them—the ones that repeat, the ones that rhyme, the ones that quietly question our relationship with complexity. Consider what went wrong not as an indictment of technology, but as a mirror held up to the way we design, maintain, and trust the systems around us. These failures are not random; they are echoes of the same patterns playing out across decades and disciplines.

And, importantly, they are not the end of the story.

Because everything you've read in this volume-all the arithmetic mishaps, the protocol misadventures, the brittle data, the illusions of safety and resilience-serves as nothing more than the groundwork. These are the *foundations*. Flawed, fascinating, occasionally absurd, but still only foundations.

Before we leave these pages, I want to add one more thing. I hope that somewhere between the trajectories gone wrong, the misbehaving routers, and the heroic-but-hopeless backups, you found moments that made you smile—or at least smirk. I hope you were never bored for too long, and that amid the irony and the acronyms, something here managed to stay with you. If even one idea from this book helps you understand the next headline, question an assumption, or see complexity a little more clearly, then the journey through these foundations was worth it.

In **Volume II**, we step onto the structures we built on top of them: algorithms, automations, open-source supply chains, machine-learning systems, UX disasters, and the increasingly tangled relationships between data, inference, and human intention. If the ground floor wobbles, you can imagine what the higher stories look like.

Or perhaps you can't. And that's exactly the point. When the basics are this fragile, the systems built on them inherit the fragility and amplify it. What emerges is a world where mistakes scale faster than understanding, and where "unexpected behavior" becomes not an exception but a design pattern.

So take a breath. And hold onto the thought that the digital world we trust every day is both more remarkable and more precarious than it seems.

If the foundations of our digital civilization can surprise us this much, just wait until you see what happens when we start adding floors.

BIBLIOGRAPHY:
(OR: WHY I REFUSE TO TORTURE YOU)

This book is built on data. Specifically, over **500 verified sources**—incident reports, postmortems, RFCs, and archived snapshots from the early internet.

I ran the numbers. Printing a proper academic bibliography would add roughly **40 pages** to this volume.

That is a small forest sacrificed for a list of URLs that are functionally useless on paper. Asking you to manually re-type a 180-character Wayback Machine link into a browser address bar is a violation of user experience principles that borders on a Geneva Convention breach.

Furthermore, paper has a terrible refresh rate. The internet rots. Domains expire. Companies scrub their shameful outage reports. By keeping the bibliography digital, I can fix dead links when they inevitably turn into 404, ensuring the sources remain useful long after this book is printed.

So, for the sake of the trees, your sanity, and data persistence—the bibliography is hosted where it belongs: online.

Click here to verify my work: ↵
https://adamkorga.com/books/fuckup-almanac/vol1/sources/

APPENDICES
(OR: WHY THERE ARE NONE)

Originally, this book was supposed to end with the usual extras: an alphabetical list of companies, a catalog of concepts, maybe a tidy index — the kind that signals *"don't worry, this is Serious and Academic"* before anyone actually checks.

I seriously considered it. I even sketched a few versions. And then I realized that most of them would do more harm than good.

An alphabetical list of organizations, in particular, felt like a trap. In a book about failure, such a list would almost inevitably be read as a *list of shame* — a quiet hall of fame for corporate screw-ups — instead of what this book is actually about: recurring patterns, incentives, blind spots, and systems that were already broken long before a logo entered the frame. That framing would be catchy, shareable, and completely wrong.

A glossary-style list of concepts didn't fare much better. If you want to use *The Fuckup Almanac* as a friendly guide to certain ideas, there's a good chance the book's structure will serve you better than memorizing terminology. This isn't a vocabulary quiz. The chapters are organized around failure modes and mechanisms, not around definitions you can point at and say "aha, page 317."

Besides, if you're the kind of reader who enjoys coming back to books, you probably already have your own system for marking what mattered to you: highlights, sticky notes, margin scribbles, a separate notebook, color codes, dog-eared pages, or some personal ritual that looks mildly unhinged to everyone else. I've tried some of these approaches, never fully mastered any of them, and I'm not going to pretend I can replace habits people refine over years of reading.

And even if you don't have such a system, there's a simpler and more honest option. Bookmark the digital bibliography (link in previous section). It's intentionally organized, mirrors how I think about the structure of these failures, and — perhaps most importantly — it is powered by the ancient, battle-tested technology known as **Ctrl + F**.

Now that we've mapped the bedrock of the digital world —the compute, networking, and storage foundations where the most brutal disasters are born—it's time to look upward. You've seen how the ground can shift; now see how the structures we build on top of it can crumble.

Fuckup Almanac vol. 2 shifts focus to the higher layers: the supply chains that bind us, the algorithms that drive us, and the complex logic that connects it all. It's a deeper dive into the high-level chaos of the modern tech stack. If you thought the "foundations" were messy, wait until you see the architecture.Once the foundations are in place, it's time to look up.

P.S. Yes, there's going to be plenty of AI-driven madness.

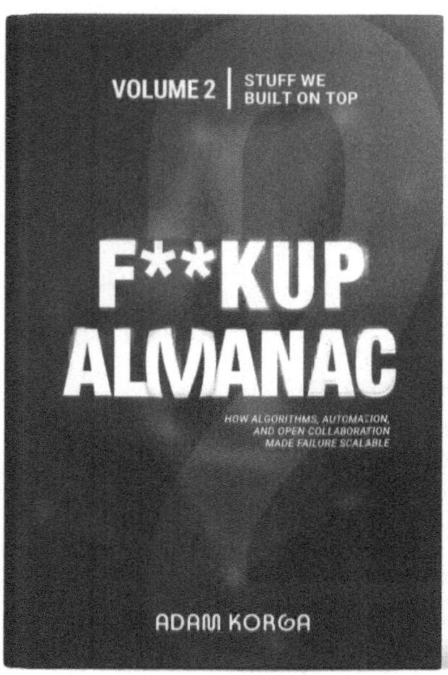

THIS IS WHERE FAILURE LEARNED TO SCALE

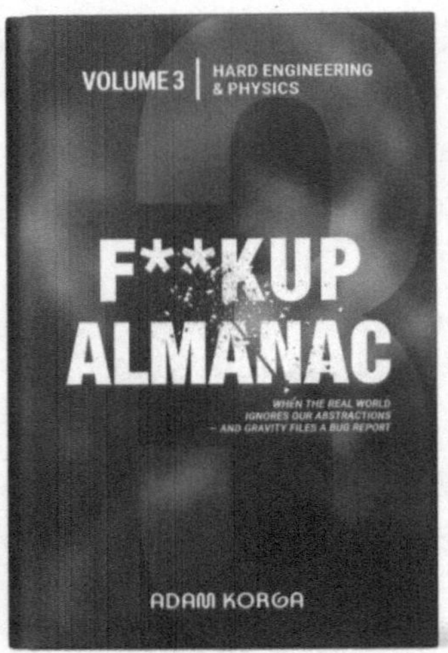

VOLUME III WILL SHIFT THE SPOTLIGHT FROM CODE TO CONCRETE.

Bridges, aircraft, reactors, and industrial systems take center stage as abstractions collide with gravity, pressure, and resonance. Same failure patterns — just measured in tons, not bytes.

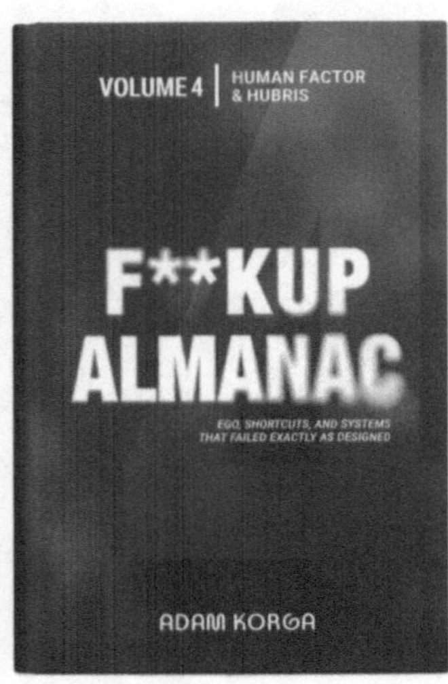

VOLUME IV WILL TURN THE LENS ON US.

Ego, shortcuts, cost-cutting, and stories we tell ourselves take center stage. From procedural drift to outright fraud, this volume is going to show how systems fail exactly as designed—by the humans running them.

IT Dictionary is not a textbook and not a career guide. It's a satire of the IT industry — written as a dictionary, read like group therapy.

For seasoned professionals, it's catharsis: finally naming the absurdities everyone recognizes but rarely admits out loud. For newcomers, it's a warning label — a map of incentives, rituals, and corporate theater hiding behind familiar buzzwords.

You won't learn how to be a better engineer. You might learn how to survive the industry without losing your mind.

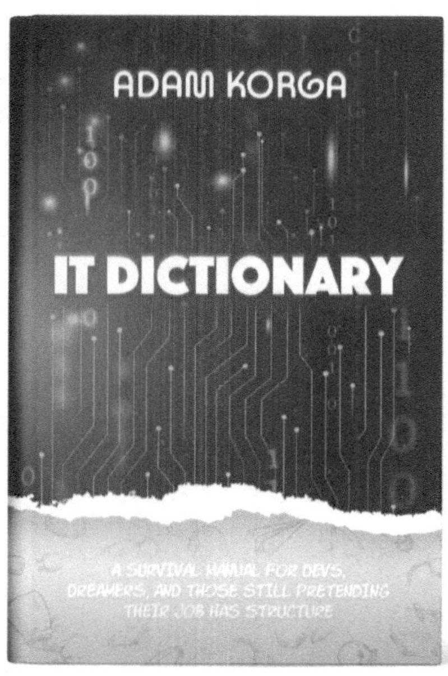

THE INDUSTRY'S UNWRITTEN RULES, FINALLY WRITTEN DOWN.

One of Independent Book Review's Best Books We Read in 2025.